# Contents

# Clio's Favorites

# Introduction

by Robert Allen Rutland

Clio, the Greek muse vested with the inspiration of history, has been reigning for a long time in places as diverse as New Haven, Cambridge, Oxford, Paris, Bologna, and Berkeley. If there is something grandiose in claiming that we have found Clio's outstanding practitioners in American history, forgive us for overstatement. But here we go.

Historians talk about each other's work all the time but have a reluctance to record their thoughts concerning colleagues. Hence the entire twentieth century passed by with only a handful of books devoted to the historical profession in the United States. The landmark work was the 1937 publication, *The Marcus W. Jernegan Essays in American Historiography,* written by former students of their teacher at the University of Chicago and edited by William T. Hutchinson. This festschrift became a kind of Bible for a generation or so of graduate students, who went into their oral examinations with trepidation and a copy of *Jernegan* nearby. *Pastmasters,* published in 1969 and edited by Marcus Cunliffe and Robin Winks, brought the story up to date. Both books reached back to Francis Parkman's time. None of the historians covered by the 1937 book is in this work, but from the Cunliffe-Winks collection we find four historians who still command respect—Richard Hofstadter, David M. Potter, Arthur M. Schlesinger, Jr., and C. Vann Woodward. Eight new faces—those of Bernard Bailyn, Merle Curti, David Herbert Donald, John Hope Franklin, Howard Lamar, Arthur S. Link, Gerda Lerner and Edmund S. Morgan—complete our roll call of excellence. Initially, there were thirteen historians who made "the final cut," but the person who accepted one assignment never turned in his essay, and deadlines cannot be stretched forever. Our "Contributors" section notes that essays on five of the chosen twelve have been written by former students.

How did some historians make the honored list and others not? Earlier essays took professional recognition as their guide but included non-historians (Perry Miller and Vernon Parrington). For this book some twenty-five historians served as jurors in an informal poll taken during the summer of 1999. They were asked to name the leading historians of American history active since the end of World War II. The criteria were the quality (not the volume) of the historians' work, their influence in their field of study, the importance of their graduate and undergraduate teaching; their public recognition as indicated by awards, honors, involvement in public service; and, last, personality traits that were worth noting. Most of the chosen historians also broke new ground.

The twelve historians whose careers are studied here met these standards with acclaim. And with regret we have to say that some excellent men and women barely fell short of inclusion. Indeed, I trust that in due course essays will appear to honor such worthies as Joyce Appleby, Carl Degler, Jack Greene, Oscar Handlin, Michael Kammen, Linda Kerber, Leonard Levy, Merrill Peterson, Kenneth Stampp, and Gordon Wood. The list could go on and on, but I believe we have harvested the cream of the crop, and as a president of the United States once reminded us, the buck must stop here. Now it stops as I carry out my final duties as editor.

America and the world surely underwent profound changes after August 1945. The atomic bomb signaled a new era in which technology makes old ideas invalid. The historical schools of Frederick Jackson Turner and Charles A. Beard were challenged by a group of historians who thought narrative history passé; instead of using musty letters or diaries for grist, they looked for evidence in polling records, census returns, or export and import lists. Then the Cold War marked the appearance of "consensus history" as American military and economic might was in need of home-front moral reinforcement.

Was the American Century comparable to the Golden Age of Pericles? Nobody was certain, but historians such as Daniel Boorstin, as the Librarian of Congress, and Arthur Schlesinger, Jr., serving at the White House, turned out books that reflected a confidence the American public readily accepted. David Potter, on the other hand, was not sure that American ideas were as important to the rest of the world as was Yankee affluence, represented in automobiles, refrigerators, and other creature comforts.

In the early sixties there was a winner of the Pulitzer Prize in the White House, and after his death another major shift in American history took place. President John F. Kennedy's assassination proved to be a historical watershed, followed by more assassinations, the Vietnam War, a White House scandal, and a presidential resignation. Such dark events troubled the nation and its historians—for who could explain these tragedies befalling a country founded on self-evident truths? Politics mattered more than some historians cared to admit; and Richard Hofstadter reminded us that progressivism was a hope, not an achievement, and the roots of anti-intellectualism were far deeper than most cared to admit.

Old areas of historical study were reopened by new insights. Bernard Bailyn showed that ideas were of great importance in fomenting the American Revolution, just as Edmund S. Morgan reexamined the Stamp Act crisis as a turning point in Anglo-American relations before 1776. And John Hope Franklin's studies on slavery broke new ground and led to the publisher's dream of more than a million copies in sales. C. Vann Woodward dissected racism since the Civil War and tore apart old notions about Reconstruction. Not long afterward came David Herbert Donald's reexamination of the Civil War and Reconstruction, and then his remarkable biography of Lincoln, which may have done more to help us understand the Great Emancipator than any other previous work.

Nor could historians ignore Gerda Lerner's bombshells in women's history, even though this field was suddenly full of prodigies and programs. Arthur Link outshone all previous editors of presidential papers with his Woodrow Wilson volumes, masterfully annotated. Merle Curti produced his provocative studies in what came to be called "intellectual history," and Howard Lamar's books and graduate students broke away from the Turner thesis with gusto as they rewrote the themes of western or frontier history.

Looking into the backgrounds of our twelve historians, it may be more than coincidence that six were born in the South but flourished in the North. One was a refugee from Nazi oppression. Most taught at Ivy League universities, but those based at Chicago and Wisconsin also made their mark. There was growing evidence in the final decade of the century that centers of learning on the Pacific Coast were an increasing force in the profession.

Good historical writing is never outdated. Thucydides was read by the young Theodore Roosevelt, a future president (of both the nation and the American Historical Association). Thousands of readers are still fascinated by the colorful and accurate writing of Francis Parkman. Henry Adams's prodigious labors on the Jefferson and Madison administrations appeared more than a century ago, and his interpretations may have been under-read but have not been overturned.

We have come a long way since Allan Nevins, writing in a popular magazine in 1938, bemoaned "What's the Matter with History?" Nevins complained that unreadable works by "Dryasdust" historians were killing interest with the reading public. Then, in December 1941, the war spread to America. History was made every hour, and by millions of American airmen, soldiers, sailors, and Marines. With the return of peace in 1945, academic history saw a period of popularity. Returning GIs took advantage of generous legislation to crowd into colleges and universities; state legislatures mandated courses in American history from elementary school to the twelfth grade. Then cynicism came with the assassinations of the Kennedys and Martin Luther King, with Vietnam and Watergate.

Perhaps people wanted to forget such tragedies as the Kent State shooting. From the 1970s onward history courses were often dropped in public schools, and watered-down "social studies" were substituted. Jobs for doctoral students in American history were not easily obtained. National polls indicated that both teenagers and college graduates were often unable to recall the names of leading figures in American history, those once held sacred in American memory. Identities of the four presidents on the face of Mount Rushmore became blurs in students' minds.

The twelve historians covered herein are virtual heroes in the effort to revive history as an important academic discipline. All of their books are provocative, and some have become best-sellers. Most of these authors are proud to be called narrative historians. Narrative history, Vann Woodward observed, was "the end product of what historians do. . . . Other types of history—analytical, quantitative, comparative history—as important as they are, are mainly for other historians . . . [and] they mainly represent historians talking to each other." The twelve historians chosen as Clio's favorites have, of course, talked to each other over the years, but their audience has been and must be a vast and thoughtful reading public.

As readers of these essays will discern, the honors heaped on these twelve are not only deserved, they counter the claim that America is a nation where intellect is barely recognized and seldom honored. *Clio's Favorites* is a testimony to excellence. May the twenty-first century produce their equals!

# Bernard Bailyn

## by Jack N. Rakove

In 1949, at the age of twenty-seven, four years out of the U.S. Army and three years into his graduate education, Bernard Bailyn was appointed an instructor in the Department of History at Harvard University. Fifty years later, though officially retired, he was still actively teaching at Harvard, not only offering courses to entering graduate students but also conducting an ambitious seminar for younger scholars on Atlantic history—an area of research that he had pioneered at the start of his career and returned to in the 1970s.[1] In between, he garnered two Pulitzer Prizes, a National Book Award, and a Bancroft Prize; served as president of the American Historical Association in 1981; and gave the Jefferson Lecture in the Humanities in 1998.

The GI Bill of Rights (the postwar educational boon for veterans) helped thousands of servicemen. But few matched "Bud" Bailyn's accomplishments. Born on September 10, 1922, in Hartford, Connecticut, Bailyn was graduated from Williams College in 1945 (although in fact he received his degree without returning to Williams from service in the United States Army). At Harvard, Bailyn was appointed to three endowed chairs, in-

1. For biographical information, see A. Roger Ekirch, "Bernard Bailyn," in *Twentieth-Century American Historians,* ed. Clyde N. Wilson, *Dictionary of Literary Biography* (Detroit: Gale, 1983), 17:19–26, and Michael Kammen and Stanley N. Katz, "Bernard Bailyn, Historian and Teacher," in *The Transformation of Early American History: Society, Authority, and Ideology,* ed. James A. Henretta, Michael Kammen, and Stanley N. Katz (New York: Knopf, 1991), 3–15. In writing this essay about my own teacher, I should note that I draw as well upon personal impressions that date to my first encounter with Bailyn in September 1969, as well as conversations over the years with other students, especially Pauline Maier and Gordon Wood and his friend, associate, and editor at Knopf, Jane N. Garrett. I have written two previous essays on Bailyn: an overall assessment of his writings, "'How Else Could It End?': Bernard Bailyn and the Problem of Authority in Early America," in *The Transformation of Early American History,* ed. Henretta et al., 51–69; and "Encountering Bernard Bailyn," *Humanities* 19 (1998): 9–13.

cluding the Adams University Professorship; directed the Charles Warren Center for Studies in American History and edited both the John Harvard Library and the annual review, *Perspectives in American History;* chaired the Department of History and served on numerous other committees; and received an honorary doctorate in 1999.

A half century of active teaching and scholarship would be an impressive achievement for any historian, but what is more remarkable in Bailyn's case is the extent to which his teaching has always reflected his intense, ever-fresh, and always stimulating engagement with the identification and solution of new historical problems. His career as both teacher and scholar coincided with, and deeply influenced, the transformation of the entire field of early American history, from the foundation of the English colonies in North America to the adoption of the Federal Constitution. When Bailyn entered Harvard in 1946, the *William and Mary Quarterly* had just begun to provide a forum that would help make early American history a major field of research.[2] But it would take more than a forum to demonstrate that the first two centuries of American history were more than a mere prologue to the more exciting and momentous developments that presumably got under way only in the nineteenth century. Along with Edmund Morgan of Yale, Bailyn was one of the two preeminent postwar scholars whose writings shaped the essential agenda of research and interpretation, and whose teaching inspired scores of students to undertake fresh projects of their own.

When Bailyn first entered the field, it already claimed several major figures whose best works were both intellectually respectable and authoritative. The four volumes of Charles McLean Andrews's *The Colonial Period of American History* provided a general framework for understanding the stages in the English colonization of North America. Perry Miller's essays and books on Puritan theology had revealed the depth and complexity of the religious convictions and concerns of the Puritans and their descendants. And the shadow of two earlier giants of progressive historiography—Arthur M. Schlesinger and Charles Beard—still dominated the interpretation of the formative political events of the Revolutionary era. At Harvard, too, Samuel Eliot Morison—"the Admiral," as he was known for

---

2. Keith Berwick, "A Peculiar Monument: The Third Series of the *William and Mary Quarterly,*" *William and Mary Quarterly,* 3d ser., 21 (1964): 3–17.

the rank he held while writing the history of American naval operations in World War II—cut an imposing figure.

Bailyn was deeply engaged with the work of these scholars, but from an early point—indeed, probably from the outset—he aspired to break new ground. Andrews's survey, for all its learning, had no real mechanism for moving beyond the organization of colonial authority to describe the process through which the deeper structures of English society were transferred to the new world. Miller's brilliance as an intellectual historian could not obscure the extraordinarily abstract nature of the ideas he was studying. The progressives' assessment of the structure of late colonial and revolutionary politics had recently been challenged by Bailyn's teacher, Oscar Handlin, and was soon to be weakened even more by Edmund Morgan's revisionist account of the Stamp Act crisis.[3] And Morison, for all his narrative gifts, was too enamored of his own personal attachments to the American past—his family and the sea—to provide an adequate framework of interpretation.

By his own account, Bailyn came to his studies with an ambitious intellectual agenda that had somehow coalesced during his undergraduate education at Williams College, his wartime service in the Army Signal Corps and the Army Security Agency, and a year spent in Paris immediately after the war. This rough agenda had three items: "the relation between European and American life . . . the transition between the premodern and modern worlds . . . [a]nd the interplay between social history and cultural or intellectual history." At Harvard, Bailyn studied under Perry Miller (whom he once described "striding across the Harvard Yard, belted up in an old Army trench coat trying to look like Humphrey Bogart")[4] and the medievalist Charles Taylor. But it was Oscar Handlin, then emerging as the dominant intellectual figure among the Harvard Americanists, with whom he formed the closest attachments.

Handlin was himself all of thirty-one when Bailyn entered Harvard, but

3. Oscar Handlin and Mary Handlin, "Radicals and Conservatives in Massachusetts after Independence," *New England Quarterly* 17 (1944): 343–55; Edmund S. Morgan and Helen M. Morgan, *The Stamp Act Crisis: Prologue to Revolution* (Chapel Hill: University of North Carolina Press, 1953).

4. Bailyn, *History and the Creative Imagination* (St. Louis: Washington University, 1985), 11 (this is the published text of a lecture Bailyn gave as the Lewin Distinguished Visiting Professor at Washington University).

he had already published his pathbreaking work of social history, *Boston's Immigrants,* and was nearing completion of *Commonwealth,* a landmark study of the political economy of Massachusetts (coauthored with Mary Handlin).[5] Under Handlin's "direction" (one uses the term advisedly, for Handlin—very much like Bailyn—left his students free to make their own way intellectually), Bailyn undertook the research that eventuated in his first monograph, *The New England Merchants in the Seventeenth Century,* published by Harvard University Press in 1955. Although that book owed a little to Perry Miller's concern with the economic forces that fueled "declension in a Bible commonwealth," and something to Admiral Morison's maritime interests, Handlin's efforts to map the lives, ambitions, and experiences of Boston's immigrant workers offered a far more salient model of social history.

In tracing the origins and composition of the New England merchants—in writing their collective biography—Bailyn found inspiration beyond the precincts of American history in the prosopographical studies done by two other imaginatively creative historians: Ronald Syme, who had reconstructed the entrance of provincial notables into the ancient Roman elite, and Lewis Namier, who had offered a new portrait of eighteenth-century English politics by unraveling the complexities of the patronage system. Bailyn long remained fascinated by the ability of these two historians (and others, such as Miller and Andrews) to discover an entire world of relationships that other scholars, looking at the same material, had simply failed to perceive. These remarkable historians set an agenda of research that younger acolytes would pursue by expanding the scope of interpretation until it encountered its own boundaries or exposed its own structural weaknesses.[6]

Bailyn's efforts to use the colonial merchants as a prism through which to look afresh at the structure of colonial society had another, more personal source. In 1952, Bailyn married Lotte Lazarsfeld, the daughter of Paul Lazarsfeld, one of the many distinguished scholars, largely of Jewish ori-

---

5. *Boston's Immigrants, 1790–1865: A Study in Acculturation* (Cambridge: Harvard University Press, 1941); *Commonwealth: A Study of the Role of Government in the American Economy: Massachusetts, 1774–1861,* rev. ed. (Cambridge: Harvard University Press, 1969 [1947]).

6. See, again, Bailyn's *History and the Creative Imagination* and the commentary on this lecture in Gordon Wood, "The Creative Imagination of Bernard Bailyn," in *Transformation of Early American History,* ed. Henretta et al., 16–50.

gin, who had fled Nazi Germany or Austria before 1939. Their exodus brought to the United States a brilliant group of thinkers who transformed American intellectual life. Through Lotte (who has also enjoyed a distinguished professorial career in the Sloan School of Management at the Massachusetts Institute of Technology), Bailyn gained access to this circle of refugee scholars, whose writings in sociology and social theory offered a powerful analytical framework for approaching problems of social organization.[7]

Like Syme and Namier, Bailyn was intrigued by the process through which an elite segment of a society comes into existence.[8] While rejecting the rigid view of class embraced by the progressive historians, *New England Merchants* was nonetheless concerned with the creation of an elite with in-

7. See the concluding observations in Bailyn's *From Protestant Peasants to Jewish Intellectuals: The Germans in the Peopling of America,* German Historical Institute, Washington, Annual Lecture No. 1 (New York: Berg, 1988), 9–12. At a 1989 conference tied to the preparation of his festschrift, Bailyn regaled his students with an account of the trepidation a visit with his father-in-law could evoke. It was Lazarsfeld's wont, he noted, to ask his son-in-law odd questions about any obscure aspect of American history, such as, if you went into a store in 1830 and wanted to buy something, what currency would you pull out of your pocket to pay for your purchase. Lotte Bailyn has written a brief but engaging memoir about the women in her own family (*Four Generations: A Memoir of Women's Lives* [Cambridge: Harvard University Press, 1997]). Bailyn's interest in the impact of the refugee intellectuals was evident in the second volume of *Perspectives in American History,* an annual publication of short monographs and articles that Bailyn coedited with his colleague Donald Fleming for the Charles Warren Center in American History at Harvard. This volume, entitled *Intellectual Migration: Europe and America, 1930–1960* (Cambridge: Harvard University Press, 1969), includes a memoir by Lazarsfeld.

8. One could speculate about another similarity between Bailyn and these two prosopographers. Syme and Namier were both knighted after distinguished academic careers (though Namier was bitterly disappointed by his failure to be called back to Oxford, where he had done his graduate studies), but Syme was a provincial outsider from New Zealand, and Namier was a member of a highly assimilated Polish-Jewish family that claimed descent from the celebrated sage of Lithuanian Jewry known as the Vilna Gaon. Bailyn's parents, Charles and Esther, were established members of the Jewish community of Hartford, and though Harvard was less resistant to the entrance of Jews into its faculty ranks than Yale or Princeton—Arthur M. Schlesinger, Sr., was a descendant of German Jews, and Bailyn's teacher, Oscar Handlin, came from the classic immigrant background he depicted so brilliantly in *The Uprooted*—Bailyn's accession to the position held by Morison, who possessed an impeccable New England pedigree, symbolizes the transformation of American university life that accompanied the entrance of Jews into faculty ranks after World War II. Numerous stories have circulated within the profession of the immense disappointment that Carl Bridenbaugh, then teaching at Berkeley, felt over Bailyn's appointment. Bridenbaugh's bitterness is transparently revealed in his grotesque presidential address to the American Historical Association, published under the title "The Great Mutation," *American Historical Review* 68 (1963).

terests distinct from those of Miller's Puritan ministers. This elite found its authority challenged after midcentury by an influx of new English traders and imperial officials, and the gap that opened between the original Puritan merchants and the interlopers was destined to have lasting consequences, Bailyn concluded, for the entire structure of authority in Massachusetts. The most successful merchants may have occupied the top rungs of colonial society, but that alone did not grant them the authority and power enjoyed by others with better connections to the sources of political power and influence of the larger empire. Four years after his first book appeared, Bailyn published a briefer study of a different colonial elite—the emerging planter aristocracy of colonial Virginia—that reached the same conclusion. This much-reprinted essay, "Politics and Social Structure in Virginia," concluded with a general interpretation of the underlying problem of authority throughout the colonies. "The divergence between social and political leadership at the topmost level created an area of permanent conflict," Bailyn wrote, producing a "strangely shaped" structure of authority in which the traditional sources of superiority—wealth and political power—no longer coincided. "Herein lay the origins of a new political system," Bailyn concluded, somewhat oracularly.[9]

During these same years of the 1950s, Bailyn was developing the legendary seminar from which he regularly recruited unsuspecting students into his field. Perhaps all students of great professors boast similar memories, but Bailyn's roughly four-score doctoral students from several generations have good reason to think they shared one of the most memorable seminars any American historian—or, for that matter, any scholar—has ever given. Not that it taught them anything about the mechanics of doing research: the use of finding aids or catalogs, the development of bibliographies, or the selection of proper note cards.[10] That was the student's job to figure out—and if he couldn't, too bad. Instead, Bailyn assigned a bewildering array of readings, often having little to do with each other or

---

9. "Politics and Social Structure in Virginia," in *Seventeenth-Century America,* ed. James Morton Smith (Chapel Hill: University of North Carolina Press, 1959), 90–115. According to Ekirch, this essay was reprinted no fewer than seventeen times.

10. Bailyn loves to tell the story of one such course he took, in which the professor explained in excruciating detail exactly what type of note card to use for each type of data. His own refinement on this introduction took the form of repeating each of these carefully detailed steps, but adding one other: "And, then, you throw the whole thing out the window." Bailyn, *On the Teaching and Writing of History* (Hanover, N.H.: University Press of New England, 1996), 84.

even early American history: moldy monographs like Harlan Updegraff's justly neglected *The Origin of the Moving School in Massachusetts;* materials that seemed to have wandered into the syllabus on their own, like Lord Denning's report on the Profumo spy scandal of 1963; or intriguing books from exotic fields, such as E. H. Carr's *Romantic Exiles,* an account of Alexander Herzen and his circle of exiled Russian liberals. Hardly anything that Bailyn assigned would qualify as the "cutting-edge" scholarship of the day.

To Bailyn's students that did not matter. The universal experience of confusion—"shaking our heads and wondering what on earth did he want us to read this for," as Gordon Wood recalled; "a droll yet apprehensive guessing game," as Michael Kammen and Stanley Katz put it[11]—gave way, in the course of discussion, to a gradual appreciation of some underlying problem of historical analysis or exposition. Often this had to do with learning how to tell a well-defined historical problem from a bad one, or a clearly stated causal thesis from one that muddled the mechanism of change. Sometimes it had to with something as simple as the proper use of adjectives or the importance of transitions in the construction of a readable historical narrative.

Bailyn's role in developing these points was often so passive as to border on the inert—until, that is, an imperious "Look!" summoned students to the real issue at hand. It was at once a mystifying and exhilarating two hours, and most who took the seminar came away from it with a much more potent sense of what the writing of good analytical history entailed.[12] Over the years the readings changed, but written evidence and oral testimony indicate that the experience remained the same.

In 1958, Harvard promoted Bailyn to the rank of associate professor of history with tenure; three years later, he was named full professor. In 1959, as an outgrowth of his first book, he and Lotte Bailyn published an intensively researched quantitative study entitled *Massachusetts Shipping, 1697–1714,* a work that demonstrated how remarkably active colonial shipbuilders and merchants had been in creating their own merchant marine. The work was notable for another reason: its use of the counter-sorter to tabulate data gave it a pioneering place in the annals of quantitative history. Bailyn's growing reputation in the profession, however, owed more

11. Wood, "Creative Imagination," 19; Kammen and Katz, "Bernard Bailyn," 12–13; Rakove, "Encountering Bernard Bailyn," 9–13.

12. For the professor's own reflections on the method of the seminar, see Bailyn, *On the Teaching and Writing of History,* 13–14.

to several other papers he completed and published as the age of Eisenhower was giving way to the New Frontier shaped by a different kind of Harvard historian—John F. Kennedy.

The first of these papers was the suggestive study of the Virginia planter elite, already discussed; the next was the introductory essay to a slim volume, *Education in the Forming of American Society*, ostensibly devoted to the historiography of education, a subject most historians avoided. In the mid-1950s, Bailyn had also taught in the School of Education at Harvard, and this essay was in part a product of that involvement.[13] But it was essentially the work of someone consciously positioning himself outside the accepted boundaries of the field, for Bailyn argued that the conventional approach to the history of American education had been skewed (at least for the colonial era) by its dominant tendency to treat all aspects of that story as a prelude to the eventual establishment of mass public education.

Bailyn believed such an approach led inevitably and fatally to anachronism—the one sin for which he reserved his hottest criticism. In Bailyn's alternative view, education was better conceived as the larger process whereby a society transfers its cultural values from one generation to the next, principally through the family. Thus, in the case of the American colonies, the challenge was to determine whether the family structures painfully taking root in the new world were up to the task. In his view, they had fallen short. The extended families of the old world, so densely interwoven with the larger community that children often did not "know where the family left off and the greater society began," were unsuited to the disruptive conditions of the American wilderness. The origins of institutional education in the American colonies, then, could only be understood within the larger context of the history of colonial society.[14]

Bailyn wrote this essay unaware of the pioneering work on the history of the early modern English family then being done by Peter Laslett and John Harrison and their associates, which called into question his own basic assumptions about the deep stability of the old world family. Moreover, when other scholars, including his own student, Philip Greven, began examining the history of the colonial family—particularly in New England, the one region where education early became a subject of offi-

13. The story always told at Harvard was that Bailyn was placed there for safekeeping pending the retirement of Morison.

14. Bailyn, *Education and the Forming of American Society: Needs and Opportunities for Further Study* (Chapel Hill: University of North Carolina Press, 1960), quotation at p. 18.

cial concern—they discovered that Bailyn's assumptions about its struggles and fate in the New World were not well grounded. Even so, this essay had an impact on scholarly thinking out of all proportion to its diminutive size and speculative nature. Indeed, Bailyn had found a way to rethink an entire subject, and in doing so he focused on the need to understand exactly what had happened to the family structure in its transplantation from Europe to America.

In the 1960s and 1970s, the reconstruction of family history in New England and the Chesapeake became the hottest topic in "the new history" of colonial society, and Bailyn's *Education* first established the framework of inquiry. The creation of such a framework was the subject of a brief comment that Bailyn contributed to a collection of papers entitled *Philosophy and History*. The conference occasioning this volume examined the logic of historical thought and explanation, but Bailyn's contribution took the form of the prosaic observations of a "working historian" who found all these speculations interesting in themselves but only tangential to what historians really do. The essence of the historian's task instead inhered, Bailyn argued, in the identification of "true historical problems," which he defined as "questions raised by the observation of (1) anomalies in the existing data, or (2) discrepancies between data and existing explanations." By "anomalies," Bailyn simply meant evidence of discontinuities in past behavior; or, more simply still, change; or, in the classic formulation often given in the seminar, the problem of how one gets from point A to point B. A good historical problem began with the recognition that something which had taken place in the past was surprising (either to its participants or to observers much later). An especially good problem was one in which existing explanations could no longer fit the available evidence (old or new).[15]

In the early 1960s, two great anomalies commanded Bailyn's attention. The first involved making sense of what Bailyn came to call "the milling factionalism" of colonial politics, that is, searching for underlying patterns and explanations to account for the recurring disputes over royal prerogative and legislative privilege that repeatedly disrupted political life. Rather than view these quarrels as mere American variations on a familiar En-

15. Bailyn, "The Problems of the Working Historian: A Comment," in *Philosophy and History: A Symposium,* ed. Sidney Hook (New York: New York University Press, 1963), 92–101. Bailyn also used this essay to stress the importance of language—especially the choice of adjectives—in historical writing.

glish theme, Bailyn understood that they were the product and reflection of the more profound fissures in the very structure of authority that he had identified in his studies of New England merchants and Virginia planters. It was his purpose, at the time, to undertake a broad study of colonial politics, one that would consider the emergence of provincial elites in conjunction with the new forces and factors introduced by the tightening bonds of empire in the eighteenth century.

In the meantime, Bailyn had also accepted an invitation from Harvard University Press to edit a multivolume collection of the pamphlet literature of the American Revolution, and that project soon eclipsed the other one. For as Bailyn proceeded, he came to the realization that the underlying structure of ideas and beliefs revealed in the pamphlets offered an explanation for a second, more profound "anomaly" of historical inquiry: how the time-worn constitutional claims that lay at the heart of the Anglo-American controversy of 1765–1776 could lead not only to the radical step of independence but also to the broader range of meliorist impulses that the Revolution unleashed.

Like Edmund Morgan some years earlier, Bailyn began with the assumption that the revolutionary controversy was best understood as a constitutional dispute; and, like Morgan, he assumed that American arguments were not merely rhetorical rationalizations of deeper material interests, but accurate expressions of convictions and principles that were the true objects of dispute. By the time Bailyn published the first of the projected four volumes of *Pamphlets of the American Revolution* in 1965, his book-length introduction (entitled "The Transforming Radicalism of the American Revolution") provided a more sweeping interpretation of the origins and significance of the Revolution than even Morgan had ventured.[16]

Bailyn's insights had a marked effect on scholars in America and Great Britain. Three great themes gave his interpretation—soon separately published as *The Ideological Origins of the American Revolution*—its extraordinary impact. First, Bailyn argued that the animating power of American political ideas did not lie solely in the familiar sources that scholars had long recognized—that is, in the writings of Enlightenment liberals, from John Locke on; or in the common-law tradition; or in the appeal of antiquity—but rather drew critical strength from a somewhat more obscure

16. Sadly, it seems unlikely the remaining three volumes will ever appear.

tradition that Americans had been absorbing since the early eighteenth century. These were the writings of the so-called Commonwealthmen[17] who remained loyal to the republican experiments of the seventeenth century and who were suspicious of the rise of ministerial power and influence in the eighteenth. From their writings, Bailyn concluded, Americans had fashioned a coherent political ideology that inclined them to view the miscues of British policy after 1763 not as a set of ill-informed but well-intended errors, but rather as proof of a deep-laid plot to strip the colonists of their fundamental rights. This ideology generated a "logic of rebellion" that ineluctably led to the decision for independence while a succession of British governments and officials continued to seek ways to bring the American colonies more firmly under imperial control.

Important as this argument was to the question of why the Revolution occurred, it did not constitute, in Bailyn's own view, his most important findings. In the two concluding chapters, which comprise the second half of *Ideological Origins,* Bailyn returned to the formal constitutional issues in dispute between Britain and America and then examined the spillover effect that the liberating impulses of the Revolutionary agitation released on seemingly unrelated issues. "Transformation," the first of these chapters, traced how the decade of "pounding controversy" after 1765 drove American polemicists to adopt more radical positions on such issues as representation, rights, the nature of a constitution, and sovereignty; but it also argued, more subtly, that these positions brought American thinking more into accord with underlying realities of politics and governance that had been evolving in the colonies since their inception. In "The Contagion of Liberty," Bailyn carried his argument a step further by describing how the Revolution challenged fundamental assumptions about the social order itself: the legitimacy of slavery, the right of the state to maintain religious establishments, and, most important, the need to require a just measure of deference to social superiors. For Bailyn, then, the political fears that drove the colonists from resistance to revolution were only the initial element in a broader thrust of revolutionary idealism, releasing forces that would have further consequences in the decades to come.

*Ideological Origins* received both the Pulitzer Prize and the Bancroft

---

17. The phrase comes from the important monograph by Caroline Robbins, *The Eighteenth-century Commonwealthman: Studies in the Transmission, Development, and Circumstance of English Liberal Thought from the Restoration of Charles II until the War with the Thirteen Colonies* (Cambridge: Harvard University Press, 1959).

Prize in 1968, and in the same year Bailyn published *The Origins of American Politics,* the principal fruit of his now sidetracked project on colonial politics.[18] Bailyn used the three lectures that composed this book to fill in a critical link left open in *Ideological Origins.* By explaining how disparities in the structure of politics in Britain and America engendered repeated conflicts between the crown and the colonial assemblies, *Origins of American Politics* also showed why the colonists proved so receptive to the radical Whig or Commonwealth ideas that had produced "the logic of rebellion." It was the history of colonial politics before 1765, that is, that revealed how Americans had absorbed the ideological view of politics that British provocations after 1765 repeatedly triggered.

Readers of these two works would have been inclined to include Bailyn in the liberal consensus historiography that came under such sustained assault in the late 1960s. In fact, Bailyn had always been scrupulously apolitical in his writings; yet it was difficult to avoid reading the final pages of *Ideological Origins* and not conclude that he deeply identified with the liberal impulses, the challenges to received authority, that the Revolution unleashed. In the late 1960s, however, such an identification was not enough. Bailyn's belief that the Revolutionary glass was half full (or more), not half empty (or less), found little sympathy among those who held that the most conspicuous legacy of the Revolution was its failure to undo the evil of slavery or the hierarchies of class. That judgment of New Left historians, circa 1970, seemed to be confirmed by Bailyn's next book, *The Ordeal of Thomas Hutchinson,* which appeared in 1974. Without apology, Bailyn offered a deeply sympathetic and moving biography of the one man whom the Revolutionaries most reviled, the traitorous royal governor of Massachusetts who believed that "some abridgment of what are called English liberties" must necessarily occur in the colonies.[19]

Bailyn had laid the groundwork for the Hutchinson biography in the closing pages of *Ideological Origins,* where he viewed the revolutionary "contagion of liberty" from the vantage point of its Loyalist critics. "What reasonable social and political order could conceivably be built and maintained," Bailyn allowed the amazed Loyalists to ask, "where authority was questioned before it was obeyed, where social differences were considered

---

18. *The Origins of American Politics* (New York: Knopf, 1968). The three lectures were first presented as the Colvin Lectures at Brown University and originally published in the inaugural volume of *Perspectives in American History.*

19. *The Ordeal of Thomas Hutchinson* (Cambridge: Harvard University Press, 1974), 227.

to be incidental rather than essential to the community order, and where superiority, suspect in principle, was not allowed to concentrate in the hands of the few but was scattered broadly through the populace?"[20] If any American figure still represented the traditional concentrated unity of social and political authority, it was Hutchinson, wealthy merchant, conscientious public servant, thoughtful historian of the Bay colony he loved, and devoted husband and father. Bailyn's Hutchinson illustrates what an American aristocracy might have become had the developments Bailyn traced in his previous writings not intervened. For Hutchinson was also the object of a malevolent jealousy he could never comprehend. His ability to make the British empire work for his own and his family's welfare blinded him to the resentment that his success engendered. His myopic views in turn left him ill prepared to meet the new political forces that swirled around him as the leading representative of imperial authority in his majesty's most turbulent province. Failing to understand those forces, Hutchinson made miscalculations that only exacerbated the problem. When royal authority in Massachusetts and America collapsed, Hutchinson was driven into exile to England, there to discover how much of an American he truly remained.

*The Ideological Origins of the American Revolution* may have been Bailyn's most important and influential book, but *The Ordeal of Thomas Hutchinson* is probably his best. Its psychological portrait of Hutchinson presents a man who is thoroughly admirable in every respect except the one that mattered most, given the context within which he was forced to act. Bailyn rescues Hutchinson from the obloquy of having cast his lot with the wrong side, and in a concluding chapter describing the bitter fruit of exile, he brings readers to understand the terrible pathos of Hutchinson's actions. Yet for all this, Hutchinson's limitations and failings finally outweigh his virtues. The American future could never have belonged to him. "Committed to small, prudential gains through an intricate, closely calculated world of status, deference, and degree," Hutchinson never understood the volatile mix of social resentments, meliorist impulses, and moral enthusiasms that could so naturally select him as a target. Failing to grasp these forces, he was destroyed.[21]

20. Bailyn, *Ideological Origins of the American Revolution* (Cambridge: Harvard University Press, 1967), 319.
21. For more sustained assessments of the key place of the Hutchinson biography in

The impact of these two seminal books, plus the lectures on colonial politics, was multiplied by the impressive number of monographs soon produced by Bailyn's students. In the short space of five years (1967–1972), no fewer than nine of his students published dissertations concerned with colonial and revolutionary politics. The most important of these books was Gordon Wood's *The Creation of the American Republic,* which in effect picked up chronologically where *Ideological Origins* had left off in 1776 and explored how the impulses of the Revolution had shaped the process of constitution making that accompanied independence.[22] But the list also includes noteworthy monographs on revolutionary politics in Massachusetts and New Hampshire by Richard D. Brown and Jere Daniell; Pauline R. Maier's study of prerevolutionary radical leaders; and Mary Beth Norton's account of the fate of the Loyalist exiles. Similar acclaim went to works by Stanley Katz, Michael G. Kammen, Thomas C. Barrow, and James A. Henretta on various aspects of Anglo-American politics before independence.[23]

As the appearance of these important books gave rise to the so-called republican paradigm that soon became so fashionable, Bailyn's own intellectual interests were moving in another direction. The late 1960s and early 1970s were in fact banner years of scholarship in both of the main

---

Bailyn's oeuvre, see Wood, "Creative Imagination," 42–47, and Rakove, "'How Else Could It End?'" 58–64.

22. *The Creation of the American Republic, 1776–1787* (Chapel Hill: University of North Carolina Press, 1969). Wood had already published an intriguing essay attempting to explain to early Americanists the significance of Bailyn's "Transforming Radicalism": "Rhetoric and Reality in the American Revolution," *William and Mary Quarterly,* 3d ser., 23 (1966): 3–32. Some years later, Wood quietly modified some of his concluding reflections on the sources of ideological politics in "Conspiracy and the Paranoid Style: Causality and Deceit in the Eighteenth Century," *William and Mary Quarterly,* 3d. ser., 39 (1982): 401–41.

23. Brown, *Revolutionary Politics in Massachusetts: The Boston Committee of Correspondence and the Towns* (Cambridge: Harvard University Press, 1970); Daniell, *Experiment in Independence: New Hampshire Politics and the American Revolution, 1741–1794* (Cambridge: Harvard University Press, 1970); Maier, *From Resistance to Revolution: Colonial Radicals and the Development of American Opposition to Britain, 1765–1776* (New York: Knopf, 1972); Norton, *The British Americans: The Loyalist Exiles in England, 1774–1789* (Boston: Little Brown, 1972); Katz, *Newcastle's New York: Anglo-American Politics, 1732–1753* (Cambridge: Harvard University Press, 1968); Kammen, *A Rope of Sand: The Colonial Agents, British Politics, and the American Revolution* (Ithaca: Cornell University Pres, 1968); Barrow, *Trade and Empire: The British Customs Service in Colonial America, 1660–1765* (Cambridge: Harvard University Press, 1967); Henretta, *"Salutary Neglect": Colonial Administration under the Duke of Newcastle* (Princeton: Princeton University Press, 1972).

subfields of early American history—imperial and revolutionary politics, and colonial society. For it was during this period that new approaches in family, demographic, and community history—"the new social history," as it was commonly called—transformed the study of early American society. Indeed, Bailyn's *Education* essay of 1960 had helped launch this new line of inquiry, and he had encouraged a different phalanx of his students—Richard D. Bushman, Philip J. Greven, Michael Zuckerman, Peter Wood, and Lois Green Carr—to undertake research in this area.[24] But as Bailyn returned to social history in the late 1970s, he fashioned a distinctive agenda of his own, one that built upon the substantial body of articles and monographs that seemed to grow with each passing year, but which also reflected his special concerns with problems of historical exposition, the identification of the right analytical problems, and the growing need to see the subject whole.

Bailyn used the occasion of his December 1981 presidential address to the American Historical Association, delivered in Los Angeles ("the land of the Pharaohs," as he once described it), to lay these concerns before his colleagues. Part of the address was devoted to the general crisis in historical knowledge generated by the flood of "technical" monographs that had become the stock-in-trade of social history. Bailyn feared that studies focusing on an analysis of quantifiable data constituted a threat to the historian's obligation to narrate a coherent story of change over time, in which real human beings were described as both fashioning and reacting to the anomalies of their historical experience. In Bailyn's view, "the challenge of modern historiography" was to discover narrative devices for conveying these findings in engaging and appealing forms.[25] Solving the narrative problem alone would not suffice; it was also necessary, Bailyn believed, to devise an overarching framework that would enable historians to gain interpretative control over the proliferating corpus of special-

24. Bushman, *From Puritan to Yankee; Character and Social Order in Connecticut, 1690–1765* (Cambridge: Harvard University Press, 1967); Greven, *Four Generations: Population, Land, and Family in Colonial Andover, Massachusetts* (Ithaca: Cornell University Press, 1970); Zuckerman, *Peaceable Kingdoms: New England Towns in the Eighteenth Century* (New York: Knopf, 1970); Wood, *Black Majority: Negroes in Colonial South Carolina from 1670 through the Stono Rebellion* (New York: Knopf, 1974); Carr and David W. Jordan, *Maryland's Revolution in Government, 1689–1692* (Ithaca: Cornell University Press, 1974). Carr also became an active member of the cluster of scholars working on the early settlement of the Chesapeake.

25. Bailyn, "The Challenge of Modern Historiography," *American Historical Review* 87 (1982): 1–24.

ized studies. Such a framework could be found, he proposed, in the concept of the colonization of the Americas as a process of "peopling" involving the massive transfer of population from the Old World—meaning Europe and Africa alike—to the new. Erecting this framework involved at least three main challenges: explaining why people either chose or were driven to emigrate; uncovering the linkages of Atlantic commerce and American land speculation that distributed this population across the landscape; and tracing the life histories of the migrants themselves, in order to capture the raw experience of colonization.

Bailyn was not merely preaching from on high, however; he was also hard at work on the principal research project to which he devoted himself after the Hutchinson biography.[26] In 1986, he published the first two installments of this research: *The Peopling of British North America,* an elegant set of lectures stating four hypotheses about the character of early emigration and its impact on colonial culture; and the much heftier *Voyagers to the West,* which earned Bailyn his second Pulitzer Prize for its painstakingly researched, vividly written account of a dramatic upsurge in emigration from Britain just prior to the Revolution.[27] The books share a common interest in describing a "dual migration" to America: one part consisting of luckless laborers caught up in the servant trade, the other of farming families with significant assets, rationally choosing to emigrate in response to the opportunities America promised and in reaction to encounters with the arbitrary structures of power and privilege dominating Georgian Britain.

The complicated narrative architecture of *Voyagers* provides the greatest insight into Bailyn's mature view of the historian's enterprise. *Voyagers* rests on Bailyn's discovery of the records of an inquiry conducted by the British ministry in response to its discovery of the scope of the emigration

26. The main exception to this was his decision to prepare a two-volume collection on the debates over the ratification of the Constitution, published as *The Debate on the Constitution* (New York: Library of America, 1992). In conjunction with this work, Bailyn also wrote an interpretive essay, "The Ideological Fulfillment of the American Revolution: A Commentary on the Constitution," which was first published in his volume of collected essays, *Faces of Revolution: Personalities and Themes in the Struggle for American Independence* (New York: Knopf, 1990), and then reprinted as an epilogue to an enlarged paperback edition of *Ideological Origins* (Cambridge: Harvard University Press, 1992).

27. *The Peopling of British North America: An Introduction* (New York: Knopf, 1986); *Voyagers to the West: A Passage in the Peopling of British North America on the Eve of the Revolution* (New York: Knopf, 1986).

to America. It begins, therefore, with evidence of a political response to a perceived social problem; but beneath that "manifest event" all kinds of latent forces were operating, too elusive for the government's lackeys to detect but not so elusive as to defy recapture by the historian. Bailyn explores the various mechanisms that conspired to transfer Britons across the Atlantic, from the fantastic visions of land speculators, imagining themselves lords of quasi-feudal baronies in the American woods; to the sources of colonial demand for brute labor; to the agents and entrepreneurs and ship captains who actually recruited emigrants from far-flung vales and ridings, hamlets and towns across Britain and managed, usually, to transport them to America; to the means by which these Britons were distributed from Atlantic ports among settlements that were sometimes well planned but more often bungled. In many ways, these details returned Bailyn to his original interest in the seventeenth-century merchants, for this is a story in which the sparks of entrepreneurial ambition—not to say a utopian madness—carry great interest. But in other, more subtle ways, Bailyn's concluding chapters, recounting the emigrants' search for a decent "competence," echo the concluding themes of *Ideological Origins.* For the ambitions driving these searchers—regardless of their immediate loyalties during the Revolution—are of a piece with the refusal "to truckle," to defer to authority merely because it claimed the privilege to rule, that Bailyn saw as the great enduring legacy of the Revolution.

Bailyn turned sixty-five the year after the first two volumes of the "Peopling" project appeared, and to other historians his continued productivity and activity in the years that followed were a source of amazement. Anyone conversing with him would quickly discover that Bailyn remained as captivated by the challenge of historical scholarship in his nominal retirement[28] in the 1990s as he was when he returned from Europe in 1946. In 1995, with the support of the Mellon Foundation, he launched the Atlantic History Seminar at Harvard, which he used to promote workshops and conferences, primarily for the benefit of younger scholars working on topics relating not only to North America but also to the history of Europe, Africa, the West Indies, and the mainland Iberian settlements. Noth-

---

28. Bailyn's birthday placed him a few months on the wrong side of the cutoff date when universities lost the legal right to impose mandatory retirement ages on their faculties.

ing better illustrates how much Bailyn's own expansive view of early American history has pushed this field beyond its once parochial boundaries than the variety of projects the Atlantic seminar has sought to encourage. More noteworthy still, nothing better illustrates the inherent interest and demonstrated importance of this field of American history since 1945 than the acclaimed contributions of "Bud" Bailyn.

# Merle Curti

## by Paul K. Conkin

**M**erle Eugene Curti was one of the most distinguished historians of the twentieth century. He lived for most of that century, dying at the age of nearly one hundred in 1997. He was the most influential pioneer in, if not the founder of, what are now three distinct fields of historical scholarship—intellectual, cultural, and social. He received almost all the honors available in his discipline. In three consecutive years (1952–1954) he served as president of the Mississippi Valley Historical Association, the American Historical Association, and the American Studies Association. He held chairs at Smith College, Teachers College of Columbia University, and the University of Wisconsin. In 1943, he won the Pulitzer Prize. He received numerous research grants, including a Guggenheim Fellowship when he was only thirty-two years old. He also spent two years abroad, teaching first in India and then in Japan. He was honored by membership in the American Academy of Arts and Science and the American Philosophical Society.

Above all, Curti became one of America's most prolific historians. For over half a century he worked at his task as a teacher and scholar, writing books and articles in many historical fields. He was interested in all aspects of the human past. He exemplified a single-minded commitment to the hard work and sometimes drudgery involved in telling the story of that past. Other historians surpassed Curti in eloquence, in striking insights, in controversial interpretations, in intensive analysis, and of course in the mastery of highly specialized topics, but no one contributed as much of high quality in as many areas of historical knowledge. He had an insatiable curiosity and thus the pioneer's zest for moving on, for scholarly homesteading on completely new territory. He was amazingly industrious. His eye was ever on the rail, his hand on the throttle, at work day after day, year after year, with the help of a hundred archives, the endless, appreciative scanning of thousands of books and articles, the evaluation of millions of documents, and, in snatches of precious time, the writing of more than six thousand pages of text.

Curti lived a long time. In his youth he listened to speeches by Theodore Roosevelt, Woodrow Wilson, and Eugene Debs; studied with Albert Bushnell Hart and Frederick Jackson Turner; conversed with Willa Cather; took tea at Concord with the two daughters of Ralph Waldo Emerson; and attended the Wild West show of Buffalo Bill Cody. As a lad he made use of local livery stables before he ever saw an automobile.

Born in 1897 in Papillion, Nebraska, just south and west of Omaha, young Merle was from Nebraska but not quite of it. Memories of Nebraska helped shape the adult. He was also shaped by a serious, dutiful father, who was not a failure but not as successful as his own father, a Swiss immigrant and physician. Merle's mother was counterpoint—warm, personable, socially adept, and from distant Vermont. Curti would never forget the delightful summers he spent with her and her family near Burlington—green mountains, peaceful meadows, a shimmering Lake Champlain, and the acceptance and support of relatives. Thus, Curti had an ambivalent heritage—Sodbuster and Yankee, Populist and Puritan. He never repudiated either. He had an enduring affection for the expansive great plains, for the immigrants and their struggle, for beleaguered farmers, for communal solidarity. One finds echoes of his favorite novelist—*My Antonia; O Pioneers!* But spiritually he was not quite at home in Nebraska, even as he would never be quite at home in Wisconsin. He chose Harvard, not exactly to escape Nebraska, but to get a better education, to become part of a more genteel culture. Later, he would escape the pressures of Wisconsin by spending summers on his beloved farm at Lyme Center, New Hampshire, and in his study at Dartmouth's library. In a sense, he went back to his roots.

Curti's high school years in Omaha were a period of self-discovery. His academic and social skills blossomed. Excellent history teachers provided food for his natural curiosity. Immune to boredom, he loved the excitement of discovery. He dared apply for, and won, a scholarship to Harvard. Harvard wanted provincials. And, for the first time, he was challenged to his intellectual limits. His response—a lifelong one—was to work as hard as he could, to gain good grades, to become a success. The Curti ego was already visible, as were his unrelenting demands upon himself, his almost impossible standards. He also needed people, wanted to please, to have friends. The drive, the effort, solidified into habits. For Curti, no achieve-ment was ever quite enough; no prizes, no recognition, ever stilled the intense drive. He never developed a tough skin, never became cynical. Criticism continued to hurt. He took it so seriously. Everyone's opinion counted. And he kept at his task, job after job, book after book, with all the ego-bruising hazards—hostile readers, inept copy editors, unfair re-viewers. Thus the agony, the pain, and the rare appreciation. And no rest.

At Harvard, Curti first encountered the history profession. This must have been disillusioning—like that first history convention attended by an idealistic graduate student. Harvard had more than its share of the hundred or so well-known, respected, publishing scholars who made up the profession in the World War I era. Yet even at Harvard some were fakes, with poor teaching skills and inflated egos. In fact, the profession before World War I was elitist, an exclusive club of gentlemen, all white, nearly all Anglo-Saxon. Curti absorbed some of the gentility but hated the ex-clusiveness. For him—a Nebraska lad among the Brahmans—only one of the professors, Frederick Jackson Turner, from Wisconsin, seemed like home folk—simple, direct, courteous, shy, and with a career-long inter-est in the West that Curti knew firsthand.

Curti was never tempted to be a western historian. He was interested in all fields but wanted to be a pioneer rather than write about them. His interests were broadly cultural, and thus he was later, as a graduate stu-dent, able to talk Turner into an early dissertation topic on American cul-tural nationalism in the nineteenth century, virtually a thesis on Ameri-can self-consciousness. It was as audacious a proposal as Lord Acton's ever uncompleted history of liberty, but Turner let him proceed. Curti, unlike Acton, never let audacious topics intimidate him. He finished them all, from a first, unpublished draft on national self-consciousness, which informed his later *Roots of American Loyalty,* to his final book on human nature.

World War I intruded into Curti's undergraduate years at Harvard. He had no enthusiasm for the great crusade and was pacifist in inclinations, although not to the point of conscientious objection. He joined the Stu-dent Army Training Corps and proved appropriately inept in the silly drill that was supposed to make one a soldier. He took his B.A. in 1920, stayed on for a 1921 M.A., and then to earn money accepted a one-year appoint-ment at Beloit College—a year he later made famous among colleagues by telling his stories of overwork, exploitation, unjustified elitism, and sexism. He saved money and escaped back to Ph.D. work at Harvard, with another year of teaching at Simmons College to pay bills. Newly married, he enjoyed a near idyllic research year in Europe, and only in Paris found a professor with a consuming interest in American literature. Turner had by now retired (Curti later wrote an essay on Turner and knew him better in retirement than as a mentor). Arthur M. Schlesinger became his new adviser. After rejecting Curti's cosmic topic, Schlesinger approved a small subject almost lost within it (the American Peace Movement), and at a distance he approved Curti's dissertation work but did not really supervise it. For, in 1925, Curti took a position at Smith College, two years before receiving his Ph.D. in 1927, at age thirty.

In many ways, the six years at Smith were golden ones for Curti. He liked the college and the all-female student body and proved an innovative teacher. He was a happy family man, soon with two daughters. He had time for research and writing, publishing his dissertation (*The American Peace Crusade, 1815–1860*) and two monographs (one on William Jennings Bryan and world peace and another on Austria and the United States), even as he rose quickly to the rank of full professor. He rejoiced in his teaching, in 1925 developed the first course taught anywhere on the history of American thought, and joined in interdisciplinary seminars that would later be called American studies. In brief, he quickly established himself as one of the ablest young historians in the country and an expert on the peace movement. He won a Guggenheim. In his developing philosophical outlook, he moved close to the position of John Dewey, the one person whose beliefs most critically influenced Curti and, of some note, a lad from Burlington, Vermont. Also like Dewey, Curti slowly and without great trauma moved beyond the Christianity of his youth, leaving the Episcopal Church but retaining a taste for the beauty of its music and liturgy, which joined his lifelong affection for serious music and most of the fine arts.

Dewey, admired from a distance, became a colleague in 1931, when Curti took a position in both the Teachers College and the Graduate School of Columbia University. He soon reacted, in anger and despair, to the ravages of the Great Depression. At Columbia he completed a study for the American Historical Association, published as *The Social Ideals of American Educators* (1935), even as he began work on his magnum opus, *The Growth of American Thought*. Few who read Curti's later books would guess the reform zeal, the anger, the class analysis that informed his books written at Smith and at Columbia. His anger came through in his book on educators—at times a heavy-handed indictment of the captivity of American educators to wealth and privilege—and in a survey of the peace movement—*Peace or War* (1936)—in which he castigated pacifists for their failure to appreciate the major economic changes—the repudiation of competitive capitalism and imperial greed—that would be necessary for peace. Curti left Columbia in 1942. He was tired of multiple tasks, taught too many graduate students (among these were Richard Hofstadter and Lawrence Cremin), and attended too many meetings. Such overwork, and a growing alienation from professional education, helped persuade him to accept an offer from the University of Wisconsin (later Columbia tried to woo him back).

Wisconsin: opportunity indeed. But a gentle lamb moved into a den of wolves. The Wisconsin Department of History did not have anyone with the scholarly talents of Curti. He replaced John Hicks, who went to Berkeley, and thus had to cover the whole second half of American history. Curtis Nettels, soon to leave, did the first half, and William Hesseltine covered the South and sectionalism.

It was a department full of strong characters—a showman in Hesseltine, at times a near tyrant in chairman Paul Knaplund. Soon they were joined by a neurotic Howard Beale. At its worst, the department was racist, sexist, and anti-Semitic. Even at its best, it was intensely political, full of aggressive types, self-promoters, and empire builders. Factionalism and petty conflict were endemic. Curti, slender, formally dressed, mild speaking, and courteous to a fault, never matched the departmental culture. He was too busy, too refined, too modest. But he quickly put his colleagues to shame, including even such new and able additions as James Harvey Harrington and Merrill Jensen. He worked harder, wrote more, won more awards and prizes, turned down more appealing outside offers, and enjoyed more national eminence than anyone else in the department.

Both Knaplund and the university appreciated Curti, rewarded him, and thus kept him. They gave him one of the department's first two endowed chairs, the well-named Frederick Jackson Turner professorship, to keep him from moving to Berkeley. The department also reduced his teaching load, gave him needed research support, stepped in to administer his several major grants, even as Curti magnified, exploited, and used as a protective tool his alleged practical ineptitude. But no one could protect him from himself, from his generosity, his egalitarian ideals, and his ego. He admitted almost anyone who applied to his graduate seminar, could not bring himself to fail anyone, and gave too much of his time to ill-prepared students, even as he rejoiced in the achievements of such able graduate students as John Higham and David Nobel. During his career, Curti directed more than eighty dissertations and was second reader on scores of others. He had to flee back to New Hampshire, or escape on sabbaticals, to keep at his own writing. And write he did, completing a book every two or three years in what has to be one of the most productive eras in American historical scholarship—Curti's next twenty years at Wisconsin, 1942–1962. During those twenty years he completed at least eight scholarly books, coauthored both a college and a high school text, and wrote dozens of articles or chapters in books.

Curti's two decades of exemplary scholarship began with the wartime publication in 1943 of *Growth,* the Pulitzer Prize–winning book that he twice revised. He completed his early work on nationalism in *The Roots of American Loyalty* (1946). He joined a colleague, Vernon R. Carstensen, in writing the first volume of the history of the University of Wisconsin (1949). In 1959 he directed a collaborative study of Trempealeau County in western Wisconsin (*The Making of an American Community: A Case Study of Democracy in a Frontier County*)—a pioneer work that was heralded as a new approach to new social history.

Now in his sixties, Curti published another monumental book, *American Philanthropy Abroad* (1963) and with Roderick Nash coauthored a more modest book on philanthropy and American higher education. Beginning in 1956 he had published his lectures on the American paradox (the conflict between thought and action), which he followed with the 1968 publication of his lectures on human nature in American historical thought. Curti's energy seemed inexhaustible.

Curti's role in the Wisconsin history department correlated closely with his goals as a historian. In the department he remained aloof, detached from most factional and personal conflict. With the exception of Howard Beale, Curti was able to be a friend of, and to befriend, every colleague. He found much to admire in people on all sides of controverted issues. But in his quiet way he tried to improve the department and, by implication, condemned many attitudes and practices within it. He thought it too parochial. Because of his broad interests, and influenced by his foreign teaching and lecture tours, he helped gain support for a spectrum of new courses and new fields, particularly on the Third World. From the beginning, he nourished interdisciplinary programs and created an American studies option in the history department.

Above all, Curti advocated pluralism and equality. He welcomed Jewish colleagues, led a campaign to open University Club rooms to black graduate students, and long encouraged the appointment of at least one woman in an insufferably male bastion. As president of the Mississippi Valley Historical Association in 1952, he forced its council to cancel a planned meeting in New Orleans, and move the convention to Chicago, when the contracted hotel refused to host black members. For this he suffered the ire of an insensitive minority on the council, even as his colleague Howard Beale cruelly castigated him because he had not publicized this incident and made himself a martyr to civil rights.

In all his duties, Curti tried to live up to an ideal that he shared with John Dewey, an ideal that provides the clearest theme in his historical writing. Both Dewey and Curti usually labeled this ideal "democracy." This was a rich word even as far back as the twenties and at the time Curti used it not yet completely vulgarized by overuse; into the thirties, many of the most prophetic Americans still vested their highest aspirations in the word, in the same way that a few Americans, and many Europeans, vested the same ideals, the same soaring hopes, in such words as *socialism* and *communism.*

In the writings of John Dewey, *democracy* was a prophetic term. It stood for the ever unfulfilled promise of America, a promise that could never be fully specified, for ideals grow as people change. Thus the word *democracy* primarily denoted a process, a means for people to solve collective problems, and certain institutional prerequisites for such a process. Its use required a repudiation of competitive individualism, acceptance of a type of cooperation and of social responsibility, and confidence in problem-solving methods already raised to the level of an art in the sciences. It is no accident that the word *social* was most prominent in Curti's historical vocabulary.

Democracy, in such a rich and broad Deweyan sense, requires for everyone an opportunity for fulfilling participation in collective life, not only in political choice but also in education and above all in economic management. The concrete realities of life must, above all else, fulfill the ideal of equal worth, even for those with limited abilities. From the elementary school curriculum on up, people should have a real, effective, informed voice in the decisions that most affect their lives. By this type of social involvement, by participation in the choice of both means and ends, more and more areas of life can partake of artistry and yield a type of beauty.

Always the optimist, Curti reflected this outlook. It excludes no one, particularly not because of ethnic, racial, gender, occupational, or ability differences. The very process of collective decision making should lead even diverse people toward functional communities, of the type at least prefigured by Vermont towns, by Papillion, or by the frontier settlements that Curti studied in Trempealeau County. Such functional communities should, at least in part, help bridge the tension if not the conflict between pluralistic accommodation, liberty, and tolerance on one hand, and equality and communal solidarity on the other.

Curti's historical writing is so diverse that, on first glance, it seems to lack any common themes. Not so. From first to last he tried to understand, and evaluate, the cultural achievements of Americans—all of them, through all their history. The canvas is thus vast, the broad contours alone clear, the technical distinctions often lost in the shadows. As so many American historians became in the fifties, Curti all along had been intensely identity oriented. Who are we as Americans? What have we so far achieved as a distinctive culture or civilization? What is unique about us? How much have we failed to realize our potential, or to attain our stated ideals? Assumed, in the background, are our unchallengeable economical and technical achievements, even our more stable political institutions. Other historians had dealt with those topics. Curti rarely wrote about, or was even very sympathetic with, the practical movers and shakers, the entrepreneurs, managers, and bosses. Instead, Curti focused on our cultural arbiters, those who have had the skills, the influence, or the opportunities to make American civilization what it is—the educators, philanthropists, reformers, critics, journalists, and novelists. Or, in brief, those who have contributed to that vague entity "American thought," to the shaping of attitudes, beliefs, and values, particularly those shared widely if not nationally, those that have been part of our group life, and thus what Curti called social thought. In his book on Trempealeau County, with its pioneering use of massed data and sophisticated statistical tests, the chapter that most showed Curti in his element was the one on the "social creed," in which he in a microcosm followed the pattern and method of almost all his books—a wide sampling, and selective quoting and paraphrasing, of literate opinion, of journalists, correspondents, teachers, and ministers.

Although his preferred subject was usually what might be called our cultural elite, Curti remained a democrat, in the broad Deweyan sense. He stressed the proper marriage of intellect and action. He repudiated not only the insufferably practical person, the brash American who denied the role of careful thought, but also cultural snobs, who wanted to monopolize art and artistry rather than help all people appreciate artistic excellence. In his books written in the thirties he often reflected an angry, near Marxist class partisanship. It all seemed simpler then—the democratic ideal clearer and more compelling, the enemies more easily identified. With Dewey, he then tried to identify the guardians of the old, authoritarian past, those who jealously held on to privilege and power, whether capitalists or clergymen. Later, it did not seem so clear. The harsh realities of our recent past qualified, and made more realistic and ironic, his goals, but to Curti this did not justify cynicism. Even in his last book—on human nature—Curti still gently chastised those who ignored inequities, resisted needed changes, or wallowed in pessimism because of lingering conceptions of human depravity or original sin. Even conceptions of human nature had been political weapons. To the end, Curti retained his belief in human plasticity, in ever new possibilities. He thus remained an optimist.

Curti's books are distinguished not only by their scope but also by the enormous amount of research they required. He had to become a connoisseur of libraries and manuscript collections, of books, articles, newspapers, and private papers. Several of his books have the scope of texts or even encyclopedias, most of all his *Growth* and his *American Philanthropy Abroad.* Because both broke new ground, he had to do most of the primary research. His research strategy became almost a habit—to scan and sample as much opinion as possible, and then to draw his story from it, as a pioneer who had to survey the terrain for the first time. Obviously, he could not get all the contours right. Some of the details turned out wrong, but not many. He could not avoid oversimplification, but I am constantly amazed at how close he was to what later, more detailed investigations would disclose. In a sense, he completed the geologic survey, and left the rest for all the graduate student homesteaders, who have now drawn the boundaries of almost every quarter section. Out of his surveys would come hundreds of dissertations.

Almost all historians aspire to less than Curti, and almost all have done less. Most published historians, even those with high rank and title, have published only one or two major, pioneering books. All the rest has been coasting—anthologies, collected articles, textbooks, interpretive essays. Others have detoured away from scholarship into administration, committee work, editorial work, or professional involvements. The path to wealth and power and even prestige lies outside serious scholarship. And even those who have kept at it, who have kept launching new, time-consuming research efforts, have almost always stayed in the same specialized field, on familiar turf, with familiar sources and methods. Curti rejected all these easier or more tempting strategies. Of course, most of us do not have the synoptic talents or the energy of a Curti.

But how many today even aspire to so much? Who is willing to do all the work? Who has the courage? What is the cost of such virtuosity, of daring to be a generalist, a word that long had a pejorative meaning at Wisconsin? Curti's choices meant that he could not become an authority on any narrowly specialized topic. His broadest surveys had a certain elusive generality for those who wanted a close-up, fully nuanced view. For uncongenial subjects—evangelical religion, the South, the mentality of businessmen, technical topics in science and philosophy—Curti almost always had to skate on the surface of received opinion, and thus in these areas his work has worn least well. His synoptic view warred against any monolithic theme or interpretation, particularly an ambiguous or outrageous one of the sort that often does more to insure professional immortality than a mass of completed and rigorous scholarship. Look at Turner. All historians face the pitfalls of changing fashions. Sooner or later we will all be dismissed, not for a lack of brilliance in answering questions, but for asking the wrong ones. Curti's absorbing interest in a national culture, in American identity, best fit the fashions of the fifties, which was his most productive decade, and not so much the fads since then. His moral orientation, his sense of American possibilities and thus unfulfilled promise, has not fared well since the sixties, with the gradual loss of almost all moral passion. He was both too optimistic and too demanding.

In retrospect, most historians list Curti among a somewhat vague group called the "progressive" historians. What best exemplified the usual definition of "progressive" was the class bite in his early books, his commitment to reform, his investment in a more complete democracy, and his moral passion. Yet, Curti once told me he did not like this label, possibly because it placed him in too narrow a cubbyhole. It did.

His most enduring influence was on a new and rather amorphous field which, at the end of World War II, gained the label of social, cultural, and intellectual history. His *Growth of American Thought* would have enormous influence on this developing field. Dozens of young professors, as they tried to develop brand-new courses in this area, used Curti's book as a model or as a text. I was one of those young professors. But soon some of the younger scholars branched out in new directions, and Curti sometimes felt inadequate, left behind, and was often apologetic about his own work. He made clear what he wanted to achieve in *Growth*. It was to be a social history of thought, not a history of ideas. He wanted to understand the cultural context that supported even the most technical thinking, to assess the cultural institutions, such as education, that made even the most rigorous inquiry possible, and above all to understand the consequences of such thinking upon the larger society. He did this well, but later he sometimes apologized for not doing enough with myths and symbols, or not penetrating deeply enough into what he called the interior of thought. He tried to make gestures in this direction in his later editions and rejoiced in finding much there already; but fortunately he did not change the basic orientation of his book. Curti did not have the type of mind, the specialized skills, and possibly the interest to do interior analysis. He could not unravel all the philosophical intricacies of his hero, John Dewey, and was much more revealing in his evaluation of the influence of Darwin than in his explication of Darwin's beliefs.

In such a scholarly accounting, so many of the subtle contributions of Curti are missed. It so easily conceals the vital and generous person who wrote all these books. His greatest legacy will remain in the people he directly touched—the recipients of his kindness and generosity. This includes all the struggling graduate students who remember the kind word, the appreciation for their less-than-perfect papers, the continuing interest, the paternal pride in all their later achievements. It includes the courtesy he extended to almost anyone in the profession, such as the young scholar, dismayed by some of the inevitably hostile reviews to her first book, who received an unexpected note—the brief but telling compliment—from an eminent historian she had never met. Hundreds of young scholars had similar experiences. All of this meant that, at times, Curti was too soft. He had difficulty unleashing his critical skills. He never wrote an unkind letter of recommendation.

Curti retired at Wisconsin in 1968. He continued his scholarship. He published his last book in 1980, at the age of eighty-three. For years, he made almost daily trips to the Wisconsin Historical Society Library or to his office in the new history department quarters in the Humanities Building. But in many ways his life was sad. His first wife died. He had a happy second marriage, but he had to give up his home and move into a retirement apartment in downtown Madison. It was an attractive apartment, but Curti at times felt like he was in jail. When his second wife died, he was all alone. Almost all his former friends and colleagues, the boys of his youth, were now gone. I last talked to Curti, by telephone, about a year before his death. He reported, with great sadness, that he had just returned from the funeral of one of his two daughters. Such is one of the costs of living so long.

Curti was intellectually active throughout his long retirement. He continued to read what seemed almost every book published in American history, corresponded widely, attended the First Unitarian Society and as many cultural and musical events as he could, and became what he had so often written about—a philanthropist. Through much of his career, academic salaries were low. In his busiest years, in World War II and just afterward, full professors at Wisconsin, or anywhere else, rarely made more than five thousand dollars a year. His scholarly books never brought him many royalties, not even *Growth*. But he had an unending flow of royalties from a high school textbook, one that continued to gain wide adoptions long after Curti had any real impact on its numerous revisions. He was generous to his church, to the Department of History at Wisconsin (underwriting the annual Curti lectures), and to the broader profession (providing for the Merle Curti awards in social and intellectual history offered by the Organization of American Historians). These gifts are only a final example of his enduring legacy.

# David Herbert Donald

## by Robert Allen Rutland

When looking for adventure in postwar Europe during the 1950s, most Fulbright professors sought out museums, theatrical districts, or national landmarks. But when David Herbert Donald, a bespectacled, slightly built scholar, took time off from his duties at the University of North Wales in 1953–1954, he preferred whizzing about the Welsh countryside, Cornwall, and Devonshire on a noisy used motorcycle. His second book was out, he was a footloose bachelor, and the narrow roads were an irresistible challenge.

With the motorcycle venture out of his system, Donald moved comfortably into American academic life for the next four decades, before finally slowing down a bit after his seventy-fourth birthday and the publication of his biography, *Lincoln*, in 1995. By then Donald had taught at Smith, Princeton, Oxford, Johns Hopkins, Columbia, and Harvard; had trained dozens of graduate students; and among many honors had twice won the Pulitzer Prize in Biography.

From his first days as a student at Millsaps College, Donald seemed to have definite ideas about where his future lay. Born on October 1, 1920, on what was once called a plantation in the environs of Goodman, Mississippi, Donald earned his bachelor's degree in the spring of 1941. He read obsessively, admired Thomas Wolfe as a companion soul, and has told friends that he burned the midnight oil repeatedly as he pored over the works of Reinhold Niebuhr to reaffirm his deep roots in Christianity. Some of his college friends headed for the ministry, but Donald looked in another direction. History appealed to him, and the next logical step was graduate training that would prepare him for a career in college teaching.

After a brief stint as a graduate student at the University of Illinois, he transferred to the University of North Carolina, but he was soon back at Illinois, where he became a teaching assistant and graduate student working with the noted Lincoln scholar James G. Randall. Their professor-student relationship was based on Donald's respect for Randall and Randall's recognition of the young Mississippian's talents. With Randall's encouragement, Donald was a confident graduate student when he submitted an article, "The Scalawags in Mississippi Reconstruction in Mississippi," which was accepted by the editors of the *Journal of Southern History* in 1944.[1]

After graduating from Illinois with his Ph.D. in 1945, Donald stayed at the university as a research associate in the history department, polished his dissertation (on Lincoln's law partner, William Herndon), and waited for the right opportunity. In 1947 he was offered an instructor's post at Columbia University. Randall's strong endorsement of Donald carried considerable weight at Columbia, and for two years Donald's time was spent preparing lectures, polishing his manuscript, and fitting into the routine of an Ivy League history department.

The publication of Donald's revised dissertation in 1948, when the author was twenty-eight, had a major impact in professional circles. *Lincoln's Herndon* was a deftly researched, heavily annotated, and skillfully written biography of the junior partner in Lincoln's law firm. Herndon, little known except among Lincoln scholars, was the senior partner's trusted aide until Lincoln became president and, ultimately, was Lincoln's biographer. In his introduction, Carl Sandburg, the poet and Lincoln biographer, hailed Donald's book as the answer to scholars' prayers: "When is someone going to do the life of Bill Herndon. Isn't it about time? Now the question is out."

Herndon's multivolumed life of Lincoln, which Donald believes to be "the most controversial Lincoln biography ever written," had been praised and damned since its first appearance in 1889. Encouraged by Randall, Donald determined to write a biography of Herndon that would enlighten readers, expose the flaws of Herndon's memory, and show that Herndon wrote readable prose but was given to "obscure pronouncements and cryptic remarks." As Donald studied Herndon he perceived the man's many character flaws and rendered a mature judgment. "The tragedy was that Herndon himself was fundamentally decent," Donald noted as he saw in one man the weaknesses of mankind writ large. He concluded that

---

1. *Journal of Southern History* 10 (1944): 447–60.

Herndon helped create the legendary Lincoln he decried and "stands, in the backward glance of history, [as] myth-maker and truth-teller."[2]

Lincoln scholars hailed Donald's book as a historical breakthrough. Reviewer Otto Eisenschiml noted in the *American Historical Review* that Donald "has followed every lead which may point to the truth" and went on to say Donald had shown that Herndon "was as full of ideals as he was of failings." The reviewer noted several "grammatical aberrations," but said these were insignificant "when compared to the generally magnificent style with which the author has presented his absorbing and important theme."[3]

Other laudatory reviews brought Donald to the attention of the history department at Smith, and within a year he was an associate professor on the Northampton campus. His stay at Smith was short, however, for in 1952 Donald went back to Columbia as a tenured member of the history faculty, joining fellow Mississippian Dumas Malone and other distinguished colleagues—Richard Hofstadter, Allan Nevins, Henry Steele Commager, and Richard B. Morris. With a laugh, Malone recalled that he welcomed Donald because the department was then dominated by colleagues from north of the Mason-Dixon line. "But David never had a southern accent as bad as mine," Malone jested.

Never idle, Donald looked at hundreds of Civil War photographs and composed a lengthy essay to accompany the best work of Matthew Brady and other lensemen who had chronicled the bitter aftermath of bloody battles. When published in 1952, *Divided We Fought: A Pictorial History of the War, 1861–1865* struck reviewers as a well-documented blend of text and pictures portraying the awful tragedies of war. In that same year, a poll of historians on "recently published American history and biography" showed that Donald's book on Herndon had received many votes from his peers as one of the outstanding biographies published between 1920 and 1950.[4]

Donald was the logical choice when the *American Historical Review* book editor sought a reviewer for *The Collected Works of Abraham Lincoln,* edited by Roy Basler, published in 1952. The nine-volume work had long

2. *Lincoln's Herndon* (New York: Alfred Knopf, 1948), 373.
3. *American Historical Review* 54 (1948–1949): 623–24.
4. John W. Caughey, "Historians' Choice: Results of a Poll on Recently Published History and Biography," *Mississippi Valley Historical Review* 39 (1952): 301–2.

been anticipated by the scholarly world, and Donald's assessment of the volumes was bound to reverberate with the huge academic community that had awaited the Basler edition as the "definitive collection" of Lincoln's writings.

Donald's assessment of the collection, published in October 1953, was a model for others who would be reviewing the increasing flow of printed editions of presidential papers. Donald praised the work for meeting "the highest expectations of Civil War scholars." But there were flaws. For example, in dealing with the provenance for the Gettysburg Address manuscript, the editor had failed to note that the document was in the Library of Congress. For the document labeled "Memorandum on Fort Sumter" Donald was skeptical of the attribution to Lincoln. He noted that "the document itself is not located among the Lincoln Papers but instead is in the Gideon Welles manuscripts."

Drawing on his own vast research in the Lincoln Papers, Donald also noted that a letter purportedly written by Lincoln to Gen. James S. Wadsworth in 1864 "if authentic . . . would require a complete reconsideration of Lincoln's reconstruction policy." But, Donald added, the provenance of the Wadsworth letter was "distressingly dubious," and he was led to conclude: "Unauthenticated in origin and un-Lincoln in phrasing and in ideas, the Wadsworth letter cannot be accepted as genuine." Donald went on, however, with soothing words for the edition's overall accuracy. "The degree of textual accuracy is simply incredible," he wrote.

There was still a warning signal Donald seemed obliged to post. The annotations accompanying the Lincoln documents, Donald suggested, constituted "the least satisfactory part" of the volumes because the footnotes regrettably contained "a great many errors, each inconsequential in itself but cumulatively a good deal of importance." Finally, Donald noted that the editorial headnotes were "often partial or incomplete." He cited the note on "The Proclamation Concerning Reconstruction" as giving "careful explanations of everything but the one essential thing—that this was a pocket-veto of the Wade-Davis bill." Donald applied some balm as he concluded: "Congratulations are due all around."[5] The scholarly world knew better; Donald's courtly manners had kept him from being more direct.

Then came the offer of a Fulbright professorship at the University of North Wales in 1953–1954, when the urge to see more of Great Britain led

---

5. *American Historical Review* 59 (1953): 142–49.

to the motorcycle purchase. Donald returned to Columbia in the fall of 1954 and before long began corresponding with Aida DiPace, whom he had met as a winsome Columbia graduate student and who was now pursuing a doctoral degree at the University of Rochester. A year later, Donald and Aida were married.

In the interim, Donald's typewriter was not quiet. Intrigued by the chronicles kept by Secretary of the Treasury Salmon P. Chase, who served in Lincoln's cabinet, Donald had transcribed the records and in 1954 published *Inside Lincoln's Cabinet: The Civil War Diaries of Salmon P. Chase.* Judiciously edited, with helpful but not smothering annotations, the work reaffirmed Donald's reputation as a leading scholar of the Lincoln administration. Reviewer Charles R. Wilson observed that the Chase diaries were a challenge that only "a competent scholar" could handle. "David Donald has obliged," Wilson adjudged as he noted the editor's swipe at Chase's reputation. Chase had served in all three branches of the federal government, and his "public services . . . were unquestionably important," Donald wrote, "but whether they were admirable is a matter upon which neither contemporaries nor later historians have agreed."[6]

Summers offered no respite from research for Donald. If he was not probing files in the Manuscripts Division of the Library of Congress, he was off to the Huntington Library in Pasadena or making notes at the New York Public Library. Nine of his essays were published in 1956 as *Lincoln Reconsidered: Essays on the Civil War Era.* In 1959 he contributed to another Civil War collection of essays (edited by Norman Graebner) with a penetrating portrait of Abraham Lincoln. A decade after his Herndon book was published, Donald ranked in the forefront of Civil War scholarship.

Graduate students who studied at Columbia during those years found Donald a firm but friendly seminar director. One of his students, Ari Hoogenboom, remembered Donald for his careful attention to students' papers, which were returned with a plethora of comments scribbled in the margins. Donald analyzed the papers, stressed the need for writing skills, and taught the value of topic sentences. A growing number of doctoral candidates began affectionately to call him "D.D." and found his office door usually open for stimulating conversation.[7] When students ap-

6. *American Historical Review* 60 (1954): 130–31.

7. Ari Hoogenboom, "David Herbert Donald: A Celebration," in *A Master's Due: Essays in Honor of David Herbert Donald,* ed. William J. Cooper, Jr., et al. (Baton Rouge: Louisiana State University Press, 1985), 1–15.

proached their qualifying examinations with great trepidation, Donald would coach them on the kinds of questions they might encounter. Appropriately, these sessions often turned into great learning experiences.

At Columbia and his other academic posts, Donald did not neglect his students with the excuse that his writing or research might suffer. A formidable group of his graduate students (including Jean H. Baker, William J. Cooper, Jr., Michael Holt, and Hoogenboom) remember having their seminar papers and dissertations returned with copious marginal notes. Many recall Donald as a fair but driving taskmaster. His undergraduate lectures on the Civil War and Reconstruction were crowded, and a teaching assistant recalled their content as "stunning." And there were moments of genuine vicarious satisfaction, such as the 1965 announcement that his graduate student at Columbia, Irwin Unger, had won the Pulitzer Prize in history for his book, *The Greenback Era.*

Always, it seemed, there was a book in the works. Donald edited a collection of essays on Civil War themes that finally took shape in 1960. Published by Louisiana State University Press, the book included Donald's article on the flaws of the Confederacy, "Died of Democracy," and bore the provocative title *Why the North Won the Civil War.*

As the productive decade was about to end, Donald was beckoned to move. After the birth of a son in 1958, Donald was lured to Princeton with the offer of a professorship. He took up his duties at Princeton in the fall of 1959 and soon learned that there was more formality there than at Columbia—for example, the mailboxes in the history department were arranged by seniority, rather than alphabetically. But part of the arrangement was that Donald could go to Oxford for the 1959–1960 term as the Harmsworth Professor of American History. In England, Donald found his duties at Queen's College light, with an occasional lecture (some twenty-eight during the year, usually on slavery and secession), pleasant meals at the High Table, and enjoyable camaraderie with British colleagues.

Before departing for England, Donald had been asked to review Stanley Elkins's *Slavery: A Problem in American Institutional and Intellectual Life.* This was no easy assignment. Book reviews for scholarly journals take precious time away from research, but the Elkins book provoked considerable praise and some consternation, and Donald felt a professional obligation to undertake the assignment. In the July 1960 edition of the *American Historical Review,* Donald lauded Elkins for his "high seriousness of purpose [and] his praiseworthy willingness to tackle large historical problems." *Slavery,* however, he noted, "is marred by faulty logic, an infelicitous style," and digressions on irrelevant topics (ranging from Edmund Burke's views on the American Revolution to Harry Stack Sullivan's opinions on "the significant other").

There was also a major flaw, Donald said, in Elkins's comparison of southern slaves (the stereotyped "Sambo") who accepted a servile status to listless prisoners in German concentration camps during World War II. The analogy was based on "poor taste" and "worse logic," Donald wrote as he concluded that the book was lacking in basic research. "The final judgment," Donald noted, "must be negative" as he agreed with the author's statement that the book "does not pretend to be a history."[8]

Reviewing books was not Donald's favorite pastime, but he considered such chores part of a professional historian's duty. At Oxford, he managed to review several important books and still have time to work on his next project, a study of the forbidding abolitionist senator Charles Sumner. Donald moved with dispatch into a field where other scholars had trod lightly, for Sumner was remembered as a radical abolitionist who had been whipped on the Senate floor, nearly killed, and then recovered his health but not his power.

The publication of *Charles Sumner and the Coming of the Civil War* in 1960 was greeted with enthusiasm by scholars who found Sumner's Senate career a gigantic enigma. Historian David M. Potter of Yale reviewed the work and hailed Donald's skill in treating Sumner without prejudice. Sumner's "arrogant self-righteousness . . . made him one of the best-hated men in American history," Potter noted, and "no figure would lend himself less readily to biographical impartiality." Yet Donald had demonstrated "a remarkable talent for discerning and disclosing what lies behind the distortions of human personality." Potter, whose own credentials as a Lincoln scholar gave his words authority, said Donald's book portrayed "Sumner as a man with acute psychological inadequacies" and exposed Sumner's "facade of pompous rectitude." Donald's evenhanded approach to his subject, Potter observed, was a model for biographers working with a difficult subject. "If it does not make Sumner attractive [the book] certainly makes him understandable." Great books abound in insights, and Potter was struck by Donald's ability to reveal "the hostility to Sumner in Massachusetts and the bitterness of his quarrels with other antislavery

8. *American Historical Review* 65 (1960): 921–22.

men."[9] Jurors on the Pulitzer Prize awards committee were impressed, too, and gave the Sumner study the 1961 award for biography.

There was no time for a letup in Donald's schedule, however. His mentor, James G. Randall, had died before completing a revision of his standard work, *The Civil War and Reconstruction*. While in England, with encouragement from Randall's widow, Donald incorporated into a revised edition the recent scholarship and new interpretations needed to keep the book abreast of current trends. Mainly used as a text in college courses across the nation, the new edition appeared in 1961 and quickly became a useful classroom tool. A shorter version, with Randall listed as the coauthor, appeared as *The Divided Union* late in 1961.

Access to the Library of Congress, which Donald used incessantly in his search for primary materials, may have influenced his decision to accept an offer at Johns Hopkins University in 1962. Baltimore was within working distance of the Library where so many major collections were housed, and for the next ten years Donald directed dissertations and served as director of the Institute of Southern History on the Hopkins campus. Donald wanted to make the Hopkins department into the strong force it had once been, and while he was there such major historians as Jack Greene, Ron Walters, David Cohen, Alfred D. Chandler, and John Higham joined the faculty. He also sought cooperation with neighboring all-black institutions—Morgan State and Coppin State—and welcomed historian Benjamin Quarles for his first visit to the Hopkins campus.

During this interval his wife edited the first two volumes of *The Diary of Charles Frances Adams* (with some help from Donald as the deadline approached). Donald also gave the Walter Fleming memorial lectures at Louisiana State University, which were published in 1965 as *The Politics of Reconstruction, 1863–1867*.

Indeed, Donald's energy and insights were phenomenal. Honorary degrees came his way from Millsaps and Oxford, and he was sought out to review far more books than he could handle. When Kenneth Stampp's *The Era of Reconstruction, 1865–1877* appeared in 1965, however, Donald eagerly undertook a review assignment. In the *American Historical Review* Donald made no bones about his admiration for Stampp's bold interpretation of the period. "This is the best book ever published on the Reconstruction period," Donald wrote, which was noteworthy praise from Ran-

9. *American Historical Review* 66 (1961): 1062–63.

dall's protégé. Donald determined that the book was "the new version of Reconstruction, and it has never before been sketched with such succinctness, clarity, and eloquence."[10] As Donald predicted, Stampp's work became a classic and was still in print at the century's end.

Reconstruction themes attracted Donald, and his revisionist work with Randall's study opened new avenues. Donald was elected president of the Southern Historical Association in 1969 and had his research supported by a fellowship from the American Council of Learned Societies.

In 1970 Donald finished his second volume on Sumner, entitled *Charles Sumner and the Rights of Man,* completing a self-appointed task begun more than a decade earlier. Published in the midst of the Vietnam War, which had caused turmoil on many college campuses and created doubts about American policy in the U.S. Senate, a book on a Senate icon from the past seemed timely. In the *American Historical Review* the book was acclaimed as "one of the masterworks of American biography." A much larger work than the first Sumner volume, this account covered Sumner's return to the Senate as head of the powerful Foreign Relations Committee. The reviewer, Don Fehrenbacher, called the volume "a fascinating account of what happens when an inveterate dissident becomes associated with the establishment." Sumner became friendly with Lincoln, whom "he regarded . . . as his inferior" and treated "at times with condescension, but that was the fate of most men who crossed Charles Sumner's path." Fehrenbacher also noted that "certain neo-abolitionists" had criticized Donald's earlier volume on Sumner for what they called the author's "determined hostility to his subject." In his second volume, the reviewer observed, "Donald has tried hard to be fair and with greater success, I believe, than most biographers."[11] Civil War scholars welcomed the new Sumner volume as evidence of Donald's growth as a premier student of the period, but rumors that a second Pulitzer Prize was likely proved unfounded.

At the age of fifty-three, Donald made his final academic move. In 1973 he accepted the Charles Warren professorship in American History at Harvard. For the next eighteen years his career as a teacher and author was centered on the Cambridge campus, with some time off for the Commonwealth lectureship at University College in London, the second of two

10. *American Historical Review* 71 (1966): 700–701.
11. *American Historical Review* 76 (1971): 1605–6.

Guggenheim Fellowships, as well as more honorary degrees and similar honors. He edited the Civil War memoirs of an enlisted man, helped write a section of the monumental *The Great Republic: A History of the American People,* and wrote a sweeping study on his own—*Liberty and Union: The Crisis of Popular Government, 1830–1890.* Reviewed in the *Journal of American History* by David Grimsted, *Liberty and Union* was classified as "a good period textbook" that fell into the "consensus" category as major historians probed for evidence that would validate American power during the Cold War era (1946–1987). Donald's statement that "Northerners and Southerners showed themselves to be fundamentally similar" was questioned by Grimsted, who regarded the book as of a piece with the "consensus" school of thought and accordingly disapproved.[12] "Consensus proved by similar tactics in a course of attempted mutual murder may be conflict enough for most of us," Grimsted wrote.[13]

For most of the next decade Donald's research interests were pursued in a different direction. At Harvard he had served as chairman of a graduate program in the history of American civilization, and during his six-year stint he had directed dissertations on southern writers Erskine Caldwell and Allen Tate. The relationship between history and literature was never far from his mind, and he had been planning to write a study on southern society and literature in the Reconstruction era. Then, while vacationing in North Carolina, Donald happened to visit the boyhood home of Thomas Wolfe, which was open to the public in Asheville, Wolfe's hometown. Like so many college students of his generation, Donald had read *Look Homeward, Angel* and at that time "was certain that Thomas Wolfe had told my life story.... I was convinced—without any just cause—that I too was misunderstood." Over the years, Donald read more of Wolfe, but in time he had lost interest in Wolfe and his novels.

Then, with the visit to Wolfe's home, Donald became so intrigued by the North Carolinian's peripatetic life that he began a serious study of Wolfe's works and its impact on the social history of the United States

12. After World War II some historians and political scientists spoke of "consensus history" as an explanation for the nation's social and political progress. Daniel Boorstin, Louis Hartz, and Richard Hofstadter (among others) were identified with this group of scholars who held "that America owed more—and particularly more of its successes—to a tradition of consensus about fundamental principles than to a tradition of internal conflict" (J. R. Pole in *Pastmasters: Some Essays on American Historians,* ed. Marcus Cunliffe and Robin W. Winks [New York: Harper and Row, 1969], 211).

13. *Journal of American History* 66 (1979–1980): 410.

"during the first four decades of the twentieth century." Eventually, the interest in Wolfe led Donald to decide that he must write a biography of his college-days hero. The voluminous materials were at hand, in Harvard's Houghton Library, in the files of the Wolfe estate, and at scattered collections along the Atlantic seaboard.

Once Donald fixed his focus, he shifted through thousands of Wolfe documents (as a boy and as a man, Wolfe seems to have never discarded any piece of paper with writing on it) and decided to concentrate on "a study of the creative process, the story of Thomas Wolfe's evolution as a writer." After almost eight years of research and writing, Donald's book on Wolfe was published in 1987. "I have tried to tell a story . . . without a hero and without a villain," he told readers in his preface. He also wanted readers to learn of "the ambivalent relationship that necessarily exists between authors and their publishers." Mainly, however, Wolfe's story was of a troubled genius who was "tragically limited and brilliantly gifted."[14]

Donald's leap from nineteenth-century history into the maelstrom of twentieth-century American literature was a calculated risk. But with the publication of *Look Homeward: A Life of Thomas Wolfe* the gamble paid off. A prodigious researcher all his life, Donald left no Wolfe manuscript untouched, and as his heavy documentation showed (the sources and notes section comprises fifty-six pages), valid insights and interpretations require an enormous depth of knowledge. Rarely has a Civil War historian captured the attention of the academic literati in English departments, at bookstores, and in conversation around the dinner table as did Donald with *Wolfe.*

Reviewers examined *Wolfe* with feelings ranging from awe to surprise. Harold Bloom, in the *New York Times Sunday Book Section,* did not know exactly what to make of the book. He agreed with Donald that Wolfe had written "more bad prose than any other major writer I can think of" but was concerned that such a poor writer could acquire "so major a reputation, even for a time." Donald's book, Bloom decided, ought to be called a "critical biography," but still Wolfe remained "a really difficult and unpleasant personality," unredeemed by Donald.[15]

Other critics were more charitable. In the *London Times Literary Sup-*

14. David Herbert Donald, *Look Homeward: A Life of Thomas Wolfe* (Boston: Little, Brown and Co., 1987), xi–xiii, xix.

15. *New York Times,* February 8, 1988.

*plement,* British critic Hugh Kenner praised the depth of Donald's research. "'Adequate' proves to be a feeble word for the resources David Herbert Donald has sifted through," the British scholar noted. Kenner was impressed by Donald's way of dealing with Wolfe's many weaknesses with a "headlong narrative." Donald's style seemed a perfect fit for the subject, Kenner suggested, as he cited Donald's treatment of the breakup of Wolfe's affair with his married mistress as exemplary. "In a quite different way he is as talented a writer as Wolfe, as proved by the fact that, [when] the Bernstein episode ended, we don't feel that Wolfe needs kicking."[16]

This time, rumors that another Pulitzer Prize was in the offing proved correct. In 1988 the award for biography went to Donald for the second time amid applause from colleagues as well as former students, who were now scattered from coast to coast.

In July 1991, his seventieth year, Donald decided that it was time to retire from teaching, but not from writing. He already had mountains of research notes on the life of Lincoln, and he determined that what was needed was a different kind of biography about the martyred president. As Donald saw it, his life of Lincoln would "present a story-line, much as in a modern novel, with a minimum of what I think of as historiographical throat-clearing and without heavy-handed authorial intervention and editorializing."[17] In short, Donald thought, his biography of Lincoln would be different and appeal to a wider audience.

*Lincoln* was published in 1995 and quickly became a best-seller. In the *Atlantic Monthly,* Princeton historian James McPherson observed that Donald "negotiates the potential pitfalls for Lincoln biographers with surefooted grace." Donald was at his best in the sections dealing with Lincoln the politician, McPherson wrote, and was "on less sure ground in his discussion of Lincoln as commander-in-chief."[18] Columbia historian Eric Foner reviewed *Lincoln* for *Nation* magazine and flatly declared it "the best account we have of the course of Lincoln's life." Much ground was familiar, Foner wrote, but the book "sheds new light on a number of topics, especially Lincoln's prewar legal career, thanks to material gathered from local newspapers and county courthouses." (As Donald had acknowledged, he benefited enormously from access to the Lincoln Legal Papers project

16. *Times Literary Supplement,* April 17, 1987.
17. Donald to author, January 16, 2000.
18. *Atlantic Monthly,* November 1995, p. 134.

then underway in Illinois.) Foner went on to say that "much about the man and the President remains elusive. . . . The reader is left to wonder about the meaning of Lincoln's life and the quality of his greatness."[19]

Less taken with Donald's approach was historian William Hanchett, who questioned the author's methodology in the *Journal of American History:* "What a disappointment . . . to read in the first page of Lincoln that Donald would present, not his views of Lincoln, but Lincoln's views of himself." By eschewing a broad interpretation of Lincoln's career, Hanchett suggested, Donald had left his readers in the lurch. Insights, judgments, and evaluations were "precisely what was wanted from one of Donald's stature and experience." The book was "partially redeemed by its rich and detailed examination of Lincoln the politician," Hanchett concluded, but as a commander in chief Lincoln "was not sufficiently forceful."[20]

As a plethora of honors was heaped on Donald for *Lincoln* (including the 1996 Lincoln Prize, with its $40,000 check), perhaps the best judgment on the book came from retired historian Richard N. Current. Writing in the *Times Literary Supplement* for a worldwide audience, Current was no caustic critic. "This book must be considered the best biography of Lincoln ever published," he observed. "It is not a flattering portrait; it is 'more grainy than most,' as Donald points out," but the biography was superior on all counts. As in the view of the nineteenth-century historian George Bancroft, Donald's *Lincoln* was a president who "did not lead but followed the people." The sixteenth president "was more a military bungler than a military genius," and he "was a fatalist all along." Yet if the lives of 600,000 soldiers had to be sacrificed, the guilt was not his. "The burden had been shifted from his shoulders to those of a Higher Power."[21]

Was it time for Donald to settle down now, read all the books still unread, and take trips long postponed? He was not ready to call it quits, for his mind was still active, and he still had a vast audience with most of his fourteen books remaining in print. Thus in 1996 he turned out a biography of Charles Sumner (a work combining the most significant parts of his two previous Sumner books), and as the century ended he wrote *Lincoln at Home,* an affectionate portrait of the husband-father often neglected by previous biographers.

---

19. *The Nation,* November 20, 1995, p. 622.
20. *Journal of American History* 83 (1996): 216–18.
21. *Times Literary Supplement,* March 8, 1996.

In retrospect, Donald's career was marked by a willingness to explore other fields of study and ally them with history. His interests in sociology, psychology, and psychoanalysis were evident in the Sumner biographies; and his abiding love of literature finally came to the fore in the Wolfe biography. Certainly a historian-biographer who has won two Pulitzer Prizes has done something rather exceptional. Donald labored over every sentence he wrote and was sometimes disappointed that reviewers of his books wrote about their content but overlooked their graceful literary style.

As the century ebbed to a close, Donald was living in Massachusetts, not too far from the Harvard libraries, and his files still bulged with research notes. As they had for decades, his friends and former students speculated as the year 2000 dawned: "What's Professor Donald up to now?"

# John Hope Franklin

## by Paul Finkelman

In the fall of 1971, I headed off for the University of Chicago to begin a Ph.D. in history. From my parents' home in upstate New York, the fastest route was to cross into Canada at Niagara Falls and then reenter the United States at Detroit. Long-haired, bearded, and with all my possessions stuffed into an aging car, I fully expect to be hassled at both crossings.

Entering Canada turned out to be pretty simple. I was just passing through, and Canadian customs went smoothly. I sped on through southern Ontario, simultaneously excited and apprehensive at the prospect of graduate study. Crossing back to the United States at Detroit was another matter. At the height of the Vietnam War, I was precisely the kind of blue-jeaned, work-shirted, scruffy kid the customs officials could have fun with. As I pulled up to the boarder, the customs officer sternly asked me who I was, where I was coming from, and where I was headed with all that "stuff" in my car. I proudly told him I was headed for the University of Chicago to start graduate school in history. The guard scrutinized me for a moment and then asked, "Do you know John Hope Franklin?" The question astounded me. "He will be my adviser," I answered, as I reached for the letter in my briefcase confirming this fact. He looked at me a moment longer and then waved me on.

Thus, before I even arrived at graduate school I had learned something of the mysterious power of John Hope Franklin.

## The Scholar as Public Figure

John Hope Franklin ranks as one of our greatest historians. He is, as Stanford's George M. Fredrickson noted, "a historian's historian, a scholar who has stuck to the ideal of a historical truth beyond ideology and done so more effectively than many whose political passions were weaker than his but whose work nevertheless suffered more from distortions resulting from partisanship of one kind or another. Refusing to endorse fashionable theories and ideologies, he has attempted to leave a legacy of reliable, truthful history."[1] That "attempt" has so far been accomplished through his writings, his influence on other scholars, and his training of graduate students. Indeed, it is likely that long after fashionable and trendy works of history have been relegated to deep storage in most academic libraries, John Hope Franklin's work will still be read, checked out of public and university libraries, and available for purchase. Indeed, one of the most remarkable aspects of his career is that, with the forthcoming reprint of *The Militant South,* all of his major books will remain in print, some of them more than forty or fifty years after their first appearance.

Franklin is not simply one of the greatest scholars and historians of our century. He is a public man of great eminence; a public servant; a tireless advocate for racial justice; and a humane mentor who is adored, even worshiped, by his students. He is graceful, easygoing, and yet positively regal in speech and manner. He is kind and gentle to graduate students, teaching by example and by suggestion. One never gets the sense that he pulls out a red pen in anger, but at the same time his comments in class and on a seminar paper make a deep impression on anyone fortunate enough to be in his class. Getting back a mediocre (at best) paper from him, I felt that I had failed him in my work, and that his was the greater disappointment in my poor showing.

Franklin provides an example of rare scholarly dedication. His publications fill a good-sized shelf. He has written twelve books and edited ten more. They have been translated into German, French, Portuguese, Chinese, and Japanese. At last count, he had also published 115 scholarly articles. In the grand tradition of mentors, the books of his students are prominently displayed in the living room of his home in North Carolina, filling a few more shelves. One of his most recent books, *Runaway Slaves: Rebels on the Plantation,* is coauthored with his student Loren Schweninger. He was eighty-four when this book came out, and, like much of his other scholarship, it won a prize. His honorary degrees—around 110 at last count—would fill the walls of a large apartment. He has been president of the American Studies Association (ASA), the Organization of

1. "Pioneer," *New York Review of Books,* September 23, 1993, p. 33.

American Historians (OAH), the Southern Historical Association (SHA), the American Historical Association (AHA), and the United Chapters of Phi Beta Kappa. He has served on the boards of universities, museums, cultural institutions, foundations, and corporations. He was chairman of the Board of Trustees of his undergraduate alma mater, Fisk University.

Stories about him appear in the most likely and unlikely places: the *New York Times,* the *New York Review of Books,* the *Atlanta Constitution,* the *L.A. Times, People Magazine,* and even *Modern Maturity.* At age sixty-seven he retired, for the first time, from the University of Chicago, where he had been chairman of the history department (1967–1970) and held the John Matthews Manly Distinguished Service Chair. He then became the James B. Duke Professor of History at Duke University. Emeritus from two schools, from 1985 to 1992 he was a professor of legal history at Duke Law School. In 1997, at the age of eighty-two, he accepted an appointment from President Clinton to be chairman of the Advisory Board to the President's Initiative on Race. He has yet to retire. At eighty-five he has more projects in the works—including an autobiography—than most scholars plan in a lifetime and continues to indulge with enthusiasm in his passion for the cultivation of rare species of orchids. Perhaps this stems from his lifelong interest in challenges, for orchid-growing requires patience and concentration, although he insists, "Orchids are not nearly as delicate as most people think."

Franklin has been *everywhere.* Some scholars can talk about where they have lectured. For Franklin the list might be shorter if he were to list where he has *not* lectured or taught. Africa, Asia, South America, Europe, Australia, New Zealand, Hawaii—he has covered all the populated continents and many island groups. He was the Pitt Professor at Cambridge but declined a similar chair at Oxford, believing such honors should be available to as many deserving scholars as possible. In 1976 the National Endowment for the Humanities selected him as the Jefferson Lecturer. He has dined with presidents at home and abroad and even flown on *Air Force One.*

His house is filled with evidence of fame and the memorabilia of a life dedicated to scholarship, history, and making the world a better place: a bust of Lincoln from the Civil War Round Table, seemingly endless plaques and awards for book prizes, a certificate of membership in the Oklahoma Hall of Fame, a Great Educators Award from Miller Brewing Company, a golden plate from the American Academy of Achievement.

He has enough medals to qualify as a general in chief of academics and activists: a heavy bronze medal with Jefferson on it from the American Philosophical Society; the Spingarn Medal from the NAACP, the highest accolade of the nation's oldest civil rights organization; the Cleanth Brooks Medal for Distinguished Achievement in Southern Letters; the UCLA Medal; the Schomburg Medal of the New York Public Library; and the Smithsonian Bicentennial Medal. On his lapel, if one looks carefully, is the Presidential Medal of Freedom, the highest civilian award America can offer. Franklin has not only won awards but has also had awards named for him, including a distinguished lectureship at one university, a professorship at another, a research institute at Duke University, and a publication prize given by the ASA.[2]

His leadership transcends the academic world. He has served on the boards of corporate and civic organizations ranging from Illinois Bell Telephone to the Orchestral Association of Chicago. He was appointed to the Presidential Advisory Board on Ambassadorial Appointments, the U.S. Advisory Commission on Public Diplomacy, and the National Council of Humanities, in addition to serving as chairman of the Advisory Board to the President's Initiative on Race.

While doing so much outside academia, he has managed to train countless students and has produced a stunning amount of scholarship. His first book, *The Free Negro in North Carolina* (1941), remains in print after nearly sixty years. So, too, does his most influential book, *From Slavery to Freedom,* which was first published in 1947 and is now in its eighth edition.

Franklin is noted for the many "firsts" in his career. But three stand out above all others, not merely as firsts, but as "onlies." He is probably the only historian in our nation's history to have an orchid named for him (*Phalaenopsis* 'John Hope Franklin'); the only scholar to be president of the OAH, SHA, AHA, ASA, and Phi Beta Kappa; the only historian to have a street named for him, Tulsa's John Hope Franklin Boulevard; and doubtless the only historian to have the first edition of one of his books become a collectible in his lifetime. The 1947 edition of *From Slavery to Freedom* is now rare and expensive. While the old books of most scholars end up on the remainder table, Franklin's often go to the auction block.

---

2. The University of Tulsa College of Law has just named an annual lecture for Franklin's father. John Hope Franklin was tapped to give the first Buck Colbert Franklin lecture.

## Obstacles on a Black Historian's Road

Franklin's journey to greatness as a historian was unusual. In part he encountered as many roadblocks as roads. The roadblocks were always a function of race and racism. Sometimes the roadblocks slowed him down, but they never deterred him. Doubtless, the process of avoiding the roadblocks of racism helped sharpen Franklin's skills, although one can imagine far less painful ways to sharpen skills. Much of his career was spent describing, analyzing, and explaining the history of these roadblocks. His greatest book, *From Slavery to Freedom,* is in many ways the telling of their history. Another component of his career was his contribution to the fight against such roadblocks. Indeed, his very presence and prominence in the academy were in effect a battle against racism.

Franklin was born in 1915 in Rentiesville, Oklahoma, an all-black village of two hundred people near Tulsa. In his early years, his family lacked electricity or indoor plumbing. In Rentiesville he developed a lifelong passion for fishing, although at the time it was more of a necessity than a sport —a good catch made a good dinner. His father, Buck Colbert Franklin, had practiced law in Ardmore, Oklahoma, and once had to travel on behalf of a client to Louisiana, where a local judge told him "that no 'nigger lawyer' could represent clients in his court." It was after this experience that the Franklins moved to Rentiesville, where they hoped to avoid the pervasive racism of the age and region. There, Buck Franklin was a lawyer, postmaster, justice of the peace, farmer, newspaper editor, and small businessman. Franklin's mother taught school. With daycare unknown, John Hope went to work each day with his mother, patiently sitting in the back of the classroom, drawing pictures. Soon, however, he was also copying his mother's lessons on the paper. By age five he was reading and writing. As he later noted, "from that point on, I would endeavor to write, and through the written word, to communicate my thoughts to others."[3]

Just before John Hope turned eleven the family moved to Tulsa, where his father practiced law and his mother no longer worked outside the home. The family had expected to move in 1921, when John Hope was six, but shortly before the planned move the Tulsa race riot—probably the

3. All quotations in this section are from John Hope Franklin, "John Hope Franklin: A Life of Learning," in *Race and History: Selected Essays, 1938–1998* (Baton Rouge: Louisiana State University Press, 1989), 277–91, and John Hope Franklin, *Vintage Years: The First Decade* (Washington, D.C.: Cosmos Club, 1994).

most murderous in American history—intervened, destroying the building his father was planning to buy and temporarily derailing the family's
plans. Once in Tulsa, John Hope entered Booker T. Washington, the city's
segregated high school. The young child thought it an incredible edifice,
until he saw the all-white Central High. While living in Rentiesville, Franklin had faced segregation only when he left town. But in Tulsa segregation
was ubiquitous, forcing Franklin to make hard choices. To hear sym-
phonic music or opera, which he loved, he had to sit in the Jim Crow section of Tulsa's Convention Hall. More than six decades later, the indig-
nity of voluntarily submitting to this racism still bothers him.

Racism was more obvious, and more painful, in Nashville, where John
Hope entered Fisk University in 1931. He faced segregation everywhere in
Nashville, enforced by abusive white petty tyrants. While John Hope was
in college, the lynching of a young black man, whose "crime" consisted of
a baseless rumor that he had offended a white woman, underscored the
fragility of black life in the American south of the 1930s.

Despite the racism, and working multiple jobs to cover his living ex-
penses, Franklin thrived at Fisk, serving as president of the student body
and achieving a superb academic record. With the backing of a white
professor, Theodore Currier, he became the first graduate of a historically black college to be admitted to Harvard's graduate history program. Admission did not come with financial aid, however, so Professor
Currier borrowed five hundred dollars to send his protégé off to Cambridge.

At Harvard, Franklin encountered the more genteel and polished racism
of the Ivy League. Samuel Eliot Morison, one of the most senior faculty
members, bragged about his abolitionist ancestry, implying he would treat
the young graduate student fairly, despite his race. Perhaps Morison did
so, but clearly he did so with extraordinary condescension, and in his subsequent writings on slavery and abolition he revealed a continuing insen-
sitivity to the plight of blacks and a hostility to their white allies that denied his own antislavery roots.

Harvard in the 1930s was not an entirely segregated place. As Franklin
later recalled, "there were a few blacks at Harvard in those days. One was
completing his work in French history as I entered. As in Noah's Ark, there
were two in the law school, two in zoology, and two in the college. There
was one in English and one in comparative literature; there were none in
the Medical School and none in the Business School." Tokenism was a new

sort of discrimination—not as dangerous as lynching, but surely, in its own way, as humiliating as being asked to sit at the back of the bus.

While at Harvard, Franklin learned of an entirely different kind of racism when his fellow graduate students opposed electing a Jewish student, whom Franklin had nominated, as president of the Henry Adams Club. This student was, in Franklin's mind, the best in the class, and he went on to be Pulitzer Prize–winning scholar of great distinction. But, for the Harvard graduate students of that time, his Jewishness was a barrier to acceptance. This encounter with anti-Semitism helped shape Franklin as an egalitarian for all seasons, for all cultures, for all people.

Franklin left Cambridge in 1939, anxious to teach and eager to escape the stifling atmosphere of Harvard. In 1941 he finished his Ph.D., writing a dissertation that would be published in 1943 as *The Free Negro in North Carolina* (reprinted in 1969 and 1994).

## The Creation of Black History

Franklin did not begin his career as a "black" historian. At Harvard he studied under a southern historian, Paul Buck, and throughout most of his career he consciously identified himself as a "southern" historian. Three of his books—*The Militant South: 1800–1861* (1956), *Reconstruction: After the Civil War* (1961), and *A Southern Odyssey: Travelers in the Antebellum North* (1976)—deal with southern history. A fourth, *The Emancipation Proclamation* (1963), is about national politics and its impact on the South. All four books deal with race and slavery. But African American history, as it was understood then and now, is not a central theme.

At another level, these books demonstrate that the African American experience is central to both the history of the South and the history of the nation, as does Franklin's dissertation, on free blacks in antebellum North Carolina. That book is about the South, and it is about blacks.

Franklin understood, more than many white scholars, that American history, especially southern history, was always about blacks and Indians, as much as it was about whites. Indeed, one of Franklin's most significant (but least recognized) scholarly contributions was his subtle, but relentless, drive to integrate southern history. Franklin cannot take sole credit for this, and in his typically modest way he would probably claim no credit at all. In fact, his scholarship, especially *The Militant South,* was part of a new approach to understanding how much race and slavery affected the development of the white south. Similarly, his *Reconstruction: After the Civil War* forced the scholarly community to confront the violence of the white South toward former slaves in the years following the Civil War. Indeed, scholars today take for granted the incredible violence of the South, and especially the racial violence. For younger scholars and students it seems almost impossible to remember when historians could write about the South and yet remain almost oblivious to the presence of slaves, free blacks, or, after the war, former slaves, and the violence perpetrated against them.

Similarly, Franklin has worked to integrate black history into mainstream American history. Ironically, the author of *From Slavery to Freedom* never considered himself a "black historian." When African American studies was coming into its own, he refused the chairmanship of the new program at Harvard, telling a stunned recruiter that he was a "historian" and would not consider serving in another department.[4] As August Meier and Elliott Rudwick noted in their important work, *Black History and the Historical Profession, 1915–1980*, Franklin has "constantly striven to make black history not a Jim Crow specialty, but an integral part of the fabric of American history-writing." At the same time, his scholarship has been a model of restrained prose and careful analysis. His commitment to the craft of the historian has led him to avoid polemics, even when polemics seemed to dominate scholarship on race.

While Franklin did not intend to be a historian of the African American experience, that is where his career started and where it will probably end. It is also what he is most famous for. His first book, *The Free Negro in North Carolina* (1941), is clearly an examination of African American history, as much as it is an examination of southern history. His most recent book, *Runaway Slaves: Rebels on the Plantation,* is similarly about blacks in the antebellum South. It is black history and southern history. And *From Slavery to Freedom* remains, more than half a century after its first publication, and now in its eighth edition, the most important single work in African American history. It is, indeed, the book that, more than any single work, created that field.

To be sure, Franklin was not the first to write about black history. In the antebellum period the black abolitionist William C. Nell wrote a book

4. Late in life, he remained a historian but did teach in Duke University's Law School, having "retired" from the history departments at both Chicago and Duke.

about African Americans in the Revolution. After the Civil War, George Washington Williams wrote his monumental work on the subject, *The History of the Negro Race in America* (1882). Significantly, late in his career Franklin wrote a prize-winning biography of this pioneering scholar, *George Washington Williams: A Biography* (1985). Another pioneer, W. E. B. Du Bois, added important scholarship on blacks starting with his Harvard dissertation in 1895 on the suppression of the African slave trade. In 1913 Benjamin Brawley, who studied at the University of Chicago (where Franklin would later teach), published a second history of blacks, *Short History of the American Negro.* Alongside the work of George Washington Williams, this book provided a basic text for the subject, and by the 1920s a few historically black colleges offered courses in Negro history (as it was then called).

The professionalization of black history began in 1915 and 1916, when Carter G. Woodson founded the Association for the Study of Negro Life and History and began editing the first journal devoted to the subject, the *Journal of Negro History.* After World War I a number of significant black scholars, including Charles H. Wesley, Luther Jackson Porter, Lorenzo Greene, Rayford Logan, and Benjamin Quarles,[5] and a few whites, such as Frederic Bancroft and Herbert Aptheker, began publishing in the field. These scholars were, however, hardly in the mainstream. In a segregated nation the history of blacks was segregated out of most history books. When blacks did appear, they were caricatures. One popular textbook, written by Ivy League scholars, began its chapter on slavery, "And now for Sambo."

When Franklin entered Harvard for graduate study in 1935, the historiography of the three most important topics affecting blacks—slavery, abolition, and reconstruction—was mostly in the hands of whites who were at best merely unsympathetic to African Americans and their history. Many were openly racist. Since the turn of the century the study of slavery had been dominated by Yale professor Ulrich B. Phillips and his students. Phillips, the grandson of a Georgia slaveowner and planter, did not defend slavery per se. He admitted it was wrong, but in the same breath he described blacks as childlike and unfit for self-determination.

Meanwhile, the work of William A. Dunning and his disciples domi-

---

5. Others included W. Sherman Savage, James Hugo Johnston, and Alrutheus A. Taylor.

nated Reconstruction scholarship. In their version of Reconstruction ignorant blacks in league with corrupt carpetbaggers and scalawags rode roughshod over the white South. They might admit slavery was a tragedy, but for the Dunning school, Reconstruction was the greater tragedy because it imposed "black rule" on the white South. The scholars in the Dunning school ignored, almost completely, the violence of the Ku Klux Klan and other white terrorist groups. Scholars in this period viewed the Civil War itself as the result of a blundering generation that was pushed into war by radical abolitionists who destroyed a viable political system. Slavery, in their minds, could not have been the cause of the war because they could not conceive of white Americans fighting over the subjugation of blacks. Thus, their history justified the segregation then present everywhere in America.

*From Slavery to Freedom,* first published in 1947, forced a fundamental rethinking of the place of race in American society. For the first time a scholarly work presented a framework for teaching black history. The book received a mixed reception. Wisconsin professor William Hesseltine, writing in the *American Historical Review,* could not quite figure out how to approach it. He began by attacking all previous work on "Negro history" as "at best" having "the trappings of scholarship" over a "thin veneer of overemotionalism." He praised Franklin's book as a "single competent, coherent volume" on the subject with "a minimum of emotion-charged words," "restrained in diction, lucid in expression." But Hesseltine seemed shocked that a black man could write so well and mystified by the very publication of such a book. He rejected the need for the first few chapters on Africa, essentially arguing that African Americans had no African past that they remembered, or perhaps that was worth remembering. He concluded the whole book was "a highly intelligent piece of overemphasis on the Negro's role in American history."

For Hesseltine, Franklin's sympathetic portrayal of slaves compounded his "overemphasis" on blacks. Hesseltine complained the book paid "excessive attention to slave insurrections" and that Franklin confused criminals and simply lazy blacks with "'protestors' against the slave 'system.'" It never dawned on Hesseltine that "lazy" slaves were simply, subtly, and safely protesting their bondage. Significantly, starting with Kenneth Stampp's *The Peculiar Institution* (1956), scholars of slavery would expand on Franklin's insights on slave resistance, often without acknowledging them or even knowing where they originated.

Like many historians at the end of World War II, Hesseltine did not see slavery as such a terrible institution. He complained of Franklin's failure to "discuss slavery as an instrument of social control," implying that black people needed to be controlled by whites. He argued that Franklin failed to understand that the harshness of slavery was "more the result of necessary agricultural labor under frontier conditions than the product of the innate brutality of the slaveowners." Yet he could not have offered examples of frontier whites whipping their free white farmhands, or selling the children of their laborers to make extra money. He found an "overemphasis" on the African background as well as on the lives of significant blacks and their contributions to American life and culture.[6]

In contrast to Hesseltine's anger and annoyance at the tying of African history to American history, Bell I. Wiley, then teaching at Louisiana State University and writing in the *Journal of Southern History,* praised Franklin for his insights. Wiley, like most other white reviewers, also hailed Franklin for his "impressive clarity," "cohesiveness," and "felicitous" style. Wiley found the book "outstanding" and likened Franklin in his balanced approach to both Lincoln and Booker T. Washington. But these were safe topics, especially for a white southern academic in the age of segregation. Despite such praise, the book rankled southern white scholars when it challenged too directly southern myths, especially about contented slaves, Confederate treatment of black soldiers, and the valor of blacks serving in World War II. Wiley complained that Franklin used "biased sources" in his discussion of the Fort Pillow massacre—when troops led by Gen. Nathan Bedford Forrest murdered black prisoners of war. Doubtless, the bias was in not keeping to the proper southern white view of Confederate chivalry. Like Hesseltine, Wiley also complained of Franklin's chauvinism, while not recognizing his own southern/confederate prejudice. Other scholars, both black and white, failed to see the chauvinism in Franklin's book. The *Catholic Historical Review* noted that Franklin was "interested neither in the achievement of outstanding Negroes nor in apologetics for the race."[7]

The contrast between these reviews is striking. Hesseltine saw excessive chauvinism because for him, and perhaps most white historians, any discussion of black achievements was excessive. This was the world in which

6. Hesseltine in *American Historical Review* 54 (1948): 155–56.
7. Wiley in *Journal of Southern History* 14 (1948): 264–66; Peter E. Hogan, in *Catholic Historical Review* 34 (1948) 343–44.

Franklin wrote, and also the world Franklin helped to change, by a life-time of careful scholarship and judicious writing. While never conceding a point to racism or racists, Franklin avoided letting the evil of segrega-tion and racism poison his judgment, research, or tone. The Hesseltines of the world might complain about too much emphasis on blacks in a book about blacks, but they could never lay a glove on Franklin's scholar-ship or style.

Franklin demonstrated the fundamental wrongness of slavery, segre-gation, and racism not by attacking the perpetrators of such injustices but simply by describing in clear and uncontrovertible detail what had actu-ally occurred. In both *The Militant South* (1956) and *Reconstruction: After the Civil War* (1961) Franklin would return to the themes of racial violence as a way of illustrating all the evils created by slavery. Again, it is worth noting that this theme has now been accepted by historians, but many younger scholars have no idea that it originated in these three works by Franklin.

The profession that Franklin wrote for was rigidly, although not com-pletely, segregated. Almost all blacks teaching history were on the faculties of historically black colleges. Franklin worked his way up the roster of black colleges, from St. Augustine to North Carolina College for Negroes (now North Carolina Central University) to Howard University, the pre-mier black institution in segregated America. It was a segregated collegiate world where history was dominated by whites who were nearly oblivious to their black colleagues. Blacks did not publish in the *American Histori-cal Review,* the *Mississippi Valley Historical Review,* or the *Journal of South-ern History.* They did not give papers at meetings of the sponsoring orga-nizations. As strange as it now seems, in 1946 the SHA had a panel on free blacks that did not include a single African American.

In 1949 Franklin became the first black to appear on a panel of the SHA. In 1956 he moved to a white institution, Brooklyn College, entering as de-partment chair. It is perhaps no accident that his first job in a historically white school was in a department dominated by Jews, many of whom were refugees from the Holocaust. As he had learned as a graduate student at Harvard, Blacks and Jews were indeed soul mates in the universal strug-gle against racism. In 1964 he moved to the University of Chicago, be-coming the first black historian to teach at an elite school.

In 1970 Franklin became the first black president of the SHA. While there are many "firsts" in his life, this was perhaps the most significant. By this time African American history was a serious field, taught in many universities, and soon Franklin was the chairman of the history department at the University of Chicago. *From Slavery to Freedom* was in its third edition, and all but the most retrograde historians understood that the book had helped create a new field of study. More important, it was also transforming mainstream "white" history. Indeed, many younger scholars had come to understand that there was no such thing as "white" history or "black" history, but that U.S. history was the history of people of various races and cultures. Franklin's scholarship made this understanding possible, by beginning the movement to recover the history of African Americans and to place that history in the context of American history.

Another aspect of this transformation was Franklin's small but extremely influential *Reconstruction: After the Civil War* (1961). In a mighty contribution to the reconstruction of Reconstruction history, Franklin refocused the attention of scholars on the importance of race and the ending of slavery. As was true in all his scholarship, he accomplished this with forceful but for the most part dispassionate analysis of the development of Reconstruction. He reminded readers that slavery had been a key cause of the Civil War, and that the remaking of race relations, as much as the reconstitution of the Union, was a goal of Reconstruction.

While the Dunning school of Reconstruction had bemoaned the depredations of "black rule," Franklin showed there had never been "black rule." A simple table of delegates to the state constitutional conventions, something Dunning and his followers could have prepared but did not, showed that only in South Carolina were blacks ever in the majority in any state convention. The same analysis revealed that the "so-called carpetbaggers were in the minority in every state except Mississippi." His book drove home the point that few United States soldiers actually occupied the South, and that it was the Ku Klux Klan and other white terrorist organizations, not the U.S. government or the Republican-controlled state governments, that threatened fundamental concepts of democracy in the postwar South. As Michael Perman has noted in a volume dedicated to Franklin, his book on Reconstruction "was one of the first studies of the Reconstruction era to be quite categorical about the importance of violence. That chapter that examined the nature and the methods of the opposition to Reconstruction was called 'Counter Reconstruction,' and it was devoted entirely to violence and the Ku Klux Klan." As Perman notes, "violence and force were at the heart of the counterattack on Reconstruction."[8] At the heart of the historical profession's awakening to this idea was Franklin's scholarship, especially *Reconstruction: After the Civil War.*

While the Dunning school stressed the ignorance of former slaves, Franklin stressed the "eagerness of Negroes at the close of the war to secure an education" and the importance of the Reconstruction governments in creating the first public school systems in the South. Franklin, in the end, zeroed in on the great complaint of most southern whites—and by implication most white Reconstruction scholars—that the period led to the "disappearance of the white man's government."[9]

In some ways, what Franklin taught Americans was not new. W. E. B. Du Bois had made similar points in *Black Reconstruction.* But Franklin's approach was a study in dispassion—what one reviewer called his "remarkable restraint" and his lack of "special pleading." Another reviewer praised the book as "readable, and meticulously balanced."[10] Perhaps indicative of the strength of Franklin's book was the response of two hostile critics, Avery Craven and Eric L. McKitrick. The aging Craven, writing in the *Journal of Southern History* and teaching at the University of South Carolina, could not accept the arguments of Franklin. Nor could he find any evidence or arguments to oppose them. Rather, he ignored the book altogether, never mentioning Franklin by name or even referring in the review to "the author." Instead, Craven ranted against an emerging scholarship where "the emphasis, one sincerely regrets to find, is always on how the Negro fared in this or that situation." The fact that Franklin's book was not solely focused on this subject was irrelevant to Craven, who seemed offended that a black scholar was writing about Reconstruction at all. Instead of analyzing the book, he complained that "scholars sitting in Northern libraries reading the official documents are not reconstructing Reconstruction in a very realistic way." Columbia University professor Eric McKitrick accused Franklin of adding nothing new to the debate over Reconstruction, but rather repeating "'revisionist' formulas that we all accepted years ago." McKitrick complained that the book was too short to

8. "Counter Reconstruction: The Role of Violence in Southern Redemption," in *The Facts of Reconstruction: Essays in Honor of John Hope Franklin,* ed. Eric Anderson and Alfred A. Moss, Jr. (Baton Rouge: Louisiana State University Press, 1991), 121.

9. *Reconstruction after the Civil War* (Chicago: University of Chicago Press, 1961), 102, 108, 118.

10. Hans Tresfousse, in *American Historical Review* 67 (1962): 745–46. William D. Miller, in *Catholic Historical Review* 48 (1963): 554–55.

do justice to the period, while condemning Franklin for starting a chapter with a discussion of the founding of Fisk University. McKitrick, aligning himself with the "old-fashioned" historians, could not understand the importance of race or slavery to the sectional conflict and did not see, as Franklin did, that the creation of a black institution of higher learning was as important in the evolution of American society as was any specific statute passed or vetoed.[11]

The balance of Franklin's scholarship, his often dispassionate writing, seemed conservative and even reactionary to some blacks and to white radicals in the mid-1960s and 1970s. His refusal to embrace scholarly fads made him seem "old-fashioned" to younger scholars. In some important recent scholarship on Reconstruction these scholars fail even to cite his work, although they have in fact adopted his thesis on Reconstruction without either realizing or acknowledging where it originated.

The civil rights movement of the 1950s and early 1960s and the black power movement in the late 1960s and 1970s radicalized college campuses, forcing stodgy departments to suddenly seek out black professors and instantly add courses on black history, to be taught by blacks if possible, by whites if necessary. This remarkable change would doubtless have happened without Franklin; but his scholarship, and his training of undergraduates at Brooklyn College and of graduate students at Chicago, was critical to its success.

Because of Franklin, more than any other individual, there was a textbook to teach from and a growing body of monographic literature (often done by his protégés and students) to expand the literature. In addition, he had taught many scholars as undergraduates and graduates who either were able to teach African American history or were at least sympathetic to the field. Some, like his Brooklyn College undergraduate Richard Polenberg, were not in the field but were more sympathetic to the field be-

---

11. Craven, in *Journal of Southern History* 28 (1962): 256–57; McKitrick, in *Mississippi Valley Historical Review* 49 (1962–1963): 153–54. In the nine-hundred-page *The Age of Federalism: The Early American Republic, 1788–1800* (New York: Oxford University Press, 1993) McKitrick and his coauthor, Stanley Elkins, managed to completely ignore slavery and race, barely mentioning the issue in passing, despite significant discussions of the African slave trade and the adoption of the first fugitive slave law during this period. Thus it is perhaps not surprising that he was unsympathetic to Franklin's emphasis on race during Reconstruction. See Paul Finkelman, "The Problem of Slavery in the Age of Federalism," in *Federalists Reconsidered,* ed. Doron Ben-Atar and Barbara Olberg (Charlottesville: University Press of Virginia, 1998), 135.

cause of Franklin. Similarly, young teachers at Brooklyn College when Franklin was chairman, like Melvyn Dubofsky, learned the importance of the field, even if they did not enter it. He had greater influence on the graduate students he taught while visiting at the University of Wisconsin, including Herbert Gutman and William McKee. Then there were his many graduate students at Chicago, including Genna Rae McNeil, Michael Homel, Roberta Alexander, Michael Perman, Carl Moneyhon, William Poole, Juliet Walker, Ablie Burke, Barbara J. Flint, Martin J. Hardeman, Michael Lanza, Loren Schweninger, Richard Beeman, Richard Fuke, Woody Farrar, Frances Keller, Carl Osthaus, Eric Anderson, Nancy Grant, Howard Rabinowitz, Christie Pope, and Alfred A. Moss: some black, some white, all interested in African American history for its own sake, and also interested in integrating American history in more fundamental ways. He also affected other young scholars, even if they had never met him. The first book Carl Degler bought as a graduate student was Franklin's *From Slavery to Freedom*. Degler would later win the Pulitzer Prize for his work on comparative race relations in the United States and Brazil.

## A Public Intellectual

Much of the transformation of American history in the 1960s and 1970s was due to the civil rights movement and the vast social transition of the 1950s and 1960s. The demand for Negro history, then black history, then African American history, came from black and white students who believed that such a history was a key to understanding the past, the present, and the solutions to their own social concerns. Indeed, I stumbled into studying the history of slavery and abolition because I was seeking a usable past that might explain the world around me. Like Carl Degler, one of the first books I acquired as an undergraduate that was not on a reading list was the third edition of *From Slavery to Freedom*. This book, and Franklin's growing corpus of scholarship, made it possible to study black history even before my undergraduate college hired a specialist in the field, who (as it turned out) was the first black to have gone through Harvard's Ph.D. program after Franklin.

Franklin of course, was a pioneer at Harvard, as he was in the profession. In this sense, from almost the beginning of his career Franklin has been an activist as well as a scholar. In his own quiet way, he has been on the front lines in the battles against segregation and discrimination. His life story is in part the embodiment of the struggle against racism. He was the first graduate of an all-black college to go directly into Harvard's graduate history program; the first black chairman of a history department of a historically white school (Brooklyn College); the first black president of the SHA, AHA, OAH, and ASA. Some firsts are more astounding than others. When he came to Chicago 1964 he was the first black to *ever* teach in the history department at an elite, white, Ph.D.-granting institution.

Many of the "firsts" in Franklin's career represented important symbolic victories over racism. That he was the first black to serve on a program at the SHA—in 1949—was important. But more important was the meaning of that appearance to the larger profession. As blacks began to appear at professional meetings, program committees had to begin to consider where to hold a meeting. Some places in the South would allow an integrated meeting; most would not. Yet the transition was slow. In the late 1950s Franklin served on the SHA's program committee, but he refused to attend the meeting, which had been booked, years before, into a segregated hotel in Louisville.[12]

Simultaneously, Franklin was involved in larger struggles against segregation. He served as an expert witness in the lawsuit that desegregated the University of Kentucky's graduate program in history. In the summer and fall of 1953 he worked quietly, behind the scenes with Thurgood Marshall, Jack Greenberg, and the rest of the NAACP legal staff, preparing the briefs for the final arguments in *Brown v. Board of Education* (1954).

Here Franklin found a direct use for his years as a scholar. He described the result as a detailed history of how "Southerners defied, ignored, and worked against every conception of equality laid down in the Fourteenth Amendment and subsequent legislation." In their own brief to the Supreme Court, South Carolina's attorneys specifically complained about "this catalogue of inflammatory labels."[13] In many ways the South Carolina brief, prepared in 1953–1954, reflected the earlier response to Franklin's work by traditional scholars. Today historians read Franklin's inhouse papers for the NAACP and find nothing remarkable about them. They might even seem tame and restrained. But, for lawyers representing

---

12. Tom Chaffin, "A Quite Scholar Changed the Way America Sees Its Bitter Racial Past," *Atlanta Constitution*, July 28, 1991, Dixie Living, sec. M, p. 1.

13. Richard Kluger, *Simple Justice* (New York: Random House, 1975), 624.

a segregated South Carolina, the catalog of statutes and events in the South's racist past was intolerable.

Franklin also worked, along with historians Alfred Kelly and C. Vann Woodward and legal scholar Howard Jay Graham, on developing a fuller understanding of the goals of the Republican congressmen and scholars who wrote the Fourteenth Amendment. Here they attacked, head-on, the Dunning school of Reconstruction and the "horrors" of "black rule." Much of this effort for the *Brown* case was eventually incorporated into *Reconstruction: After the Civil War.*

In the *Brown* case Franklin's goal as a historian was ambiguous. Lawyers often seek certainty. They often want from historians ammunition for a jurisprudence of original intention that will "decide" the case.[14] As Franklin knew, history cannot be legitimately shaped, and reshaped, to please lawyers, judges, or activists. In *Brown,* however, Franklin and his fellow historians were able to achieve some success by adhering to the inherent ambiguities of their craft. The court had asked for reargument, in part to determine what the framers of the Fourteenth Amendment might have intended about segregation in general, and school segregation in particular. For historians today there is no completely satisfactory answer to the question. Some members of the Congress, including leaders like Thaddeus Stevens and Charles Sumner, were clearly racial egalitarians, while others were not. Such an answer is acceptable to historians, who constantly work with ambiguity and nuance. The lawyers wanted answers that historians, if faithful to their craft, could not give.

In the end, the ambiguity was enough. Franklin and his colleagues raised questions and doubts in the NAACP briefs that undermined the certainty of the southern advocates, who had relied solely on the work of Dunning and his followers, scholars unaffected by the insights of black scholars from George Washington Williams to W. E. B. Du Bois to Carter Woodson to John Hope Franklin. In a subtle tribute to Franklin, Kelly, Woodward, Graham, and the other scholars, Chief Justice Earl Warren concluded that history alone could not settle the question of school desegregation or integration. Summarizing the issue, he declared: "This discussion and our own investigation," which of course was informed by the briefs the histo-

---

14. On the weakness of this jurisprudence, and its dangers for serious historians, see Paul Finkelman, "The Constitution and the Intentions of the Framers: The Limits of Historical Analysis," *University of Pittsburgh Law Review* 50 (1989): 349–98.

rians helped write, "convince us that, although these sources cast some light, it is not enough to resolve the problem with which we are faced. At best, they are inconclusive."[15]

While any graduate student might shudder at being told his or her research was "as best . . . inconclusive," this was exactly the comment these scholars wanted to hear. "Inconclusive" was a huge victory against the white supremacist view of Reconstruction that had so long dominated American historiography.

The victory in *Brown* also set the stage for a major rethinking of Reconstruction history and the place of African Americans in the making of America. Since even before 1954, but certainly after that critical year, John Hope Franklin, through his books, articles, and very presence in the profession, has been at the very center of that rethinking.

15. *Brown v. Board of Education*, 347 U.S. 483 (1954).

# Richard Hofstadter

## by Jack Pole

Walking away from the Columbia University campus, soon after crossing Broadway you come to Claremont Avenue, where, at No. 25, Richard Hofstadter did most of his work. The internal arrangement of the (rent-supported) apartment was symbolically and literally characteristic of the man and his method; the living room, which looked down onto the avenue, was divided only by a long settee. In front was the general living area; behind, the wide desk and book-lined shelves: the study. This spatial plan was more than symbolic; it was how Richard Hofstadter lived. Not until he reached his early fifties did he move to the East Side and acquire the symbolic luxury of a separate study. The move would be a sign of deeper changes.

Through his most productive period, the historian's work shared its space with that of his daily life. Hofstadter loved company and joined in the after-dinner social life, indulging in irreverent mimicry, throwing out aphorisms in which penetrating observation was often wrapped in verbal wit, always listening attentively to others, conversing joyously with Gustin (for Augustin, and pronounced as in French), his much loved little terrier. His conversation, usually animated, often hilarious, but seldom merely frivolous, was, for an academic, singularly devoid of small talk; there was always much to say and hear. But late at night, when all the others had gone to bed, he passed behind the settee, sat down again at his desk, and began (or resumed) his long day's work. He was frequently there at three or four in the morning, and asleep while others began breakfast. Of course this was not his only working space. *The American Political Tradition* was begun at the University of Maryland, at the bedside of his first wife, who was dying of cancer; later, whenever they went on holiday to their retreat in Wellfleet, Massachusetts, or even to the Caribbean, until the end of his own foreshortened life, he always took work with him.

Working in these spaces, at this pace, year by year, between the late 1940s and the late summer of 1970, he wrote, compiled, or edited about a dozen books (two of which won Pulitzer Prizes) and innumerable essays, lectures, and speeches, exerting a deeper influence on his profession, and a wider public influence, than any other American historian (possibly excepting Arthur M. Schlesinger, Jr., and C. Vann Woodward) during the same span of time.

As an undergraduate at his hometown University of Buffalo, Hofstadter majored in philosophy but learned the historical craft from Julius Pratt, a diplomatic historian with the Progressives' taste for realism. Pratt had challenged the conventional, ideologically based interpretation of the War of 1812 with a sectional analysis based on the distribution of the congressional vote for war. The approach was in keeping with the new emphasis on material interests rather than ideals as the driving forces of historical change. Hofstadter, by contrast, invariably treated ideas as realities in their own right. But Pratt clearly had an eye for quality, and Hofstadter always spoke of him with respect.

To many of Hofstadter's generation, it appeared that democratic capitalism had broken down, and by the late 1930s, when he and his first wife, Felice, moved to New York, it was still uncertain how far the New Deal had succeeded in rescuing it. The move was symbolic, though Hofstadter could not yet know it, of a wider shift in historical perspective. Save for a few eminent Bostonians, most American historians had written from the perspectives afforded by small towns; the United States had a capital but no metropolis. Richard Hofstadter's background was urban (his father was Jewish), and he let New York take possession of him, feeling not the slightest need or inclination to defer to the social or moral preeminence of agriculture, the farmer, the countryside, or the west. As a historian, he legitimized the city.

A paradox that might have pleased him could be framed around the observation that only America could have produced New York, yet New York was utterly different from any other American city. Its linguistic variety exfoliated into newspapers in more than 230 languages. The ferment of left-wing politics was fought out in fierce ideological attachments; Hofstadter briefly joined the Communists but had little taste for political activity based on overheated ideological speculation and was disgusted by the Moscow trials and the Nazi-Soviet pact of August 1939. His disenchantment exposed a residual conservatism of temperament, while leaving him almost depoliticized.

At Columbia, under the guidance of Merle Curti, he undertook a dissertation not so much in the history of systematic political philosophy as in the reconstruction of collective mentalités, which always seemed to him among the most important of problems for the historian. No historian had yet analyzed the implications of applying to human society Charles Darwin's concept of the natural world's evolutionary struggle for survival. Hofstadter saw the opportunity and embarked on the dissertation that quickly became his first book, *Social Darwinism in American Thought.*[1]

By far the most prominent exponent of "Social Darwinism," the doctrine that animal survival strategies as observed by Darwin carried object lessons for human behavior, was the English publicist Herbert Spencer. But Spencer believed that the logic of his view called for complete self-restraint by government; it was the most extreme version of laissez-faire yet seen. The idea, known to Spencerites as "the survival of the fittest," was briefly adopted as the creed of certain self-appointed American spokesmen for unrestricted business competition. But if the evolutionary process was to be an end in itself, making no claim to serve any communal purpose, or to put any valuation on who or what survived, the argument could escape tautology only by claiming moral superiority for whatever or whoever trampled the rest underfoot. By the end of the nineteenth century, the doctrine had virtually blown itself out—a rare example in intellectual history of a bad idea losing an argument.

Hofstadter's monograph announced the arrival of an unusual new talent possessed of a brilliant clarity of style in which lucid exposition combined with incisive comment. The range of his sources, moreover, was uncommonly wide, so that the book was an education in intellectual history. From its initial publication in 1944 to the Beacon Press edition in 1992, the book sold two hundred thousand copies. Yet it had some of a first book's limitations; although the author was searching for a new way to reconstruct collective states of mind, his epistemological method did not venture far from a formal Marxist basis or break into new territory in the sociology of past knowledge. Ideas were still determined by the interests they served.

1. *Social Darwinism in American Thought* (1944), new introduction by Eric Foner (Boston: Beacon, 1992). Much of what follows is indebted to Foner's introduction; also to Stanley Elkins and Eric McKitrick, "Richard Hofstadter: A Progress," in their *The Hofstadter Aegis* (New York: Knopf, 1974), 300–367.

These problems, however, proved to be Hofstadter's abiding interest, to which he would return to make methodological advances in later work.

Disenchantment had fed some of the young scholar's doubts about many of the more popular legends of American history. He was greatly impressed by Charles A. and Mary R. Beard's *Rise of American Civilization,*[2] a vast and sweeping survey written from the Progressive standpoint, dominated by the conviction that American history was driven by conflicts between great economic and social forces, representing progress against reaction. That the historian ought to be on the side of progress was implicit in the teleology. He seems to have found the Beards' relentless attribution of events and motivations to material interests too reductionist to be satisfying. Without yet having a specific program, he began to draft essays on salient individuals in public life who had contributed to America's consolidating political tradition; over some four years, and with encouragement, probably personal, from Alfred Knopf, he built these into a series of twelve. The result was *The American Political Tradition and the Men Who Made It.*[3] The subjects—all Anglo-Saxon, or nearly so—ranged in time from the Founding Fathers (a collective study) to Franklin Roosevelt. But each chapter constituted a separate essay; they were not linked to form a narrative, nor—the title notwithstanding—to demonstrate a single theme. The essays had in common a distinctive tone and style: skeptical, fresh, revisionary, occasionally ironical, without being harsh or merely destructive.

More than thirty years later, and ten years after Richard Hofstadter's death, this book was reported to be selling many thousands of copies a year. It is one thing to account for its initial impact, but further research and shifting points of view have outdated many of the original conclusions, and the historians who continue to assign the book no longer defend many of its arguments. It is, therefore, another thing to explain its extraordinary record of prolonged sales and assignments. Yet any account of Hofstadter's achievement and influence calls for some attempt at explanation.

This must begin with style and approach; the reader is at once in the presence of a powerful, energetic, and self-confident mind. The fact that

---

2. *The Rise of American Civilization,* 4 vols. (New York: Macmillan, 1927–1942).
3. *The American Political Tradition and the Men Who Made It* (New York: Knopf, 1948).

the author speaks with fresh, critical skepticism so directly to his own contemporaries, addressing *their* states of mind, and questioning their sometimes cherished prejudices and convictions, has not diminished the impact of the work on later generations; on the contrary, it gives the book an
additional value as a particularly interesting source of information about
America at the end of World War II. At the very beginning, Hofstadter dis-
cerns a nostalgia, a yearning for security in a longingly contemplated but
receding past; he was particularly fond of his little joke about the view
from the observation car at the back of the transcontinental train. In this
anxious nostalgia, Hofstadter perceived "a keen feeling of insecurity."[4] He
addressed a generation which had experienced boom, crash, and depression; devastating war on ocean and land; and victory with an economic
recovery which, however, failed to inspire confidence for the future. Hofstadter's book made its first impact on Americans less self-assured than
earlier generations had been, who were more than usually vulnerable to
the kind of revisionary attack that Hofstadter launched when he proceeded to explore and reconsider the godlike effigies who studded the popular
record. All were suddenly, disturbingly transformed—disturbingly, but
plausibly, for Hofstadter also reinvented their backgrounds, which became
part of their own picture. Such subtitles as "The Aristocrat as Democrat"
for Jefferson; or the description of Jacksonian Democracy, hitherto always
"the era of the common man," as a phase in the development of liberal capitalism; or the description of Calhoun as "the Marx of the Master Class" or
of FDR as "the Patrician as Opportunist"—these characterizations might
or might not be wholly convincing, but their effect was provocative and
liberating. Through Hofstadter's book, students discovered a new freedom
to question academic authority, and to reconstruct American history for
themselves.

The word *tradition* seemed to imply some degree of institutional continuity and shared values among "the men who made it." Yet the essays, as
drafted, contained little to establish the distinctive character of an *American* political tradition; they could have been called a collection without a
theory. In response to his publisher's suggestion that the book would be
improved by the appearance of a unifying thesis, Hofstadter wrote a preface to explain his standpoint. The previous generation of historians had
recounted American history as so dominated by fierce conflicts between

4. Ibid., v.

rival interests that it was difficult to see how the whole political structure had been able to survive. Yet the leaders of opposing interests had subscribed to the republic's central institutions and the principles that sustained them; to that extent, they had contributed to a tradition, without which there could have been no republic. It was no part of Hofstadter's plan to impose a doctrine or start a school; in fact, he began to feel a need to disclaim such an intention when, a few years later, he found himself being linked as a founder of the "consensus school" with such diverse writers as Louis Hartz and Daniel J. Boorstin.

Not that they had much in common. Hartz argued that England had exported the seeds of an already liberal-bourgeois society, which had only to unfold in order to bloom on the friendly soil of America.[5] Boorstin began a three-volume general history with the sobering experience that "The colonies were a disproving ground for utopias."[6] In this elegantly written work, and in a more forensic work of political science, *The Genius of American Politics,* Boorstin attributed American success to the absence of preconceived, consistent theory. His political agenda was close to the surface; it was, of course, a rejection of Marxist theory, which developed into a dogged antipathy to theory in general, and also of history as a record of class conflict. Hofstadter would never disavow his faith in understanding the past through its opinions, or through climates of opinion (to borrow an expression from Carl Becker). In any case, he did not think highly of Boorstin and found the implied connection unflattering. But he quoted with approval an English comment on the controversy: "It may seem strange that American historians should be moved to take sides over the very question of whether there were any sides to take."[7]

In 1962 he set out his thoughts on the theme of consensus to the same English correspondent:

> My impression is that much too much has been made of the whole issue of consensus, and that it probably would not have been had it not been for the fact that the generation of Beard and Parrington put such an excessive emphasis on conflict that an antidote was needed.

5. *The Liberal Tradition in America* (New York: Harcourt, Brace, 1955).
6. *The Americans: The Colonial Experience* (1958; rpt. Harmondsworth: Penguin, 1965), 1:1.
7. *The Progressive Historians: Turner, Parrington, Beard* (New York: Knopf, 1968), 452–53, quoting J. R. Pole, "The American Past: Is It Still Usable?" *Journal of American Studies* 1 (1967).

My own approach to the matter is one of common sense. It seems to me to be clear that a political society cannot hang together at all unless there is some kind of consensus running through it, and yet that no society has such a total consensus as to be devoid of significant conflict. It is all a matter of proportion and emphasis, which is terribly important in history. Of course, obviously, we have had one total failure of consensus which led to the Civil War. One could use that as the extreme case in which consensus breaks down.

Part of the trouble with the emphasis on this issue is that it has led to the classifying together of people like Boorstin, Hartz and myself, who have some considerable differences and do not form anything that could be called a "school." I think that whatever is written on this subject ought to be more than a little comic. It is the only way to get the thing back into perspective.[8]

Commissions to write, with Columbia colleagues, historical studies of higher education in the United States and of the concept of academic freedom had significant consequences for Hofstadter's own development as a historian.[9] The political climate known broadly as McCarthyism was decidedly hostile to the freedom claimed by university teachers as an essential safeguard of their integrity, while the taxpayer was told to view this as a privileged protection for subversion and disaffection. The contention reached its height in Berkeley, California, where an extremely bitter controversy raged for more than two years over a loyalty oath ordained by the legislature to be taken by all members of the faculty. The imposition implied distrust of universities in particular, and of intellectuals in general; many of the faculty considered their academic independence as well as their dignity to be at risk, for if the legislature could do this one day, what might it do the next? Some, immigrants from Nazi Germany, felt they had seen this sort of thing before. Some of Berkeley's most distinguished figures had left before the affair had blown itself out. Many other universities were harassed and bullied by investigations sprung on them by state legislative committees.

8. Hofstadter to Pole, April 30, 1962, personal archive. See also the preface of Hofstadter's *America at 1750: A Social Portrait* (New York: Knopf, 1971).

9. Richard Hofstadter and C. DeWitt Hardy, *Development and Scope of Higher Education in the United States* (New York: Columbia University Press, 1952); Richard Hofstadter and Walter P. Metzger, *The Development of Academic Freedom in the United States* (New York: Columbia University Press, 1955).

Hofstadter kept his nerve—and also his sense of humor—attacking the New Right while steering clear of the new liberal dogma that true academic freedom required nothing less than absolute freedom of speech with value-free content. All teaching, Hofstadter perceived, must involve an element of indoctrination. The concepts of rule of law, freedom of the press, and the whole galaxy of liberal values threatened by the anti-intellectualism and intolerance of what in one famous essay he styled "the pseudo-conservative revolt" were indeed *values,* collectively forming an ideology. Even to teach these values seemed to involve an element of indoctrination, and universities, Hofstadter maintained, must not shirk their duty as custodians of intellectual liberty. Some twenty years later, he stood by the same principles when his university was occupied by demonstrators against the war in Vietnam. If McCarthyism had inculcated the need to defend the liberal conspectus against enemies on the right, the New Left could mount its own brand of intolerance, which, receding, left its scars on the intellectual landscape. The issues opened up by his work on the history of higher education and academic freedom furnished information and suggested perspectives that would remain among Hofstadter's central preoccupations.

For the historian as well as for the social analyst, the phenomenon of McCarthyism presented novel problems. Historically, serious social malaise had usually been associated with economic crisis or military defeat. The women of Paris had marched on Versailles demanding bread; the collapse of the czar's armies opened the way to the Bolsheviks. But the America that now seemed beset with self-distrust and internal accusations was the America that had contributed mightily to Allied victory, on sea and on land. Moreover, since the anticipated postwar depression had not materialized, the economy seemed to have found ways to make prosperity a normal condition (incidentally casting a retrospective glow over the incomplete achievements of the New Deal). After a generation of presidential victories, the New Deal legacy seemed to have become a way of life, to be taken for granted by the academic world. By contrast, the McCarthyite mentality revealed itself in this unexpectedly wide substratum of the American people, distrustful, anti-intellectual, and conflating academic freedom with both political subversion and social privilege. (Alger Hiss proved the leading case.) Yet America, in addition to its Ivy League, had built a system of distinguished state universities; what had gone wrong? In search of explanation, Hofstadter sought for ideas and methods in the social sciences. The present condition reverberated from the known or imagined past, from which we could surely learn. But where was the past? Who owned it? How was it to be recovered? The problem was not only to reconstruct—to *reinhabit*—past states of mind but also to explain the destabilizing pressures that brought structural changes in collective psychology.

Hofstadter was an extremely reactive historian; the keys to his historical agenda seemed to fly up from the pages of today's *New York Times*. He found in the work of Karl Mannheim, who had fled from the Nazis to a chair at the London School of Economics, one clue he needed; Mannheim had opened London intellectuals to a concept he had developed before the war: that the object of knowledge was not an absolute but a variable product of social conditions. The idea was refined by the notion of a "common climate of opinion," of ground shared even among antagonists, and this perception enabled Hofstadter to supply the unifying ingredient that held together the disparate elements of the political tradition that Americans had framed. Hofstadter later claimed to have learned from Mannheim how to connect the individual with society. But his principal gain from the sociologists, anthropologists, and others was awareness of the ever-widening range of the aspects of human life that could be open to scientific inquiry and might be of use to the historian in reconstructing a past society. He also sought enlightenment from his Columbia colleague Thomas Merton, who systematized the distinction between "manifest" and "latent" functions, the latter being unintended—or not consciously intended— consequences of policy. These procedures increased Hofstadter's analytical equipment without yielding a specific theory.[10]

That theory was to emerge from a seminar held jointly with the sociologist Seymour Martin Lipset, which addressed the problem that we might call McCarthyism in the midst of plenty, and from which grew the concept of status as a social force. Social scientists were more at home than historians with the psychology of status and the idea that grievances arising from displaced social status might drive political events or fire large-scale movements. To historians and their readers the novelty no doubt accounted for some of the initial success of Hofstadter's next major book, and his first full-scale work since *The American Political Tradition*.

10. Hofstadter, "History and the Social Sciences" in *The Varieties of History*, ed. Fritz Stern (New York: Meridian, 1957).

The appearance of *The Age of Reform: From Populism to Progressivism* proved to be a literary event of the first order. To apply all the skills and aperçus derived from years of reading and discussion in the social sciences, as well as in literature and criticism, to the agrarian protest of the Populists and then to convert the new methodology to explain the motivation and animus of the many branches of so-called progressivism was a tour de force that captured a Pulitzer Prize for history, but could as well have done for its literary accomplishments. No one is likely to comment more felicitously than Arthur M. Schlesinger, Jr.:

> Hofstadter's elaboration of this theme was a very remarkable piece of historical writing. Unfolding his argument in a series of brilliant analytical vignettes—on, for example, such subjects as the alienation of the professionals, the decline of the clergy, the rise of the professors, the shift from Mugwumpery to Progressivism, the Progressive idea of reality, the Progressive conception of the economy as a means of building individual character, the difference in political ethos between Yankees and immigrants—he showed superbly how insights derived from the social sciences and from literary criticism could illuminate without interrupting a historical narrative.[11]

Hofstadter characterized the Progressives' concept of reality as "hard": they thought in terms of steel, oil, wheat, railroad rates, the price of hogs. These were the elemental substance of politics. As Schlesinger observed, the idea of a "status revolution" worked better for the Progressives than for the Populists, whose struggle was too often for survival.[12] But on further reflection, should either movement be called a revolution? The language implied that both upheavals generated a rhetoric of protest which somehow exceeded the substance of what was being protested about, or represented more sentiment than substance.

Hofstadter recognized the stress and suffering that informed and politicized the Populist movements; but he lacked the more traditional sense of sympathetic identity and in no way shared the Populists' sense of a sort of moral *ownership* of the values of the republic. (Had not Jefferson called those who labored in the earth "the chosen people of God"?) For

---

11. "Richard Hofstadter," in *Pastmasters: Some Essays on American Historians,* ed. Marcus Cunliffe and Robin W. Winks (New York: Harper and Row, 1969), 305.
12. Ibid.

Hofstadter, they were victims of a commercialized agricultural economy rather than agrarian idealists. When he found Populist publications blaming their plight on international finance, and on banks with names like Rothschild, he detected a whiff of anti-Semitism. Rural hardship did not excuse or explain racial or religious bigotry, whose force, however, he certainly exaggerated.

Hofstadter was fascinated by the interplay and formation of public ideas; he had no appetite for the dust of archives. He failed to convince some of the Populists' ideological sympathizers, and historians who dug into the correspondence of Populist spokesmen were able to shake his more provocative findings. Anti-Semitism proved to have had little more than a minor rhetorical role in the social thought of a few; sympathy with all oppressed peoples was an equally prominent theme. And on the Progressive front, his critics found equally significant examples of "Progressive" reformers and circumstances incompatible with the "status" analysis. But if after some years it seemed that the argument had claimed more than it could sustain, *The Age of Reform* remained compulsive reading, to be absorbed, learned from, wrestled with, and simply enjoyed as literature. The status theme might not have swept the field, but it had enriched the historical vocabulary.

Hofstadter was much in demand. He had delivered the substance of *The Age of Reform* first at Chicago and later as the Commonwealth Fund Lectures at University College London. He returned to Britain in 1957 as Pitt Professor of American History at Cambridge, where a battery of great names did not wholly compensate for the minor ceremonial formalities; he greatly appreciated the immense resources available in London and felt more at home at the London School of Economics, a great institution which, he felt, responded creatively to its urban setting. A serious Dodgers fan—as were all New York intellectuals—he was appreciatively surprised to see a demonstration of one of the minor subtleties of cricket.

His readings in American history had exposed numerous traces of a propensity to anti-intellectualism, a mind-set that had grown no less virulent and, whether directed to domestic or to foreign policies, no less dangerous since the war, threatening tranquillity at home and security abroad. Of course, there were many ways of being anti-intellectual, just as there were many varieties of intellectual. Most characteristically, the attitude revealed itself in a distrust of expertise, a disposition to reject without argument the findings of scientific research, and an aversion to the practice of thinking when detached from immediate concrete objectives. Anti-intellectualism, without having an objective of its own, was an attitude always available to those who didn't want to spend public money on education or the arts. (It was beautifully delineated in Frank Capra's immensely popular film *Mr. Deeds Goes to Town.*) It was strongly averse to the patience and the compromises of diplomacy and could easily be made to condemn the outcomes of patient diplomacy as cowardice or treason. On the other hand, anti-intellectualism was hard to identify as an independent social force; nor was it likely to be consistent in character at different periods. Why had it become so widespread in a republic born of the Enlightenment?

*Anti-Intellectualism in American Life* (with which he was not himself satisfied) proved to be less a work of history than a historically informed tract for the times.[13] It traced the conscious rejection of learning to the anticlericalism of early religious revivals; it found negativity toward the hard work of learning to think in the softening process Hofstadter associated with modern educational methods. (For this trend he was particularly severe on the teacher-training profession.) The range was exceptionally wide, but the connections were not always clear. He explored the sociology of group or tribal prejudice and the authoritarian mind-set; in the historical context, however, it was hard to trace more than the most tenuous connection from eighteenth-century anticlericalism to the politicized anti-intellectualism of the 1950s.

The Pulitzer committee thought the tract important enough to merit a prize for general nonfiction—itself, no doubt, a sign of the times. As history, the book's most coherent theme was the argument that a distinct, self-consciously intellectual *class* had formed in the 1890s, which felt entitled to exert its own influence on social policy. It seems that this class—educated, sensitive, and uniquely qualified to take long views—was frustrated by the forces of anti-intellectualism from fulfilling its proper social role of public service. Intellectuals felt themselves deprived of the respect that would have been due to them in a better ordered society. Their own cast of mind was characterized by alienation from American society.

The intellectuals do not in this light appear as victims of status anxiety, but as beneficiaries of elite advantages in the "Ivy League" and other distinguished universities, the State Department, even the federal bench,

13. New York: Knopf, 1963.

sometimes adorned with tribal markings such as Dean Acheson's formal, British-style clothing (which aroused McCarthy's fury). It hardly seems surprising that they should have attracted a mixture of envy and resentment from sufferers of economic and social disadvantage.

Anti-intellectualism thus drew from its own roots in American society, to be taken into account in making public appointments and even in directing foreign policy. Since the 1890s, however, the American intellectual had responded with a self-protective attachment to this alienation from America's undereducated, consumer-oriented society. With characteristic ironic discernment, Hofstadter noticed that the intellectuals were half in love with their alienation: it preserved their sense of superiority. Any move toward a rapprochement threatened their elite status. Yet, paradoxically, he also found signs from the 1950s that many intellectuals were beginning to seek ways of recognizing the claims of mass culture and rejoining, or finding their own place in, America's mass society.

Anti-intellectualism fed the outbreaks of paranoia which periodically disfigured both city and country, leading to persecutions, irrational assessments of exaggerated dangers, and even wars, preferably short and distant. Hofstadter ascribed these and comparable phenomena to what he called a paranoid "style." This analysis included his influential view that the last decade of the nineteenth century was a period of "psychic crisis." The notion was catching and started to reappear in other historians' interpretations of unrelated episodes.

"The Paranoid Style," one of several essays devoted to the resurgence of right-wing extremism, remains a brilliant exercise which, like much of Hofstadter's work, is both a critical and a diagnostic account of the times. The "style" was characteristically given to "heated exaggeration, suspiciousness, and conspiratorial fantasy."[14] Hofstadter, who drew striking comparisons with apocalyptic fantasies in medieval Europe, noted similarities in language right down through McCarthyism to Barry Goldwater. The typical paranoid was obsessed with vast conspiracies which were held to control domestic politics, foreign policy, and, eventually, world history. Nor, Hofstadter also observed, was the extreme left free from such obsessions. These essays, we may add, were more than topical, they were timely; the extreme right had immense funds and access that gave it influ-

14. *The Paranoid Style in American Politics* (New York: Knopf, 1965), 3.

ence beyond its numbers. Military power and paranoid delusions are not a reassuring mixture.

Hofstadter had been educated in the shadow of three historians— Frederick Jackson Turner, Vernon Parrington, and Beard—whose influence he felt a need to exorcise. As a young man, Beard, who was the weightiest, had been in England at the time when irreverent historians had begun to question "the myth of Magna Carta"; it is possible that his celebrated critiques of the economic interests he discerned behind the Supreme Court and the making of the Constitution echoed this iconoclastic tone. And it is again possible to pick up the echo in Hofstadter's critical reappraisals of national icons. Beard had done much of his most influential work in the belief that concentration on ideas distracted the historian's attention from economic "realities." This unfruitful distinction, which he later abandoned, could never have appealed to Hofstadter, whose work was inspired by the need to understand history through ideas, or the states of mind in which ideas fermented. His reexamination of the progressive historians might better have been entitled "The Progressives as Historians." Yet he was uneasily conscious of their pervasive influence; and this last encounter was clearly impelled by a psychic need in Richard Hofstadter—a need for his own liberation from the more parochial constraints of the past.

Hofstadter sometimes remarked of himself that he was not so much a historian as a "historical critic." This not wholly satisfying self-description may perhaps be understood in the light of his intense interest not only in literature but also in literary criticism. He certainly wouldn't have claimed exemption from the rules of historical evidence; but he regarded criticism as a literary activity sui generis. History itself, as written, became literature; the historian should not lose sight of that aspiration. Hofstadter never lost sight of it, and was disappointed when critics blurred his finely chiseled prose, designed to convey fine and sometimes ironic distinctions, into gross simplifications.[15]

When he received from Berkeley an invitation to deliver the Jefferson Memorial Lectures, he took up a problem with which teachers of American history had long had to wrestle without having an adequate framework: why had political parties established themselves on a permanent ba-

15. Hofstadter to Pole, late summer 1967, personal archive.

sis under a constitution designed by men who opposed the very thought of parties? Ever since Queen Anne's reign, parties had formed, struggled, and dissolved both in Britain and in America. But in Hanoverian Britain, government was stabilized, and "formed" opposition became tainted with disloyalty to the throne itself. Some of this ethos washed over to the United States, where political unity was not an indigenous growth, making the threat of party divisions appear all the more dangerous to the Union. Hofstadter grasped, as previous American historians had not, the implications of British experience for George Washington and his generation. The first president's views were not all that far distant from those of George III! Against this background, Hofstadter traced with great subtlety the need for and growth of a concept of *loyal* opposition. True to his cast of mind, he saw the problem in intellectual terms; it was how to found, and legitimate, *the idea* of a party system—something its originators generally preferred to deny they were doing.[16]

*The Idea of a Party System* remains one of his most valuable contributions to American history. But something was dragging on his vitality. When his daughter Sally was young he used to tell her an endless story of an American Indian family in which the father's name was Tired-After-Four and the mother's was How-Much-of-This-Can-I-Take? His chronic disposition to hypochondria could no longer be summoned to immunize him against his increasing malaise. Meanwhile, his sense of place in American history was changing; he was moving further back, seeking deeper roots in an understanding of the less immediate past (he was fascinated by the discovery that in the mid-eighteenth century mariners approaching the New England coast could smell the pine forests from 180 nautical miles away). Hofstadter now planned for a disappearing future—to spend eighteen years on a three-volume work of American history on the old, grand scale.

A passage from his letter explaining the concept to Knopf also casts some light on his more general vision of his historical role: "What I hope to accomplish is a large-scale history that will deviate from conventional general histories to the extent that a primarily interpretive focus will govern the inclusion of narrative material."[17] The idea was to illustrate "the meaning of historical events" through "the exploration of decisive

---

16. *The Idea of a Party System* (Berkeley: University of California Press, 1969).
17. *America at 1750*, vii–ix.

episodes." Hofstadter himself, of course, would determine the meaning of the "meaning."

Funds were obtained; work began. Beginning with what he knew best, and writing now with an eloquent, sometimes melancholy simplicity, Hofstadter described, often in visual terms, the filling up of the population by white servitude and the forced movement of slaves from the African interior. He included chapters on religious awakenings and the emerging culture of a genuine colonial middle class—all this was by way of descriptive foundation, in which free will and individual happiness were often found to have been subordinate to force, domination, and fear. His main thrust aimed to be political. Then he paused, and began a preface, which suddenly stopped. Without naming leukemia, he admitted half comically that he was not manufacturing enough platelets, though he had only just learned that this had been his practice. He had worked into the early fall of 1970, occasionally pausing to write letters of encouragement to friends. He died in New York on October 24.

*America at 1750: A Social Portrait,* which was published in 1971—lucid, eloquent in transmitting both the human achievement in America and its human costs—was an ultimate vindication of Richard Hofstadter's faith in history as a literary art. His wife, Beatrice, who throughout their life together had made editorial contributions that will forever be incalculable, completed with consummate craftsmanship what he had left, handing on a virtually seamless fabric to commemorate an unfinished life.

A new book from Richard Hofstadter's hands always proved to be an event in the intellectual world. His influence extended far beyond the circle of professional historians and university students. His impact was immediate; his influence, both subtle and extensive, cannot be dismissed as ephemeral. No doubt many of his formulations have been superseded, yet the quality of his insight into both his own times and past times continues to fill his writings with a sense of immediacy that makes them exciting to read. He had exposed the "paranoid style." As an alternative he offered to Americans a style that was critical without being destructive, at once imaginative, rational, and responsibly ironic. It is no paradox to suggest that his contribution to the mental climate of his own lifetime may be a lasting achievement, for it will continue to be a wellspring for later generations.

# Howard Roberts Lamar

## by Lewis L. Gould

**M**any historians combine excellent scholarship with outstanding teaching, but few have been able to transform their major field of study through both their own writings and the impact of the books and articles of their students. Howard Roberts Lamar has performed that double feat for the history of the American West. He stands as both an inheritor of the tradition of Frederick Jackson Turner and the godfather of the "New Western History" that rejects so much of Turner's intellectual legacy. That Lamar has been both a conservator of the grand tradition of western history and an iconoclast for an often dormant field attests to his central place in determining how the American western experience has been studied and understood during the second half of the twentieth century.

A native of Alabama, Lamar was born in Tuskegee on November 18, 1923, one of two sons of John Howard Lamar and Elma Roberts Lamar. His father raised cotton on the family farm and built highways for the county. After difficult times in the Depression, the Lamars prospered during the 1940s.

Howard Lamar grew up in an atmosphere suffused with history. He was aware of the distinguished heritage of the Lamar family, which included two members of the United States Supreme Court, Lucius Quintus Cincinnatus Lamar and Joseph Rucker Lamar, and the second president of the Republic of Texas, Mirabeau B. Lamar. An intellectually inclined aunt and two grandmothers dedicated to historical study also influenced the young Lamar.[1]

Educated at Tuskegee High School, Lamar attended Emory University

---

1. Interview with Howard R. Lamar, November 16, 1999; Howard R. Lamar, curriculum vitae, 1999. For a brief biographical essay on Lamar, see Homer E. Socolofsky, Richard Etulain, and Patricia Nelson Limerick, "Western History Association Prize Recipient, 1992: Howard R. Lamar," *Western Historical Quarterly* 24 (May 1993): 149–50.

in Atlanta, where he studied with the historians James Harvey Young, who introduced him to Frederick Jackson Turner's frontier hypothesis, and Ross H. McLean. He graduated in 1944. Now intent on a career in history, he entered the graduate program at Yale University the following autumn. At Yale he wanted to write on the industrialization of Alabama in the Gilded Age but was having difficulty identifying source materials. He asked Professor Ralph Henry Gabriel what to do to find a viable topic and was told: "Raised in the South, educated in the East, for a dissertation, go West, young man!" When he asked how to do that, Gabriel directed him to the newly acquired William Robertson Coe Collection of Western Americana at Yale.[2]

In the Coe Collection, Lamar found fascinating letters about politics in the Dakota Territory. Although he was the "least pioneering type one could ever meet," the twenty-four-year-old Lamar hitchhiked and traveled by bus in 1947 to Pierre, South Dakota, to begin his dissertation research on territorial politics. Arriving at harvest time when accommodations were not to be had, he bunked on cots with the men bringing in the wheat crop before starting his research at the South Dakota Historical Society. Years later, recalling the descendants of pioneers that he had met, he remarked: "I came away knowing I had experienced a passing frontier."[3]

Lamar received his doctorate in 1951 for his study of the Dakota Territory, and the dissertation was awarded the George Washington Egleston Prize. Although a heart problem kept Lamar out of military service in World War II, he taught for the Army Specialized Training Program at the University of Massachusetts in 1945–1946. He then spent a year at Wesleyan University, from 1948 to 1949. Lamar was appointed an instructor in history at Yale in 1949 and an assistant professor of history five years later. During this period he revised his dissertation for publication by the Yale University Press in 1956. His active schedule also included a two-year term, from 1951 to 1953, on the New Haven Board of Aldermen, where he learned about urban politics in the Northeast from the inside. He decid-

2. Catherine McNicol Stock, "Introduction to the Institute for Regional Studies Edition," in Howard Roberts Lamar, *Dakota Territory, 1861–1889* (Fargo: Institute for Regional Studies, North Dakota State University, 1997), xiii.

3. *Writing the History of the American West: Essays and Commentary by Martin Ridge, Elizabeth A. H. John, Alvin M. Josephy, Jr., Howard R. Lamar, and Kevin Starr* (Worcester, Mass.: American Antiquarian Society, 1991), 117–18 (both quotations).

ed not to run for reelection and also declined a later offer to be a candidate for the Connecticut legislature.[4]

In 1951, the Yale Department of History asked Lamar to offer the first course on the history of the American West to be taught at Yale. Those Americanists interested in improving the offerings in western history included David M. Potter, also an Emory graduate who became a friend and mentor, and Ralph Gabriel. The faculty specified "that it was to be a small starred course only to be taken by history majors who had already had a number of 'regular' American history classes."

To prepare himself for his new teaching assignment, Lamar traveled around the American West and into Mexico for two months during the summer of 1951. His immersion in the expanse and diversity of the West convinced him that he had found a subject worthy of a lifetime's study. In the first class of History 37 that he launched that fall, two of his students were Robert A. Divine and William H. Goetzmann, both of whom would become distinguished American historians in their own right at the University of Texas at Austin. History 37 became popular with Yale undergraduates because of Lamar's engaging style as a lecturer and the wide range of perspectives on the West that he provided. His teaching assistants recall hearing many of the themes of his subsequent writings first tried out in lectures in the course. It soon lost its "starred" status and gained the friendly title "Cowboys and Indians," by which it was known among generations of Yale undergraduates.[5]

Lamar's dissertation, published by the Yale University Press in 1956 as *Dakota Territory, 1861–1889*, represented the first scholarly investigation of the politics of a territory in the Trans-Mississippi West. Earl Pomeroy had published his general study of the territories nine years earlier, but an intensive probe, based on primary sources, of a single western territory had not been written. Lamar's main point was that "a federally supported territorial government" had assumed "a primary economic importance during the region's development." The emphasis on the role of eastern institutions and values in the West would be a continuing theme of Lamar's work. In that respect, Lamar's book represented a major challenge to Frederick Jackson Turner's depiction of the frontier as an incubator of demo-

4. Lamar interview, November 16, 1999.
5. Lamar, "Much to Celebrate: The Western History Association's Twenty-Fifth Birthday," *Western Historical Quarterly* 17 (October 1986): 397.

cratic ideals. *Dakota Territory* became a major influence on Lamar's graduate students in the 1960s who were following his lead in approaching the study of the political institutions in the West.[6]

The critical success of *Dakota Territory* placed Lamar in the forefront among younger western historians during the late 1950s and early 1960s. He was actively involved in the creation of the Western History Association in 1961 and 1962, and he was beginning to attract a small but growing number of graduate students in the Yale department. In 1959 he was promoted to associate professor, and in that same year he married Doris Shirley White. The couple would have two daughters.

During these years, Lamar came to have a high regard for the scholarly ability and encouragement to pursue issues of western history of the leading Turnerian historian in the field, Ray Allen Billington. Billington invited Lamar to be a coeditor of the History of the American Frontier series, a commitment that endured after Billington's death, when Lamar worked with Martin Ridge and David Weber and later William Cronon. In 1964 Lamar was promoted to the rank of professor of history.

For his second book, Lamar embarked on a more ambitious study of four territories—Colorado, Utah, Arizona, and New Mexico—and their political development. Drawing on material from the rich resources of the Yale Western Americana Collection, he also edited volumes about western voyages and overland treks that forecast his interest in how the process of getting to the West changed the people who experienced it.[7]

*The Far Southwest, 1846–1912: A Territorial History* was published in 1966. The book solidified Lamar's reputation as a preeminent interpreter of the western experience. In addition to recounting the political history of the four territories he had examined, the book showed Lamar's growing interest in the economic role of capitalist merchants and their institu-

6. Lamar, *Dakota Territory*, 280. Earl S. Pomeroy, *The Territories and the United States* (Philadelphia: University of Pennsylvania Press, 1947); for reviews of *Dakota Territory,* see Robert W. Johannsen, *Pacific Historical Review* 26 (February 1957): 84–86, and Hebert S. Schell, *The Mississippi Valley Historical Review,* 43 (March 1957): 690–91. Lewis L. Gould, *Wyoming: A Political History, 1868–1896* (New Haven: Yale University Press, 1968); R. Hal Williams, *The Democratic Party in California Politics, 1880–1896* (Stanford: Stanford University Press, 1973).

7. Joseph T. Downey, *The Cruise of the Portsmouth: A Sailor's View of the Naval Conquest of California,* ed. Lamar (New Haven: Yale University Library, 1958); Susan S. Magoffin, *Down the Santa Fe Trail and into Old Mexico,* ed. Lamar (New Haven: Yale University Press, 1962).

tions such as Zion's Co-operative Mercantile Institution in Utah and the Goldwaters in Arizona. Lamar's interpretive focus was shifting to the economic and social history of the West. *The Far Southwest,* with its emphasis on the role of Hispanic political and economic leaders in New Mexico and Arizona, also contributed to the surge of interest about the impact of Mexican Americans in the West during the mid-1960s.[8]

At the end of the 1960s, Lamar appraised the historical legacy of Frederick Jackson Turner in a chapter for Marcus Cunliffe and Robin Winks's *Pastmasters.* For the project, Lamar did research in Turner's papers and mastered the extensive critical literature on Turner that had been produced during the previous four decades. In the essay, Lamar concluded that "Turner had posed his thesis before the facts were in." Turner had overlooked the idea of a border as a frontier between two countries, or empires, as in the case of the American West. He had not given sufficient emphasis to the role of the federal government and the extent to which settlers had looked eastward for their political and cultural values rather than innovating. Lamar did credit Turner with identifying free land as a key concept in American history. While Turner "may not have been a great historian in the orthodox sense," Lamar decided, "he was something of an intuitive genius."[9] Although respectful of Turner's achievements, Lamar was finding his own vision of the West as the 1970s began. In recognition of Lamar's scholarship, he was named the William Robertson Coe Professor of History in 1970.

Lamar's reputation in western history had reached a level that made it natural for him to be selected as the president of the Western History Association in the autumn of 1972 when the scholarly group held its annual meeting in New Haven, Connecticut. The riches of the Coe Collection added to the attractiveness of holding the meeting in the East for the first time. Lamar's presidential address proved to be a turning point in the evolution of the field. While it did not have quite the national impact of Frederick Jackson Turner's 1893 presentation, entitled "The Significance of the Frontier in American History," what Lamar had to say proved to be a catalyst for an important revitalization of the field of western history.

8. New Haven: Yale University Press, 1966; for reviews of *The Far Southwest,* see Harwood Hinton, *Pacific Historical Review* 35 (November 1966): 470–72, and John Porter Bloom, *Journal of American History* 52 (March 1967): 825–26.

9. "Frederick Jackson Turner," in *Pastmasters: Some Essays on American Historians,* ed. Marcus Cunliffe and Robin W. Winks (New York: Harper and Row, 1969), 100, 109.

Lamar's title was "Persistent Frontier: The West in the Twentieth Century," but his essay ranged into all aspects of the field and its existing research agenda. His address drew on the work that other innovative western historians, including Earl Pomeroy, had done in the preceding decade, but the remarks were delivered with Lamar's dry wit and adroit turn of phrase. At that point in the early 1970s he asserted that "the West is now more, rather than less, significant as a part of American national history." Accordingly, Lamar argued, historians of the West would benefit from "the new approaches to history" that were then in vogue in the profession.[10]

One by one, Lamar reviewed the topics that could gain in interpretive insight from fresh exploration. Among them were ethnic and racial minorities in "culturally distinct enclaved groups," urban life, the role of women in the Gold Rush and other mass western migrations, and the history of Native Americans. In common with his own evolving interest in the role of traders in the West, Lamar spent much time on the ways that trade had promoted both destructive and constructive interactions among Indians and whites. Lamar had also been thinking about a way to explain the role of western merchants and businessmen who moved from one enterprise to another. These "phase capitalists" were an important element in understanding regional economic growth. "Indeed," Lamar concluded, "one could come to know the regions of the West by the companies they kept."[11]

In the last portion of the talk and subsequent essay, Lamar looked to family history as a means of explaining how the West had been a persistent frontier. He called for "a comparative study of ethnically distinct family structures in the West" as his discussion moved from Mexican American wives in Arizona hidden away from Anglo scorn to the stories of Hamlin Garland to even the Earps and the Daltons. Finally, Lamar urged his listeners to see the West as a region where Americans both sought to reform the existing institutions and to "save America." Conservation politics, national policy toward Indians, and the homestead ideal all reflected, in Lamar's estimation, a desire to preserve the West and yet make it

---

10. "Persistent Frontier: The West in the Twentieth Century," *Western Historical Quarterly* 4 (January 1973): 5–25 (quotations on 6–7). Like all western historians, Lamar has recognized the pioneering work of Earl Pomeroy in his significant interpretive essay, "Toward a Reorientation of Western History: Continuity and Environment," *Mississippi Valley Historical Review* 41 (March 1955): 579–600.

11. "Persistent Frontier," 7, 15.

anew. As presidential addresses went, it was an ambitious road map for future research and writing. It suggested that the assembled western historians were engaged in as important and far-reaching a scholarly enterprise as anything Turner might have prescribed eight decades earlier.[12]

At the end of his talk, Lamar struck a cautionary note. "We have a duty, it seems, to avoid the pitfalls of using history to conduct crusades." He believed that all students of western history, nonprofessionals and academics, "must join in ferreting out the facets of the past and honestly appraising their meaning, even if that meaning should be unpopular." Such an approach, Lamar maintained, "might produce a new history of the Old West and a first history of the twentieth-century West which may be invaluable in redefining our national purpose." Striking a note that would not echo through the "new western history" to come, Lamar concluded that "the West continues to be as significant as Turner said it was, whether we are speaking of its past, its present, its future, or of its old meaning or its new meaning. Saddle up your typewriters, ladies and gentlemen, it is time to ride herd on these new frontiers."[13]

Lamar's talk made a major contribution to legitimizing new methods as applied to western history and to broadening the scope of what it was appropriate to study. He did so in a nonjudgmental manner and did not indict the work of his scholarly predecessors in the field. Clearly, he was convinced that western history had to be more inclusive, more aware of those individuals and movements that had been left out of previous accounts, and more humane in its focus on the victims of expansion as well as the victors. Never did Lamar approach western history with a hard ideological edge or an impatience with opposing points of view.

During the remainder of the 1970s, Lamar began to emerge as a leader in the Yale history department in his own right. His eminence as a teacher of undergraduates and graduate students grew during these years. In his lectures and seminars, Lamar made studying the West an engrossing experience. He was open to all kinds of classroom comments about the region, and one of his former graduate students recalls, "I never saw him put down or stifle even the most unimaginative student—he liked to make scholars bloom, and he certainly had an academic green thumb!"[14]

12. Ibid., 17, 19.
13. Ibid., 20.
14. These comments are based on my own experience as one of Lamar's students, and they are confirmed in e-mail messages I received from William Cronon, October 13, 1999;

Lamar's eclectic approach to western history and American history in general made him an active director of doctoral dissertations as his teaching career expanded during the 1970s and 1980s. By his own count, he supervised thirty-four dissertations in history and another thirteen in American studies. For another five to ten doctoral students at Yale he was a co-director or a very involved reader. He also devoted time to senior essays. One undergraduate in 1969, Jack Dalrymple, wanted to write about his ancestor Oliver Dalrymple and bonanza farming in the Red River Valley of Dakota. Approaching Lamar, who was then chair of the history department, Dalrymple made his case and waited for Lamar's reply. With customary openness, Lamar said: "Well, I'll be darned. Dalrymple on Dalrymple. . . . I would be honored to be part of this fascinating project."[15]

His greatest impact as a teacher was, of course, in western history, where the roster of his students forms a "who's who" of the school that has been labeled the "New Western History." He directed the work of such noteworthy practitioners in that field as Patricia Nelson Limerick, Clyde Milner, Sarah Deutsch, Martha Sandweiss, John Faragher, and William Cronon. As Cronon says of Lamar, "although others have contributed to the remarkable changes that have occurred in western history over the past quarter century, Howard Lamar's quiet leadership and influence are everywhere apparent in what has come to be called 'the New Western History.'"[16]

Despite the controversy that has surrounded the New Western History, Lamar acted as a mentor who urged his students to develop their own approaches to the field. Limerick and Cronon, for example, have diverged in their view of the relevance of the concept of the frontier to western history, but both can claim inspiration and encouragement from Lamar's training. His ability to prepare some of the best younger scholars in western history during the 1980s gave the field a surge of energy and excitement that it had lacked for many years.[17]

---

Philip Deloria October 13, 1999; and James E. Crisp, October 26, 1999. I received very helpful information on this aspect of Lamar's work from Karl Jacoby and Michael McGerr. John Faragher was also kind in letting Lamar's former students know about this project, and John D. W. Guice shared his memories of Lamar's teaching with me.

15. Lamar, letter to Gould, October 13, 1999, provides a list of his graduate students; Jack Dalrymple, "Foreword to the Institute Edition," in Lamar, *Dakota Territory,* ix.

16. Cronon, e-mail to Gould.

17. The literature on the New Western History is too large to summarize here, but see Forrest G. Robinson, ed., *The New Western History: The Territory Ahead* (Tucson: University of Arizona Press, 1997), 29–33, for some of the differing approaches among the field's

One reason Lamar attracted so many talented students during the 1980s was the continuing example of his own scholarship. In 1977 he published an important lecture under the title *The Trader on the American Frontier: Myth's Victim;* this volume placed western commerce in a broader historical and chronological context. That same year saw the publication of *The Reader's Encyclopedia of the American West,* which he had edited. The encyclopedia gave many of Lamar's students the chance to contribute to an important synthetic volume, and it put his name before an even wider public.[18]

Although he served as dean of Yale College from 1979 to 1985, Lamar continued to teach his western history course and to write on new developments in the field. He coedited *The Frontier in History: North America and South Africa Compared* (1981) with his Yale colleague Leonard Thompson. The volume grew out of Lamar's long-standing conviction that effectively understanding the West required a "comparative perspective." In addition to this book, he also wrote an article assessing regional responses in the Canadian and American West to the Great Depression of the 1930s. Lamar's commitment to both articulating new approaches and then carrying them out in practice was a major reason generations of graduate students at Yale found working with him so appealing.[19]

Lamar wrote other important studies during the 1980s, including his 1986 George W. Littlefield Lectures at the University of Texas at Austin, which were published as *Texas Crossings: The Lone Star State and the Far West* (1991). Also in 1986, he coauthored with William Cronon and two of his own graduate students an essay that explored ways in which the roles of women in western history could be made an integral part of survey

---

leading figures. See also Patricia Nelson Limerick, Clyde A. Milner II, and Charles E. Rankin, eds., *Trails: Toward a New Western History* (Lawrence: University Press of Kansas, 1991), and Gene M. Gressley, ed., *Old West/New West: Quo Vadis?* (Worland, Wyo.: High Plains Publishing Co., 1994).

18. *The Trader on the American Frontier: Myth's Victim* (College Station: Texas A&M University Press, 1977); *The Reader's Encyclopedia of the American West* (New York: Thomas Y. Crowell, 1977).

19. *The Frontier in History: North America and South Africa Compared* (New Haven: Yale University Press, 1981); "Comparing Depressions: The Great Plains and Canadian Prairie Experiences, 1929–1941," in *The Twentieth Century West: Historical Interpretations,* ed. Gerald D. Nash and Richard W. Etulain (Albuquerque: University of New Mexico Press, 1989), 175–206. Lamar also taught comparative history courses during the 1970s. One given with C. Vann Woodward compared Reconstruction in the South and the West. Another taught with Richard Morse approached frontiers in North and South America from a comparative basis.

courses in the classroom. Then he surveyed the achievements of the western historians on the occasion of the twenty-fifth birthday of the Western History Association. He called for more attention to the "mind" of the West and western Americans, and he renewed his desire to see more comparative studies of the kind he was advancing himself. In 1987 Lamar received Yale's highest honor for a faculty member when he became a Sterling Professor of History.[20]

His most influential work during the decade was a chapter that he contributed to a book coedited by one of his former students. Steven Hahn, who had worked with Lamar on agrarian radicalism in the South, and Jonathan Prude asked a number of younger scholars to contribute to a volume that was published as *The Countryside in the Age of Capitalist Transformation: Essays on the Social History of Rural America* (1985). Lamar's chapter was entitled "From Bondage to Contract: Ethnic Labor in the American West, 1600–1890." Looking at three centuries of western history, Lamar identified the experience of those who worked in the region against their will or under contractual conditions that limited their economic freedom. Moving from the situation of Indians compelled to work for their European conquerors to the labor system in Russian Alaska to the fur trade, Lamar examined numerous ethnic groups who had been required to furnish their labor for the dominant economic powers and asked whether "the American West and the Western frontier were more properly a symbol of bondage than freedom when it came to labor systems." He linked the existence of these preindustrial labor arrangements to the disruptions and labor violence that occurred when these workers encountered industrialization at the end of the nineteenth century. Once again, Lamar asked for comparisons of western labor systems to understand this larger historical process.[21]

20. *Texas Crossings: The Lone Star State and the Far West, 1836–1986* (Austin: University of Texas Press, 1991); William Cronon, Howard Lamar, Katherine G. Morrisey, and Jay Gitlin, "Women and the West: Rethinking the Western History Survey Course," *Western Historical Quarterly* 17 ( July 1986): 269–90; "Much to Celebrate," 397–416. Lamar also edited Jean-Nicolas Perlot, *Gold Seeker: Adventures of a Belgian Argonaut in California and Oregon* (New Haven: Yale University Press, 1985).

21. Chapel Hill: University of North Carolina Press, 1985. Lamar's essay was on 293–324 (quotation on 294). One of Lamar's students carried forward the lines of investigation that this essay opened. See Gunther Peck, "Reinventing Free Labor: Immigrant Padrones and Contract Laborers in North America, 1885–1925," *Journal of American History* 83 (December 1996): 848–71.

Lamar did not call this article or the other essays he wrote during the 1980s "the New Western History," but what he said proved stimulating and intriguing to still another group of graduate students who came to New Haven in the early 1990s to study with the author of these provocative works. In turn, these students began to delve into the labor relationships in the West that often belied the Turnerian vision of economic possibility and personal freedom.

The explosion of controversy about the "New Western History" during the late 1980s and early 1990s focused attention on Lamar as the mentor of many of the new scholarly voices that were reshaping western history. His year-long stint as president of Yale University in 1992–1993 further enhanced his national reputation as a scholar and educator. Although he retired from active teaching in 1994, his work as a historian continued with his usual energy.

*The Reader's Encyclopedia of the American West* had been so well received during the 1970s and 1980s that it was natural to prepare a new, revised edition, published in 1998, that reflected the upheavals that had occurred in western history since 1977. The task was a monumental one since the volume was the work of three hundred contributors and had more than twenty-four hundred entries and six hundred illustrations. Returning to the theme of his first encounter with western history, Lamar said of his career: "Born in the South, educated there and in the East, and headquartered at Yale for most of my career, I have found that the West provides a wonderful window on American history."[22]

The affection and respect with which Lamar is regarded by his former graduate students were evident in the festschrift that they edited for him in 1992. The book, *Under an Open Sky: Rethinking America's Western Past,* included a chapter by Lamar himself entitled "Westering in the Twenty-First Century: Speculations on the Future of the American Past," in which he deftly summarized the chapters in the volume and praised the authors for having pursued "the goals of accuracy and objectivity" as they aimed at "a full history of the complex matrix of western regions."[23]

22. *The New Encyclopedia of the American West* (New Haven: Yale University Press, 1998), ix.

23. "Westering in the Twenty-First Century: Speculations on the Future of the Western Past," in *Under an Open Sky: Rethinking America's Western Past,* ed. William Cronon, George Miles, and Jay Gitlin (New York: W. W. Norton, 1992), 257–74 (quotation on 274).

In the midst of his eighth decade, Lamar has remained an active participant in scholarship and research. He conducts tours of western sites for Yale alumni and others, and he is as productive as ever in looking toward new ideas and new approaches to his field. His recent articles have looked into artistic images of the West and the impact of novelists and poets who carried on the tradition of Frederick Jackson Turner in their writings. In 2000 his works in progress included a biography of Charles A. Siringo and a volume on the southern overland trails. A collection of his essays on western history was also planned.[24] In June 2000, Yale honored him by creating the Howard Roberts Lamar Center for the Study of Frontiers and Borders.

When Howard Lamar began research on the territorial history of Dakota in the 1940s, western history still stood in the shadow of Turner and the frontier thesis. Much had been written for and against Turner's formulation, but it persisted as the dominant theory of the field. While there was a good deal of value in Turner's insights, western history was largely an all-male drama in which Indians, African Americans, and women played bit parts. The federal government and eastern values seemed only distant echoes on the robust, free-spirited frontier of Turner.

Among historians of American history in general, the West was regarded as a place where the less talented among their ranks went to practice their craft in seclusion and comfort. The scholarly action was in southern history and colonial history and among such perennially hot topics as Jacksonian Democracy, the Civil War, and progressivism. To enter western history was to retire to a scholarly backwater, as if one was being relegated to the rear area of the war, where only faint reverberations of the real scholarly battles could sometimes be heard by the somnolent frontier historians.

Half a century later, western history has become a contested terrain where younger historians write about an endless variety of issues that

---

24. Lamar, "Keeping the Faith: The Forgotten Generations of Literary Turnerians, 1920–1960," in *Frontier and Region: Essays in Honor of Martin Ridge,* ed. Robert C. Ritchie and Paul Andrew Hutton (San Marino, Calif.: Huntington Library and Albuquerque: University of New Mexico Press, 1997), 231–50, and "Looking Backward, Looking Forward: Selected Themes in Western Art Since 1900," in *Discovered Lands, Invented Pasts: Transforming Visions of the American West,* ed. Jules David Prown et al. (New Haven: Yale University Press and Yale University Art Gallery, 1992), 167–92.

would have seemed out of bounds in the 1940s and 1950s. Howard Lamar was not the only advocate of change, methodological rigor, and a broader sweep of subject matter in western history during the second half of the twentieth century. Lamar has written eloquently about the role of Earl Pomeroy at the University of Oregon in defining "western history in such a way that it is freed of its parochial vision and can be used to address fundamental questions about the American character and the nature of history itself." Other major figures in the field of Lamar's generation would include Leonard Arrington, Gerald Nash, Gene Gressley, William H. Goetzmann, and many others.[25]

Howard Lamar, however, was ideally suited to be the major catalyst for positive change in the teaching and writing about the American West. His affiliation with Yale University provided him with access to the best graduate students entering the history profession. The resources of the Yale library system, particularly the Coe Collection, supplied an ample amount of research topics and potential books. Being apart from the West itself also kept Lamar and his students insulated from the parochial jealousies of the region's universities and historical societies. In such a congenial environment, recruiting students to work on western history topics was not difficult.

Not every historian makes the most of professional opportunities. Howard Lamar did so as a historian of the American West. From the moment that he identified his dissertation topic in the late 1940s, he pursued the implications of working in western history with energy and dedication. Across half a century, he remained open to new interpretations and in search of fresh insights. What began as a career in the political history of a western territory has embraced the concept of comparative frontiers as a means of understanding the West. Lamar and his students have delved deeply into the impact of preindustrial labor systems in the West and placed new emphasis on the artistic heritage of the region. Withal, Lamar has not repeated himself, or concentrated on a single productive topic. Instead, he has been a teacher and source of ideas as diverse and interesting as the West itself.

Lamar's intellectual scope made him an excellent mentor and enabled him to stimulate a generation of younger western historians to break out

25. "Earl Pomeroy: Historian's Historian," *Pacific Historical Review* 56 (November 1987): 547–60 (quotation on 549).

of the older stereotypes of the field. While the historical jury is still out on the specific merits of all aspects of "the New Western History," the lasting impact of the ferment that this school represented is now undeniable. Howard Lamar's dual role as a charismatic teacher and scholarly innovator has made an indelible mark on western history as it has been taught and practiced in the United States since 1945.

# Gerda Lerner

## by Catherine Clinton

The field of American history has been most dramatically transformed in the past half century by the changes wrought by waves of determined feminists who broke down barriers within the academic world after 1945. A dynamic generation of women historians joined the academy and provided a vast outpouring of new scholarship on women. For two decades both men and women historians collectively struggled to integrate the role of women into their explorations of the pageant of America's past. But no individual was more instrumental to the growth and development of the field of American women's history in the second half of the twentieth century than Gerda Lerner.

Lerner's creativity as a scholar,[1] energy as an organizer, and determination as a leader and champion of women's history have created a powerful legacy. Her influence has literally changed the face of American history, in a way that is immediately recognizable to anyone who attends the annual meetings of the Organization of American Historians (OAH). Lerner attended her first OAH conference in 1963 while a first-year graduate student. Her memories were dominated by images of a handful of women dotting a sea of men, the unfriendly atmosphere of "smokers," the closed circle of hiring through the "old boys' network." Alienated, but always resourceful, Lerner introduced herself to a group of nuns in attendance, and some of these (quite literally) "sister scholars" became lifelong friends.[2] Within twenty years, Lerner's impact on the profession was ac-

---

1. For a bibliography of Gerda Lerner's writing to 1995 compiled by Tom Dublin, see Linda Kerber, Alice Kessler-Harris, and Kathryn Kish Sklar, eds. *U.S. History as Women's History: New Feminist Essays* (Chapel Hill: University of North Carolina Press, 1995), 439–41.
2. Lerner, "Women among the Professors of History," in *Voices of Women Historians: The Personal, The Political, The Professional*, ed. Eileen Boris and Nupur Chaudhuri (Bloomington: Indiana University Press, 1999), 2.

knowledged and rewarded when she served as president of the OAH in 1981–1982, the first woman to head the organization in more than fifty years.

Lerner's sense of embattlement rather than entitlement fueled her remarkable academic career. Born Gerda Kronstein in 1920, one of two daughters in a middle-class family in Vienna, Austria, Lerner was deeply shaped by her early involvement in the Resistance. Her father escaped Hilter's dragnet by fleeing the country, but the eighteen-year-old Gerda and her mother were thrown in jail. Terrified that she might be shipped off to a Nazi concentration camp, Lerner organized a school for the seven inmates crowded with her into a one-man cell. Fortunately, teachers at her prestigious academy petitioned to have Gerda, a brilliant student, released so she could take her qualifying exam for university. Lerner and her mother were granted deportation papers only after her father signed away his property (from abroad) to secure his wife's and daughter's freedom. After six weeks in prison, Lerner was released. Although weak from starvation, she sat for her exam and received high marks, graduating magna cum laude.

Despite this impressive intellectual achievement, Lerner felt an outcast. This sense of "otherness" would be creatively exploited in her academic work in the years to come. Further, she had faced death at such a formative stage that her life would be forever altered by her youthful encounter with the Nazis.

At the age of nineteen, Gerda immigrated to America alone; she remembers that her passage was filled with trepidation and seasickness. Further, it was only the first of many difficult journeys. When she landed in the United States, she dreamed of becoming an accomplished writer—in English. She wrote novels while working in a series of stereotypical female jobs—as a salesgirl, waitress, and office worker. She met Carl Lerner, and they married in 1941. The couple settled in Hollywood, California, where Carl Lerner could pursue his career as a film editor.

Gerda Lerner gave birth to two children, Daniel and Stephanie, assuming the role of mother and housewife while continuing her writing. In 1943, she became a naturalized U.S. citizen. Lerner coauthored (with Eve Merriam) an off-Broadway review, *Singing of Women* (1951). She published her first novel, *No Farewell* (1955). Then in 1964, she penned the screenplay for *Black Like Me,* a film that tackled issues of race and social justice.

When the Lerners moved to New York City, Gerda Lerner began working on a novel about the Grimke sisters. Luckily for historians, she decided that "a fictionalized biography was no good, and I needed to improve my research skills."[3] At the age of thirty-eight, she enrolled at the New School for Social Research in Manhattan. She became enthralled by women's history. Her talent for challenging the academic status quo emerged when she proposed to the president of the college that he allow an undergraduate (her) to teach a course in women's history. Although the first time she proposed it the course failed to attract the requisite number of students, Lerner persisted. When she listed it again, the course survived. Lerner taught her first official women's history course while still an undergraduate. She completed her bachelor's degree in 1963.

Inspired by feminist theory, nerved by her sense of right, Lerner applied to do graduate work in history at Columbia University. During an interview following her application, Lerner was asked why she wanted to study history. She responded "without blinking an eyelash" that she "want[ed] to make women's history respectable." To which her interviewer responded, "What is women's history?" Clearly Gerda Lerner had her work cut out for her. Lerner later confessed that her lofty aims to carve out a place for women's history and to see it flourish were not something that she realistically felt she would be able to accomplish, considering her age and the temper of the times in academe. But with her combative spirit, she was committed to "work in that direction, and go down trying."[4]

Lerner entered graduate school at the age of forty-three. Within three years she had earned both her M.A. and her Ph.D. (completing her dissertation on the Grimke sisters). She confessed, "I made up for lost time." She was a lecturer at the New School for Social Research (1963–1965) before joining the faculty at Long Island University in Brooklyn, where she soon rose to the rank of associate professor with tenure. In 1967 her first work of scholarship in American women's history was published by Houghton Mifflin: *The Grimke Sisters from South Carolina: Rebels against Slavery.*

Lerner rightly complained that the 1960s was a dreadful time for women within the academy—colleagues were often hostile toward older women and mothers. The climate was chilly for feminists as well. Women unwilling to play secondary or submissive roles might be permanently out

3. Lerner, "On the Future of Our Past," *Ms.*, September 1981, p. 51.
4. Ibid.

in the cold. As late as 1969 women earned only a little more than 10 percent of the Ph.D.s awarded in history, so females were a token presence among history departments at colleges and especially universities.

In 1968 Gerda Lerner joined the faculty of Sarah Lawrence College in suburban New York City. Her years at Sarah Lawrence would prove pivotal and productive, and her organizational talents and dedication to women's history would launch an important crusade. Under Lerner's leadership, many would enlist in the battle to revitalize women's history and to force the closed institutions of higher learning to open to women educators, advocates of feminism, and curriculum reformers.

During this turning point in her career, it is difficult to disentangle Lerner's commitment to improving women's status within the historical profession from her vanguard role as a proponent of feminist approaches to the past. Just as clearly as Lerner saw these two goals as interlocking demands, so the traditional gatekeepers within the historical profession saw this assault on male privilege as a Hydra-like monster. While one school of thought might perceive Gerda Lerner's political style as akin to the mythical Medusa, others might rightly see her as more like Minerva, leaping full-blown from the skull of paternalism: her sword and her intellect constituted a double threat to her detractors.

She wielded a mighty pen during these heady years as she sliced through myths of female invisibility. Lerner challenged women's historical marginality in 1969 by publishing two important articles. "The Lady and the Mill Girl: Changes in the Status of Women in the Age of Jackson" demonstrated "how differences in class location altered women's relationships to each other and shaped their responses to technological and economic change."[5] Her second article, "New Approaches for the Study of Women in American History," hammered home the ideological beliefs she would soon put into practice.

Domestic political unrest during the Vietnam War encouraged change. By 1969 Lerner was able to find a growing cohort of fellow travelers who wanted to see history reconfigured in radical and dynamic ways. Because of her perceptions of her own "outsider" status, Lerner challenged those historians with whom she tangled by demanding sensitivity to a wider range of issues than many feminists at the time embraced. When Betty Friedan's *The Feminine Mystique* rocketed to national prominence fol-

5. In Kerber et al., eds. *U.S. History as Women's History*, 3.

lowing its publication in 1963, Lerner wrote to Friedan complaining that her book offered no insight into the lives of black women and had nothing to offer on the crucial subject of race. (Despite this conflict, Lerner and Friedan would reconcile to become founders of the National Organization for Women in 1966.)

This protest about the inclusion of race was not simply an idle ideological potshot, for Lerner herself was hard at work on an important collection that would be published in 1972: *Black Women in White America: A Documentary History.* Lerner would later tell stories about arriving in some southern town and giving the taxi driver the address of an African American church where she wanted to survey the archives, only to have the taxi driver warn her off such a destination—claiming it was too "dangerous." But Lerner was a woman on a mission, and she would not be derailed from her goal of discovering hidden caches of primary source material. Her published results would demonstrate the availability of sources that proved the vitality of black women's history. This collection inspired dozens of scholars, black and white, men and women, to include African American women in their scholarship, to reevaluate the crucial connections between gender and racial oppression. Lerner herself would publish pieces on Sarah Mapps Douglass and on the black women's club movement, as well as on the intersections of black and white women in U.S. history. At the American Historical Association (AHA) meeting in 1969, Lerner was one of seventeen people to show up at Berenice Carroll's invitation to initiate the Coordinating Committee on Women in the Historical Profession (CCWHP), a committee Carroll and Lerner would cochair. An open call gathered more than a hundred interested listeners; many welcomed and joined the organization. By 1970 the group's membership had responded to an important survey: 45 percent wanted the organization to focus on the professional status of women, and only 25 percent wanted courses in women's history to be the top priority. Once again, Lerner's work was cut out for her.

In the meantime, petitions to the AHA resulted in the formation of a standing committee on the status of women, chaired by Professor Willie Lee Rose of the University of Virginia. The OAH, the Southern Historical Association (SHA), and other professional organizations would soon follow in these pioneering footsteps. Leading history organizations surveyed women's status in the profession, in order to recommend and then implement strategies to reduce discrimination and gender inequality.

Lerner was part of the pressure group lobbying the AHA to prepare a roster of women historians and to create a register of advertisements for jobs—to break up the backroom "good-old-boy" politics of academic employment. Further protests caused historical organizations to regularize the application process for appearing on panels at professional meetings. Lerner and other feminist leaders also demanded representation for women on the advisory boards of journals and in other key positions within history organizations.

Lerner was fully committed to these efforts but was equally focused on promoting women's history. She kept up her pioneering scholarship, publishing *The Woman in American History* in 1971 and *The Female Experience: An American Documentary* in 1976, and redoubled her organizational efforts.

In 1970 CCWHP members reported that only twenty-two courses in women's history were then offered at institutions of higher learning. Lerner made it her top priority to create training programs for scholars in this nascent subdiscipline. With generous funding from the Rockefeller Foundation, in 1972 she launched a master's program in women's history at Sarah Lawrence—the first such program in the United States.

A great personal tragedy visited Lerner in 1972 when her beloved husband, Carl, was diagnosed with a brain tumor; he would die in 1973. A poignant portrait of her marriage and how Lerner dealt with the difficulty of the decline and loss of her husband is provided by one of her most compelling volumes, *A Death of One's Own* (1978). Despite her deep sense of grief, she carried on her important work in women's history.

This crusade was particularly heroic because of the persecution and ridicule such a campaign attracted. Alice Kessler-Harris points out, "Gerda was enormously courageous in the early part of the 1970s before women's history had become legitimate." Further, both Kessler-Harris and Linda Kerber (coeditors with Kathryn Kish Sklar of a volume in honor of Lerner published in 1995) emphasize the significance of Lerner's commitment to reaching out to a wider audience. Kerber points out that Lerner joined the profession only after she was well established as a writer. Kessler-Harris observes that Lerner was "the only person who forcefully articulated the need for a women's history that would speak not only to historians but to a wider public."[6]

6. Kessler-Harris, interview with the author, January 12, 2000; Kerber, interview with the author, January 4, 2000.

The atmosphere on college campuses was changing rapidly. In the summer of 1979, Lerner would bring together leaders of women's organizations from all around the country for a summer institute at Sarah Lawrence. Molly McGregor from Sacramento, California, carried across the country the idea of institutionalizing her community's local celebration of March 8 as Women's History Day. By 1980 members of this cadre had lobbied successfully for congressional passage of resolutions expanding the celebration into Women's History Week (which has now expanded to Women's History Month) and making it an annual event. Lerner was proud of this achievement and chided that "the energy of the movements on the grassroots level for the history of minority groups, as well as for women's history, needs to be recognized by academic historians and seen as a hopeful sign of the vital interest in history that exists in every community."[7]

Her sweeping study, *The Majority Finds Its Past: Placing Women in History*, published in 1979, traced Lerner's work and thought from 1960 to the late 1970s through a series of compelling essays. By now she had not only created an impressive body of historical work that challenged and redefined American history, her books were also being published by Oxford University Press, one of the nation's most prestigious publishers of scholarship. Following Oxford University Press's publication of Lerner's work, increasingly distinguished publishers have sought to publish more widely in the field of women's history, and several university presses have created important series to feature and promote American women's history.

Lerner has continued to publish major works with Oxford University Press, including her two-volume survey of women and history: *The Creation of Patriarchy* (1986) and *The Creation of Feminist Consciousness* (1993). Another volume of essays tracking her work from 1980 to 1996, *Why History Matters: Life and Thought*, appeared in 1997. Her studies not only reached scholars in her own field but have become significant to the wider academy, as indicated by the praise of historian John Demos in the *New York Times Book Review*: "There can be no doubting the deep thoughtfulness that informs [Lerner's] every page. And expressing this attitude is a firm, forceful, utterly clear and unpretentious voice. In speaking thus for women and for other historically voiceless legions, Lerner has set a standard that few of her fellow scholars will ever match." And she

7. "A View from the Women's Side," *Journal of American History* 76, no. 2 (September 1989): 456.

struck a chord with a wider public, as is indicated by the comments of a reviewer in the *New Yorker:* "Her sensitivity and scholarship shine."[8]

In 1980 Lerner accepted a position at the University of Wisconsin at Madison, where she held the Robinson-Edwards Chair for ten years. She was hired to develop a doctoral program in women's history and to carry on her important work as an exemplar, as a champion, as one of a kind in the burgeoning field of American women's history. During the years leading up to her Wisconsin appointment, she had been the primary mover and shaker for dozens of important projects that stimulated the massive outpouring of work that followed. She also contributed to the growing revitalization of the Berkshire Conference on the History of Women and of other important networks to promote the field.

In 1971 Lerner met with a group of scholars (including Anne Firor Scott, Carl Degler, and Janet James) to try to find ways to spotlight hidden resources for women's history. The AHA and OAH provided this band of strategists with institutional support to help secure funding for the Women's History Sources Survey. Clarke Chambers of Minnesota steered the project to his state, and Andrea Hinding of the Social Welfare History Archives came on board. In 1979 a two-volume survey, edited by Hinding, was published as *Women's History Sources: A Guide to the Archives and Manuscript Collections in the United States.*

In 1999, Lerner claimed that this survey was the most effective and important project in which she had ever been involved—not only because the end product gave scholars access to a vital guide but also because the survey created the opportunity for hundreds of archives and repositories to reassess their holdings and their systems for cataloging material on women. Colleges and universities undertook massive reclassification efforts to make materials on women more readily available. Scholars seeking to examine the history of U.S. women were given invaluable assistance through this program.

Lerner reported that when she developed her passion for women's history in 1960, she could find only thirteen books in print having to do with American women's history. In 1981 she would publish a pamphlet for the AHA entitled *Teaching Women's History* that would reveal the exponential growth of scholarly monographs in the field. By 1987, when she compiled

8. See *Why History Matters: Life and Thought,* (New York: Oxford University Press, 1997), 1998 paperback edition, back cover.

a revised bibliography in U.S. women's history, Lerner could list nearly three hundred titles in print and hundreds of dissertations in progress.

Indeed, Lerner had channeled women's history toward the politics of engagement. As a result, profound shifts took place in other fields within late-twentieth-century American history: social history, labor history, American Indian history, African American history, Asian American history, Hispanic and Latino history, the history of sexuality, as well as gay and lesbian history. Lerner urged colleagues to move beyond uni-dimensional feminist archetypes and to be as creative and inclusive as the evidence will bear. She suggested that teachers of American history create an "interactive contextual model which considers the ways in which factors of race, class, ethnicity and sex are expressed."[9]

Lerner's years at Wisconsin were marked by enormous productivity as she worked on her two-volume survey of women within world history. The first volume, *The Creation of Patriarchy,* provided what *Ms.* magazine called "a grand historical framework." The book won the Joan Kelly Prize from the AHA as the best book in women's history in 1986. This was an especially poignant award, as the prize had been established in 1983 to honor the late Joan Kelly, an important scholar in European history who had been one of Gerda's friends and colleagues at Sarah Lawrence.

Reviewer Catharine Stimpson compared Lerner's *The Creation of Patriarchy* favorably to Simone De Beauvoir's influential *The Second Sex.* Although Lerner acknowledged De Beauvoir's brilliance, she fundamentally disagreed with the French theorist's emphasis on women's passivity and especially with her claim that women had no history. Lerner pointed out in an interview in 1981 that De Beauvoir was frequently identified as a radical feminist, while historian Mary Beard was considered perhaps more conservative.

Lerner had been powerfully moved by Beard's *Woman as a Force in History* (1946) when she read it for the first time as an undergraduate, nearly twenty years after it was published. Despite what she felt were the book's shortcomings, Lerner connected with Beard's central tenets of faith: that women always had been active and at the center of history. Lerner went on to claim that Mary Beard was "my principal mentor as an historian."[10]

9. Ibid., 143.

10. *The Majority Finds Its Past: Placing Women in History* (New York: Oxford University Press, 1979), xxi. Perhaps Lerner was making a distinction about those who never did mentor her, her professors at Columbia.

That Lerner chose a radical outsider for a model was perhaps no surprise, nor was it surprising that for most of her career her unspoken motto was resistance. Indeed, she resisted the model tenets that elite academic history programs set forth during her graduate years: (1) senior professors train students, (2) those trained students must be properly deferential to their mentors and follow in their ideological footsteps, (3) each senior colleague sends forth a cadre of his or her own warriors to do battle on his or her behalf, (4) obedience will be rewarded and defections or dissent will result in ostracism. This is not to imply that Lerner substituted any maternalistic model of mentorship. Students who were seeking traditional academic cosseting at the University of Wisconsin were forced to look elsewhere than under Lerner's tutelage.

The word got around that Gerda Lerner did not suffer fools—gladly or at all. Only a select group of students wrote their doctoral dissertations under her no-nonsense direction. However, Lerner did have a profound and positive affect on several feminist scholars. Amy Swerdlow, who completed an M.A. in women's history at Sarah Lawrence, shares her thoughts: "In her person and accomplishments, Gerda Lerner exemplifies both the pain and joy of intellectual struggle. An insightful critical thinker, brilliantly creative and original, she can be frighteningly demanding as a teacher, but constructive and generous as a critic and friend." Swerdlow feels that Lerner's commitment to women's history "continues to shape my work and my life." When she came to Sarah Lawrence as a visiting faculty member in 1974, Alice Kessler-Harris was struck by the way in which Lerner exuded an enthusiasm that was infectious: "She had a commitment to the field and the meaning of the field that transcends her personality. It persuaded me that I should embrace the field."[11]

All of her students are unified in their acknowledgment of Lerner's passion and commitment to women's history. The topic of her personality can evoke a wide and fervent spectrum of opinion. Friends and colleagues confess she is assertive, and to those who don't share her views, she might seem abrasive.

Even among her fans, her bluntness is legendary. During a surprise tribute and "roast" at a Berkshire Conference, one of the co-conspirators who

---

11. Swerdlow, interview with the author, January 12, 2000; Kessler-Harris interview. In the 1990s Kessler-Harris joined the faculty at Columbia University, where she teaches women's history; when Lerner applied there for graduate school in the 1960s, she had to answer the question "what is women's history?"

planned the event recalled that several of the stories told about Lerner included references to her frankness, her curtness, her capacity for "edginess."[12] In response to this recurring theme, Lerner apologized graciously, but offered an explanation, holding the crowd spellbound by telling about the day the Nazis forced their way into her family's apartment, separating her from both her sister and her mother by taking them into different rooms. The Gestapo herded Gerda into her father's library and, prodding her at gunpoint, demanded that she conduct a thorough search. She mounted a ladder and had to shake out the books on her father's shelves, looking for incriminating documents hidden within. After several heart-stopping minutes of rifling through volumes, she let an armful of books fall out of her hands and onto the head of one of the armed guards. She took a calculated risk and, at that moment, felt her life hanging in the balance. But when the man in charge retreated, Lerner knew she had learned an important lesson.

Since adolescence, Lerner has been devoted to radical causes, struggling first against the Nazis, then within her adopted country for racial justice, political freedom, and women's rights. She knew these battles would not be won with politesse and was willing to fight for what she believed. She saw all these campaigns against injustice as intertwined and in no way incompatible with feminist solidarity. As early as 1949 Lerner was a leader in the Los Angeles branch of the Congress of American Women, a leftist-feminist group whose motto—"Ten women anywhere can organize anything"—doubtless contributed to her blossoming feminist consciousness.[13]

Lerner seemed to draw strength from trying to topple authoritarians from their shaky pedestals. Even though she herself would become a powerful member of the establishment by virtue of holding a chair at a prestigious university, by becoming president of the OAH, and by the acclaim accorded to her books, Lerner did not take her achievements for granted. She was well aware that if she had pursued her degrees in history in the 1950s instead of the 1960s she might never have enjoyed her prolific career. The Rose Report (the findings of the committee organized in 1970 by the AHA to assess the status of women in the historical profession, chaired by

12. Kerber interview.
13. For more on this group, see Amy Swerdlow's "The Congress of American Women: Left-Feminist Peace Politics in the Cold War," in Kerber et al., eds., *U.S. History as Women's History*.

Willie Lee Rose) offered abysmal statistics on the lost generation of women academics who had received their degrees early in the post–World War II years, underemployed despite their considerable accomplishments. Lerner wanted to insulate the field against such catastrophic intervals. (In the 1930s women comprised 20 percent of the history profession, but by the late 1960s their numbers were nearer to 10 percent.) She encouraged the proliferation of women's history well *beyond* what others envisioned; not just content to have their own courses, scholars in women's history must demand curriculum reforms and revised textbooks and altered academic requirements. Lerner deserved credit for the trickle that turned into a mighty tide of feminist renovation.

One impressive example of Lerner's considerable powers was the "Wingspread Conference," as it came to be known. In 1988, sixteen years after she began the Sarah Lawrence M.A. program, grants were obtained from the National Endowment for the Humanities and the Johnson Foundation by Lerner and her co-organizer, Kathryn Kish Sklar, to hold a conference on graduate training in women's history (held at Wingspread, in Racine, Wisconsin). The conference brought together several dozen teachers and scholars. They reported courses in women's history numbering in the hundreds, with more than sixty institutions of higher education offering M.A. and Ph.D. programs in women's history.

The establishment of both the *Journal of Women's History* and *Gender and History* illustrated the powerful draw of this dynamic discipline. Interdisciplinary journals such as *Signs* and *Feminist Studies* frequently showcased work in women's history. Thirty-five of the participants at Wingspread were directing a total of more than three hundred dissertations in women's history! These numbers demonstrated both the exponential growth of the field and its tremendous popularity. Lerner believed that this impressive foundation would insure the permanent success of the enterprise to which she had dedicated so much energy.

Beginning with her tenure as president of the OAH in 1981, Lerner has garnered a long string of honors and awards. In 1983 Sarah Lawrence established the Gerda Lerner Scholarship Fund. In 1991 she won a resident fellowship from the Rockefeller Foundation's Study and Conference Center at Bellagio, Italy, the same year the OAH established the Gerda Lerner–Anne Firor Scott Prize for the best doctoral dissertation in U.S. women's history. In 1998 she was elected to the American Academy of Arts and Sciences. She has won fellowships from the Ford Foundation, the Lilly Foundation, and the Guggenheim Foundation. She has a half dozen honorary degrees, including one from Yale University. Since her retirement from the University of Wisconsin, she has been a distinguished visitor at several places, including Duke University.

Lerner always demanded that women's history be located within a radical tradition. Certainly, the field might have made important inroads even if it had remained "compensatory history." But Lerner rejected this kind of approach and pushed her colleagues further: "women's history is not a collection of 'missing facts and views' to be incorporated into traditional categories."[14] From her earliest work in the 1970s, Lerner challenged traditional historical "periodization": the way in which designations for historical epochs were shaped by exclusively male sensibilities, rendering women less, if at all, visible. From her earliest years, she has rejected the marginalization of women, as participants within the past and as participants within the historical profession.

In 1979, in *The Majority Finds Its Past*, Lerner outlined goals:

> that a significant number of women acquire tenured professorships
>
> that traditional graduate and undergraduate curricula would include women's history and the feminist perspective
>
> that journals and university presses would publish articles and monographs by women scholars
>
> that professional organizations would accept feminist historians as valued participants and elected officers.[15]

Lerner certainly could take enormous satisfaction from the fact that not only were many of these lofty ideals fulfilled by the turn of the twenty-first century but they also were achieved in no small measure because she was able, in her own inimitable manner, to demonstrate why women's history matters.[16]

14. Judith Zinsser, *History and Feminism: A Glass Half Full* (New York: Twayne, 1993), 36.

15. Lerner, *The Majority Finds Its Past*, 59–60.

16. The author would like to thank Eileen Boris, Alice Kessler-Harris, and Amy Swerdlow for their assistance, and especially Linda Kerber for her generosity. Any errors contained within are wholly the responsibility of the author, with her deepest apology to a valued colleague, Margaret Rossiter.

# Arthur S. Link

## by John Milton Cooper, Jr.

In his 1958 presidential address to the American Historical Association, Walter Prescott Webb admonished ambitious younger historians among his listeners that "if they wish to occupy this place, they should listen attentively to my story . . . and then be extremely careful to avoid following the example of one who has done nearly everything wrong." Arthur Link, who was thirty-eight years old at the time, was one of the historians toward whom Webb aimed his admonition. If Link was not in the audience that heard those words, he almost certainly read them soon afterward in the *American Historical Review*. But no matter how the message reached Link, he did not heed it.

Link followed Webb's example rather than his advice. Just as the older man had flouted the prevailing fashions among American historians in the first half of the twentieth century, so did Arthur Link in the second half. Like Webb, Link was a southerner who received all of his higher education at the state university of his home state—in his case, North Carolina. Unlike Webb, he did not confine his scholarship almost exclusively to his home region, although he did make significant contributions to southern history. Nor did he spend his academic career in his home state or region but ventured out to teach at two front-rank institutions of higher learning—Northwestern and Princeton. Indeed, Link flouted the fashions of his time as blatantly as Webb did, and he also rose to the presidency of the American Historical Association.

Link rejected the prevailing fashion among his scholarly peers by declining to address the sweep of American history and by not aspiring to produce grand syntheses. Instead, he focused nearly all of his work on a single decade, 1910 to 1920, and on a single person, Woodrow Wilson. In maintaining such a tight focus on one era and one person, Link more closely resembled literary scholars who devote their careers to a single writer. For generations, such a course had not been the path to distinction among historians. Even before the recent vogue of bottom-up social history and fond concentration on out-groups, with its attendant denigration of elite white males, Link's devotion to Wilson and his era stood out as extraordinary and, to some historians, as a bit suspect. Even as distinguished a Civil War historian as David Herbert Donald worked around Abraham Lincoln as much as on him, and no New Deal historian has gained anywhere near comparable recognition by focusing mainly on Franklin Roosevelt. How Link built such a surpassing reputation on such a seemingly narrow and admittedly unfashionable base requires explanation.

To most observers, the key to Link's achievement lay in his preternatural productivity. The outstanding evidence of that productivity was *The Papers of Woodrow Wilson,* published under Link's editorship in sixty-nine volumes between 1966 and 1994. Unquestionably, this was an extraordinary accomplishment. His obituary in the *New York Times* in 1998 summed up what he had wrought by noting, "If Professor Link had done his work with the aid of computers, when oceans of data can be shunted and rearranged at the stroke of a few keys, his achievement would have been considered extraordinary. . . . But since Professor Link's accomplishment was attained with nothing more than pens, paper, a typewriter and note cards, it approaches the stuff of legend." Perhaps out of either ignorance or politeness, the obituary writer failed to note that the *Wilson Papers* were (and still are) the only documentary edition of such scope and scholarship that has been finished. Furthermore, the Link legend bordered on the heroic because he suffered from nearly incapacitating health problems, especially ones involving his back, during all but the first few years of his editorship.

This quasi-legendary productivity did not begin or end with the *Wilson Papers.* Before Link was the editor of Woodrow Wilson—that is, the compiler, conservator, and explicator of the record about him—he was the historian of Wilson and his era. In the space of twenty years, from the time that he received his doctorate until shortly before the appearance of the first volume of the *Wilson Papers,* he published nine books. The biggest and most significant of these were the five volumes of *Wilson,* the massive treatment of Wilson and his times that covered the period up to American entry into World War I in 1917. The first of those volumes—which was *not* Link's dissertation—appeared when he was twenty-seven. The last of them came out a year before the first volumes of the *Wilson Papers* were published.

Two other books were his most widely read works, *Woodrow Wilson and the Progressive Era, 1910–1917,* published in 1954, and *American Epoch,* published in 1955. The first was a volume in the highly regarded New American Nation series. Its deft blending of narrative and analysis made it one of the most esteemed volumes in that series, and it continues to be assigned in college history courses. The other was the first textbook in twentieth-century American history. It defined this century as a field of study, and in subsequent editions it also is still being used in college courses.

The final two books that Link wrote in those two decades were *Wilson the Diplomatist,* published in 1957, and *Woodrow Wilson: A Great Life in Brief,* published in 1958. The second was, by Link's own admission, the slightest of his books, sketching broad outlines and salient facts about its subject. It also constituted one of only two forays Link made as a writer into Wilson's life and career after 1917. The other came in *Wilson the Diplomatist,* which grew out of the Albert Shaw Lectures at Johns Hopkins University and constituted Link's only book-length think piece. This was also the only one of Link's books, aside from the textbook, that he would later revise.

In addition to those books, Link also poured out a stream of articles that were published in various journals during these two decades. Although he did not publish his dissertation as a book, much of it did eventually appear in articles that treated the Wilson presidential movement in different parts of the South; these were later reprinted in *The Higher Realism of Woodrow Wilson and Other Essays.* Of those other essays, the two most influential were a treatment of southern contributions to progressivism, which appeared in the *American Scholar,* and an analysis of the breakdown of progressivism in the 1920s, which appeared in the *American Historical Review.* This extraordinary outpouring of work, all done by the age of forty-five, prompted one of Link's Princeton colleagues, historian Robert R. Palmer, to remark: "It wasn't human. He must have had God on his side."

Palmer's remark was deeply insightful and requires further explication. But, before that, two distinctions need to be made. One regards the amount of work that Link did before he took command of the *Wilson Papers,* and the other regards the nature of that work. As impressive as the amount of work was, it did not comprise the distinctiveness of his achievement as a historian. Others among his contemporaries, most notably Arthur M. Schlesinger, Jr., and James MacGregor Burns, matched him in sheer volume of books and articles. Moreover, this volume of work, coupled with the later editorial feat, left the widespread impression that Link was a prodigiously industrious gatherer of facts and producer and compiler of words, a writer of narrative histories lacking an interpretive focus. Given that impression, some have concluded that he does not belong in the highest circle of historical honor, where the laurels go to the broad-sweeping synthesizers and interpreters. The impression is deeply misleading; and the conclusion is dead wrong.

Here is where the distinction about the nature of Link's pre-editorial work needs to be made. The five massive volumes about Wilson were Link's proudest literary products, but they were not, in an important sense, a biography. Those volumes embodied a-life-and-times treatment that stressed the times much more than the life. Link became deeply engaged with Wilson's personality only when he wrote extensive editorial notes about his early life, health, and writings in the initial volumes of the *Wilson Papers*. In all of his work before then, Link wrote more about Wilson's actions than about his thoughts or emotions. Likewise, as editor of the *Wilson Papers*, although he admitted that he came to admire Wilson greatly, Link always insisted that he had no stake in defending the man or boosting his reputation.

Those attitudes had their origin in the way that Link originally came to the study of Wilson. He did not start out as someone who admired the man or even liked him. As an undergraduate and graduate student at Chapel Hill, Link's primary interest was in southern history. He first became interested in Wilson in graduate school when a visiting professor suggested that the recent opening of Wilson's papers at the Library of Congress might make his political career a good dissertation topic. In his dissertation Link kept a foot in southern history by writing about support for and opposition to Wilson's drive for the presidency below the Potomac. Similarly, in the first volume on Wilson, Link passed quickly over his early life and academic career, claiming that the official biographer, Ray Stannard Baker, had already adequately covered those subjects. Most of that first volume treats the period of two and a half years between mid-1910 and the end of 1912, when Wilson first entered politics, was elected governor of New Jersey, and won the Democratic nomination for president and the election of 1912. In that volume and in *Woodrow Wilson and the Progressive Era,* Link's stance toward Wilson was strongly, often harshly, critical of him as an opportunistic, belated, and half-hearted convert from conservatism to progressivism.

Those origins of the work on Wilson brought both strengths and weaknesses to Link's scholarship. The strength lay in breadth. Until 1958, when he assumed the editorship of the *Wilson Papers,* Link wrote much more about politics and progressivism than he did about Wilson himself. During those years he joined George Mowry, Eric Goldman, and Richard Hofstadter in advancing penetrating interpretations of the reform movements that flourished before World War I. Link's distinctive contributions to those interpretations lay in three arguments that he was among the first to advance. One was to stress the importance of progressivism in the South and the importance of the South to progressivism nationally. The second was to locate the heart of progressivism in Theodore Roosevelt's New Nationalism, not Wilson's New Freedom, and to maintain that Wilson did not become a genuine progressive until he converted to the New Nationalism in 1916. The final argument was that progressivism collapsed after World War I because of internecine conflicts among reformers and uncertainties about how to pursue their agendas further. He also argued that progressivism was stronger in the 1920s than was generally acknowledged and that it formed the heart of the New Deal in the 1930s.

The breadth of Link's scholarship also extended beyond political interpretations of progressivism. He never minimized the role of race and racism in the South. He gave great weight to the woman suffrage movement and feminist concerns. He treated immigration and ethnicity as vital factors in shaping American society before, during, and after World War I. He was sensitive to issues of class, especially those having to do with industrial workers and labor movements. Another measure of the breadth of his interests can be found in the students who wrote dissertations under his direction at Northwestern. They included William Harbaugh, who worked on Theodore Roosevelt; Gerald Grob, who studied mental health; and George McGovern, who wrote about violence committed against striking workers. At Princeton, some of his doctoral students did work on Wilson, but others studied labor, gender politics, isolationism, and public opinion and foreign policy. In all, his early writings and his graduate teaching established Link as a broad-ranging interpreter of twentieth-century American history.

The weakness in much of his early work lay in its lack of grounding. Except in the dissertation-based articles and in the first volume on Wilson, before 1955 Link tended to write ahead of his research. He based his interpretations more on secondary and ready-to-hand primary sources than on the extensive digging in primary sources that would undergird the volumes on Wilson. When he did engage in that kind of research and later when he edited the *Wilson Papers,* he modified and sometimes repudiated his earlier arguments. One example of how Link changed his mind involved the first volume on Wilson. A substantial cache of material about Wilson's early life came to light in the late 1950s, impelling Link to recognize that neither he nor Baker had given that period the treatment it warranted. He often spoke of wanting to rewrite that volume after he finished editing the *Wilson Papers.* Another example involved his critical attitude toward Wilson's progressivism. After he studied the New Freedom legislation of 1913 and 1914 more closely and examined the supposed conversion to the New Nationalism in 1916, he quietly scrapped his earlier interpretation. Not even an echo of his earlier views can be found in Link's later volumes on Wilson.

Link also acquired a fresh interest in Wilson as a thinker, which led him to recognize that the man was more than a shallow opportunist. Some of this newfound interest arose when the *Wilson Papers* hired experts who could decipher the archaic form of shorthand that Wilson used to jot down his thoughts and draft notes for essays and speeches. This modern-day cryptography enabled Link to appreciate Wilson's intellectual dimension far better than he had before. At one meeting of the editorial advisory committee to the *Wilson Papers,* he compared a fresh rendering of one of Wilson's speeches with his own account from the first volume. "You can see how I misinterpreted Wilson," Link commented.

Those recantations and revisions occurred in private, without fanfare. Link did not acknowledge such changes of mind publicly—not from vanity, but from a lack of interest in historiography, which he regarded as a form of navel-gazing. Unusual among presidents of the major historical associations, he did not talk about the state of the field or lay out the next assignment to up-and-coming scholars. Rather he talked about specific subjects that came out of his recent work. This was Link's way of saying that he preferred to get on with the job.

On one occasion, however, he did bare his breast about what he regarded as mistakes in his earlier interpretations. This occurred in his revision of *Wilson the Diplomatist,* which was published under a new title, *Woodrow Wilson: Revolution, War, and Peace.* In the later book, Link treated such episodes as Wilson's responses to the Mexican revolution and German submarine warfare less harshly than before. He also gave Wilson higher marks as a war leader and articulator of war aims in the Fourteen Points. Most important, he reversed his previous view of the influence of Wilson's health during the peace conference at Paris and in the fight at home over ratification of the Treaty of Versailles and membership in the League of Nations. Link had previously stated that Wilson would have taken the same unbending stand against ratification with Henry Cabot Lodge's reservations if he had enjoyed perfect health. Now, in Wilson's deteriorating cardiovascular condition and massive stroke, Link found factors that swayed not only his refusal to compromise with Lodge but also his earlier actions at the peace conference and his dealings with the Senate over the treaty.

This newfound emphasis on Wilson's health sprang from several sources. One was research into his early life for the first volumes of the *Wilson Papers.* Those volumes differed from their successors in containing much more extensive editorial comment. In part, the disparity arose from the relative paucity of material about Wilson's early life, which Link believed required more extensive editorial commentary. Taken together, those notes constituted another substantial book about Wilson. Not coincidentally, Link wrote those notes during and just after the time when he completed the fourth and fifth volumes of *Wilson,* when he was wearing the two hats of historian and editor. Some reviewers criticized him for what they regarded as excessive, intrusive commentary. Link overcompensated afterward by rigorous eschewal of such notes by himself in the later volumes. He rejected the pleading of at least one member of his editorial advisory committee that he should comment on such matters as the election of 1916, the evolution of the Fourteen Points, and disputes with the Allies during the world war and at the peace conference.

Link's earliest editorial comment about Wilson's health came out of this more extensive research, which led him to speculate that an 1895 attack of paralysis in his right hand stemmed from the cardiovascular condition that culminated in the massive stroke that Wilson suffered in 1919. Link's subsequent editorial comments about Wilson's health also came out of his collaboration with Edwin Weinstein, a renowned neurologist and psychiatrist who had served on a national commission to study presidential disability. Link encouraged Weinstein to study Wilson and invited him to become an unpaid fellow of the *Wilson Papers*. Out of that experience, Weinstein wrote a prizewinning article on Wilson's neurological condition and a book-length medical and psychological biography. Link also coauthored an article with Weinstein about Wilson's political personality. Later, Link invited another neurologist to join the *Wilson Papers* advisory committee, and he included extensive notes by neurologists about Wilson's health immediately before and after his 1919 stroke.

Those ventures by Link into posthumous medical examination and speculation made it possible to know more about Wilson's physical condition than about that of any other president before the 1950s. They likewise fostered a better understanding of the worst crisis of presidential disability in American history.

Unfortunately, those ventures into medical history precipitated a miniature crisis of their own. Link was never one to duck controversy, but when he and Weinstein criticized an earlier portrayal of Wilson's political personality by Alexander and Juliette George they provoked a blistering counterattack in several scholarly journals. The Georges went beyond disagreement with Link and Weinstein's interpretations; they also denounced the notes in the *Wilson Papers* about Wilson's health and impugned the integrity of the project. Those counterattacks thoroughly rattled several officers of the sponsoring institutions, Princeton and the Woodrow Wilson Foundation. There was talk about making retractions, which prompted Link to threaten to resign. This tempest in a scholarly teapot eventually died down, but it permanently soured relations between Link and his sponsors. Princeton celebrated the completion of the *Wilson Papers* tepidly and belatedly, after other institutions and the media had already hailed this as a monumental feat. Also, with the completion of the *Papers,* Princeton diverted the funds of the Wilson Foundation to uses other than Wilson scholarship.

Such an ending to Link's work was doubly unfortunate. Not only did those hard feelings cloud what should have been an occasion for justifiable pride in a job magnificently done, but they also grossly undervalued Link's special role. Emerson's dictum that "an institution is but the lengthened shadow of one man" applied with special force and clarity to Link and the *Wilson Papers.* Someone else could have overseen the production of a scholarly edition of Wilson's papers, but, given the track record of other such editions, it is doubtful that another person or group of people would have finished the job in anywhere near the time that Link did. More important, it is inconceivable that anyone else would have so assiduously sought out material around the world and brought to bear such insight in selection, annotation, and commentary about the contents of the edition.

Herein lies the heart of the matter about Arthur Link's engagement with Woodrow Wilson and his era both as historian and as editor. The fit between scholar and subject was well-nigh perfect. Many scholars used to joke, "Link *is* Woodrow Wilson." Such jibes were often less than good-natured, and they usually sprang from superficiality and caricature. With his long jaw and seemingly stern countenance, Link did resemble popular images of Wilson. Moreover, Link's southern origins and publicly professed Presbyterianism appeared to complete the circle of identification. In fact, such notions did a disservice to both men. Like Wilson, Link was a warm family man and someone who liked to have a good time. One of his sons remarked at his funeral, "My father never met a cruise ship he didn't like." Like Wilson, Link was musical, and one of his passions was opera, which he attended regularly at the Metropolitan in New York. Also like Wilson, Link was a minister's son, although the faith of his fathers was Lutheran, not Presbyterian, and his ethnic stock was largely German, not Scots and Scotch-Irish.

The resemblances between Link and Wilson went further, although not in the ways that others usually supposed. For all their respective eminence in scholarship and university life, neither Wilson nor Link ever became completely domesticated to the academic life of his time. Link defied the folkways among his peers in several noticeable ways. He was a heavy smoker of cigarettes, almost literally to his dying day. That smoking habit killed him, inasmuch as he died of lung cancer at the age of seventy-seven. Otherwise, despite his other health problems, he was in remarkable condition for a man of his age. Likewise, Link was at times a heavy drinker, mostly of scotch whisky, rather than a temperate imbiber of wine or mineral water. He never drank during his long workdays, and much of his evening and nighttime consumption of alcohol came in an effort to dull his often excruciating back pain. Also, unlike most of his academic peers, he drove not an imported car but a big, soft-riding, fully loaded, gas-guzzling American vehicles, usually Lincolns.

Link's two principal differences from Wilson lay in his institutional loyalties and in his working habits. Even before the final unpleasantness at Princeton, he had a complicated relationship with that university. His first academic position after receiving his doctorate was there, when he was twenty-six. His three years at Princeton as a junior faculty member were not an altogether happy experience. Not only were hierarchy and a touch of intellectual snobbery the orders of the day, but rivalry also inescapably infected the lower ranks. A mutual dislike arose between Link and Eric Goldman, whose star then burned brighter at Princeton, and the two men had few good words to say about each other to the end of their lives. Northwestern, to which he moved as a tenured faculty member in 1949, suited him much better. His decade there was almost certainly the happiest time in his intellectual life. Link especially enjoyed working with such students as Harbaugh and McGovern, World War II veterans who were close to him in age, and he formed the closest friendship of his adult life with his colleague Richard Leopold.

Link's return to Princeton after 1958 was something less than an unalloyed triumph. The initiative to bring him back did not come from the history department. Rather, an influential alumnus and Wilson devotee, Raymond Fosdick, who headed the Wilson Foundation, persuaded the university administration to assume institutional sponsorship of the Wilson Papers and take over the foundation's assets to fund the project. Moreover, Link was not the first choice for the editorship and was invited only after another historian declined the offer. During the next three and a half decades, until his retirement in 1992, Link became a valued member of his department and made a number of friends, but a sense of separation from Princeton's mainline academic enterprise always remained.

One of his happiest connections with Princeton was supervising the undergraduates who wrote their senior theses under his direction. His most renowned such student was the Princeton basketball star Bill Bradley, who went on to be a Rhodes Scholar, professional basketball player, U.S. senator from New Jersey, and candidate for the Democratic presidential nomination. Bradley stayed in close touch with Link and often asked him for advice. For example, in the summer of 1983 Senator Bradley wrote to Link to ask for a summer vacation reading list. Link advised him to read *The Federalist* and John C. Calhoun's *Disquisition on Government*, adding that the first book was "extremely relevant to present-day problems." Link also told his former student: "Don't spend all of August reading. Leave a little time for just goofing off."

For his part, Link never became a professional Princetonian. Proud and loyal as he felt toward that university, he never made his association with it his main identity. Link remained in both his cultural identification and his collegiate loyalties a Tarheel. He did not buy a house in Princeton until late in his career, when he became a homeowner there mainly for financial reasons. Earlier, however, while he was at Northwestern, he bought a summer home at Montreat in the Blue Ridge Mountains of North Carolina. He also remained a passionate fan of Tarheel sports, especially basketball, and for many years his automobile license plate read "FPG," for Frank Porter Graham, the much loved man who had been president of the University of North Carolina during Link's student days at Chapel Hill.

Their Princeton careers revealed another difference between Link and Wilson: their ways of working. Curiously, it was Wilson, the university administrator and politician, who enjoyed solitude more. By contrast, it was Link, the scholar, writer, and editor, who was the more gregarious. No one could have done as much research and writing as Link did without spending long hours in lonely labor; but, except when he was writing and sometimes not even then, he hated to be alone. As his family has attested, at home he always wanted to have someone physically present with him. Off-duty, he relished conversing, driving around with companions, and taking trips with friends and family.

Even the editorial advisory committee of the *Wilson Papers* played a role in the enterprise that was more companionable than critical. One member once remarked to another, "You know, Arthur doesn't really want our advice." That was true. The committee did read each volume in manuscript, but most members had little advice to give, beyond catching an extremely rare error, raising questions about sources, and suggesting editorial commentary. Little advice was needed, because Link and his dedicated associates had done such a thorough and masterful job of editing. The committee's main function was to provide companionship to the editor, through correspondence, frequent telephone conversations, occasional individual visits to Princeton, and an annual meeting there that featured sumptuous dinners and lots of talk about all kinds of subjects, serious and light.

Link also wanted the advisory committee to give him emotional support. Despite his well-known stubbornness and sometimes staggering self-reliance, he did not have a thick skin when he came under attack. The brouhaha with the Georges over Wilson's health hurt him deeply, and, sad to say, only one member of the advisory committee rallied to his side. Several members, including those who had known Link the longest and the best, feared for the reputation of the project. They viewed the matter in an institutional light, as did officials at Princeton and the Wilson Foundation. His one defender, who was by nature more of a controversialist, viewed the matter both as a question of who had the better scholarly case (Link, unquestionably, in his view) and as an appreciation of Link's indispensability to the enterprise. This was certainly the worst moment in the life of the *Wilson Papers* and probably in Link's professional life. The controversy blew over, and in retrospect it seems unlikely that Link would have parted company with his beloved "*Papers.*"

Link's editorial productivity made him the envy of other editors who had set what might be called a leisurely pace on their projects, sometimes taking three or four years (and even longer) to produce a single volume. Delegating many editorial chores, Link kept his eye on the finished product, and Princeton University Press obligingly produced one volume, and occasionally two, each calendar year. A fellow editor who served on Link's advisory board, miffed by the output of Link's staff, once made a crack: "My project is better at keeping standards than deadlines." Link—who boasted in his introduction to each volume of the *Wilson Papers* that "our tolerance for error is zero"—let the gibe roll off his back and predicted that the other editor would soon resign from the *Wilson Papers* editorial board. Within a few months the dilatory editor sent in his exculpatory letter of resignation. With a wink, Link told fellow editors that he had accepted the resignation "with regret."

Link's devotion to the *Wilson Papers* was intensely personal and probably stemmed from his close resemblance to his subject. Like Wilson, Link possessed a religious faith that made him a cheerful fatalist and a believer in a higher calling. Consider what he wrote at the end of his entry in *Who's Who in America:* "I have no thoughts on life that do not stem from my Christian faith. I believe that God created me to be a loving, caring person to do His work in the world. I also believe that He called me to my vocation of teacher and scholar." What other distinguished professor at a leading university could have said that when Link did? Most academics in the second half of the twentieth century probably never had much religious faith or had long since forsaken what they once had, while those who did profess a faith usually cloaked it in embarrassed silence. This was why Palmer's remark about Link having "had God on his side" was so insightful. Herein lay the true source of his phenomenal productivity, his tight focus on a single person and era, and especially his steadfastness through adversity. Link believed that he was serving a cause that was larger than himself.

That belief also explains why his career fell into two distinct halves, the first as the historian of Wilson and the second as the editor of Wilson. Link did not shelve the multivolume history out of any sense of limits on his time and energy. Indeed, he did fill both roles simultaneously for a while. In his denial of limitations and obstacles, Link resembled both Wilson and such other figures in the generation between his subject and himself as Franklin Roosevelt. Such psychological denial also helped him greatly in persevering through his physical pain and through severe emotional problems involving one of his children.

Link stopped writing the volumes about Wilson—temporarily, in his view, since he talked about going back to them—for two reasons. One was scholarly calculation. He did not want to get ahead of his research again. In any future volumes, he wanted to get things right, as he was convinced he had done earlier (except in the first volume). Anyone who has worked in the years that he covered in those later volumes and has used the same materials that he did can attest to how justified that conviction was. Link missed nothing in the way of available sources, and when he wrote about the history of the time he nearly always got it right. The second reason for putting aside his own volumes was his belief that his editorship of the papers was more important. Shortly before his death, someone asked him what he thought had been his greatest accomplishment. Without hesitation, he shot back, "The *Papers!*"

Link's quick answer reflected no false modesty about his own writings, in which he took great pride. Rather, Link was saying that, excellent as he believed his own work was, it was not enough for him. He needed to serve someone greater than himself—Wilson, in his estimation—and something greater than himself—the monumental edition that illuminated both that greater person and some of the greatest events in American history. And he needed to do those things because he felt, in the root religious sense of the word, a vocation. Without a doubt, Link believed that his God had called him to the task.

When Link died in 1998, eulogies and obituary estimates of him and his work often ended with the formulaic saying, "We shall not see his like again." In his case, those overused words were more than a cliché. The academic world had seen his like during his lifetime only among survivors from the generation that stood between him and Wilson, and not often even among them. His only likeness among his elders in prodigious output based upon faith in divine calling was Samuel Eliot Morison, who also believed he was serving God by using his scholarly and literary gifts to their fullest. His only likeness in concentration on a circumscribed subject in a way that opened out into much larger realms was Walter Prescott Webb, who used his studies of his native heath of Texas and the Great Plains as the basis for interpreting half a millennium of world history.

There was a bit of both Morison and Webb in Link. Like Morison, he wrote with gusto about great persons and great events. He fondly described and analyzed Wilson, Theodore Roosevelt, William Jennings Bryan, and the rest of that galaxy of men and women who made that decade before World War I what has been called the "second golden age of American politics." At home, Link delved fearlessly and enthusiastically into the complexities of the most significant era of reform since the Civil War. Abroad, he gladly leaped into the thicket of interpreting America's responses to the greatest international events of the twentieth century—revolutions such as those in Mexico and Russia, modern industrialized and technological warfare on a global scale, and the effort to build international order on a just and humane basis through new methods of maintaining peace. Like Webb, Link accomplished his feats of scholarship not by ranging far and wide across the historical landscape but by sticking to his subject. By probing, pondering, and interpreting what it meant, he illuminated the big historical picture as well.

Yet Link did more. His valuing of the *Wilson Papers* above his own writing expressed more than humility or a sense of calling. Those papers were of a piece with his earlier work. They illuminated the thoughts and deeds of a historical figure of overweening significance. Between them, Link's writings and the *Wilson Papers* have made Wilson perhaps the most approachable president in American history. Thanks to the peculiar circumstance that in Wilson's time written communication had not yet lost immediacy and value, as it soon would, the record left about the events in which he participated is perhaps more illuminating than that for any other president. But it took Link's devoting his life to making that record available for that to happen. Moreover, inasmuch as Wilson was one of only two genuine intellectuals to become president since the Civil War (Theodore Roosevelt was the other), Link's work opened the way to understanding a great political mind at work in both accord and conflict with other political minds.

Arthur Link was neither unselfish nor selfless. He could be callous and insensitive to other people when he pursued his calling. He prided himself on his writings and saw the *Wilson Papers* as an expression of himself. Yet Link always looked beyond himself. He welcomed any scholar who entered the field and tried to facilitate her or his research. This was true even when such scholars disagreed with him or were attacking him, as in the case of the Georges. He also delighted in revision of his interpretations by others. Such an olympian attitude came easily to him both because, often, he had changed his mind already about those interpretations and because, more often, later scholars enjoyed access to material that had not been available to him. Indeed, the main reason later scholars could find such material was because Link provided it for them, through his unflagging research, through his advice and encouragement, and, above all, through the *Wilson Papers.* Among the great American historians in the second half of the twentieth century, Arthur Link stood tall. Link left a legacy that transcended his individual work and will grow for a long time to come. Uniquely among those historians, he earned the tribute that meant most to him, "Servant of God, well done."

# Edmund S. Morgan

## by John M. Murrin

E dmund S. Morgan has transformed our past. If history is the way we understand how we have become what we are, he has profoundly reshaped that history. He began in the late 1930s and 1940s by trying to understand the Puritans. Although a lifelong atheist, he has always written with compassion and affection about Puritans and, for that matter, about any people who try hard to live up to their own principles. After World War II he turned to the American Revolution, and there, too, he discovered people with serious commitments to principles, in this case political ones. In the 1960s he immersed himself in colonial Virginia and, more specifically, in the troubling relationship between slavery and freedom. His last major book explored the political "fictions" that have given meaning and substance to Anglo-American understandings of government over the last four centuries. In a sense, that is where he began, for in 1940 he believed he would write a dissertation on Puritan political thought. He never completed that project, but the issues raised by serious political thinkers have informed nearly everything else he has studied.[1]

Edmund Sears Morgan was born in Minneapolis on January 17, 1916, the second child of Edmund Morris Morgan and Elsie Smith Morgan. His father, a descendant of Welsh coal miners, taught law at the University of Minnesota. His mother had been raised in a Christian Science family of New England lineage, although she always denied being a practicing

---

1. This essay draws heavily on David T. Courtwright, "Fifty Years of American History: An Interview with Edmund S. Morgan," *William and Mary Quarterly*, 3d ser., 44 (1987): 336–69, which is the source of most of the quotations about Morgan's personal life and career; on William D. Liddle's excellent "Edmund S. Morgan (17 January 1916– )," in *Twentieth-Century American Historians*, ed. Clyde N. Wilson, *Dictionary of Literary Biography* (Detroit: Gale, 1983), 17:285–95; and on David D. Hall, John M. Murrin, and Thad Tate, eds., *Saints and Revolutionaries: Essays on Early American History* (New York: W. W. Norton, 1984), ix–xv. The essays in this volume constitute a festschrift in Morgan's honor.

Christian Scientist. Soon after the United States entered World War I, the elder Edmund Morgan moved the family to Washington, D.C., where he served as an assistant to the judge-advocate general of the United States. After the war, he accepted an appointment at the Yale Law School and then in 1925 moved to the Harvard Law School in Cambridge, Massachusetts. There, and in nearby Arlington, where the family lived, young Edmund spent the rest of his childhood. In 1933 he graduated from Belmont Hill School, where he studied Latin and French for six years but acquired little of lasting value from his history courses.

He then entered Harvard College, where he expected to major in English history and literature. Instead, in his sophomore year he took a course taught by Perry Miller and F. O. Matthieson, and he promptly changed his major to American history and literature, a new program, in order to get Miller as his tutor during his sophomore and senior years, with Matthieson during his junior year while Miller was on leave. He also remembers benefiting greatly from Samuel Eliot Morison's lecture course. After graduating, he entered the London School of Economics, largely on the advice of Felix Frankfurter, a family friend, who urged him to study with Harold Laski. In his year in England, Morgan found R. H. Tawney, Eileen Power, Branislaw Malinowski, and Karl Mannheim even more stimulating than Laski. He visited Germany not long before the Munich crisis. Although he was a pacifist and feared that another world war might well destroy all civilization, he found the Nazis terrifying.

Morgan returned to Harvard in 1938 as a counselor in Lowell House and then began graduate study in a new program on the history of American civilization a year later. Naturally he studied with Miller, whom he described in 1985 as America's "best historian in this century," as distinct from Morison, whom he rated as "the best historical writer in America in this century." In the summer of 1940, Morgan submitted a draft dissertation on Puritan political thought. To his dismay, Miller rejected it. "Try again, for God's sake," Miller advised. "What do you think this is, just an enlarged senior essay?" But Miller did like his chapter on the family, and over the next two years Morgan expanded it into a dissertation that Harvard accepted and that the Boston Public Library published, first as a series of essays and then as a book, *The Puritan Family* (1944).

On June 7, 1939, Morgan married Helen Theresa Mayer. They would have two daughters. Helen, a geologist by training, became Ed's close partner in his research and writing, including coauthorship of *The Stamp Act*

*Crisis: Prologue to Revolution,* published in 1953. In 1940, when Congress enacted the first peacetime draft in American history, Morgan filed for conscientious-objector status. After the fall of France, he decided that Hitler had to be stopped no matter the cost, and in late 1940 he withdrew his request. But he spent the war years at the MIT Radiation Laboratory as an "instrument maker," mostly fashioning sophisticated metal parts for radar equipment. He also found time to transcribe and edit the diary of Michael Wigglesworth. If *The Puritan Family* went a long way toward humanizing the Puritans for a generation that still regarded them as self-righteous prudes, Wigglesworth came alarmingly close to the stereotype. Morgan, who has always possessed a capacity for being surprised by his sources, found the diary fascinating largely for that reason.

After the war Morgan spent a year at the University of Chicago, where he taught a document-based U.S. survey course and English composition. "I think it's really impossible to teach English composition in a class," he soon concluded. "You can tell a class of students everything they can possibly learn about English composition in a year in about a half an hour. The problem is getting them to do it. You can do that by meeting with them individually, and going over their compositions, but to do it in front of twenty people or thirty people in the classroom is just a waste of time. . . . I could never think of a decent way of filling up the time. I used to wake up at night wondering, 'What in hell am I going to do in that class tomorrow?'" He found Chicago "an exciting place," but the frequency and intensity of faculty discussions about "what a liberal education was" exhausted him and left him no time for research. When Brown University offered him an appointment to teach early American history—and nothing else—he jumped at the opportunity and moved his family to Providence in 1946.

Morgan loved Brown's intellectual environment. "Henry Wriston, then President of Brown, was a Republican, and a conservative, and an *absolute* champion of academic freedom." The history department chair, James B. Hedges, "regarded his function as simply to hire people and then to protect them from outside interference by the administration, or anyone else." Hedges, as Morgan recalled, "protected you from the rest of the university—and Wriston protected you from anybody outside the university. It was absolute heaven."

At Brown, Morgan returned to his sources and again discovered that they were not saying what they were supposed to tell him. He took a long, fresh look at the coming of the American Revolution and announced his preliminary findings in "Colonial Ideas of Parliamentary Power, 1764–1766," which appeared in the *William and Mary Quarterly* in 1948. It remains one of the most important essays the *Quarterly* has ever published. The reigning progressive interpretation explained the Revolution largely as a clash of competing economic interests while dismissing what the patriots said as a pragmatic retreat from one strategic position to another until they finally embraced independence. According to this view, the colonists found "external" taxes (port duties) acceptable and objected as of 1765 only to "internal" taxes (in this controversy, that phrase meant stamp duties on legal documents and publications, but presumably it also included excises, land taxes, and head taxes). But in the Townshend Crisis (1767–1770), the colonists presumably changed their arguments. They rejected both internal and external taxes, insisting that all taxes for revenue, as against those that regulated trade, violated the constitutional precept of no taxation without consent. Finally, in 1774 the colonists insisted on no *legislation* without consent, leaving the Crown as their only legal connection to the British government. And, of course, they repudiated George III in 1776. Morgan argued, quite convincingly, that as early as 1765 the colonists emphatically rejected all taxes for revenue enacted without their consent. Their constitutional position did not shift until 1774, when Parliament claimed the power to transform the very structure of their governments without their consent.

When Ed and Helen pulled the whole story together in *The Stamp Act Crisis,* informed readers were prepared for that part of the argument but not for the rest of the book. Although the Morgans clearly sympathized with colonists who resisted Britain's new taxes, they devoted five of seventeen chapters to the victims of this resistance—to Thomas Hutchinson, whose Boston mansion was destroyed by a mob; to John Robinson, a customs collector; to Jared Ingersoll and John Hughes, who had accepted appointments as stamp distributors. Most of them emerged from the crisis with ruined lives. Yet the Morgans described them and their plights with great sympathy. These men were decent people trapped on the wrong side of a great historical divide. The Morgans resolved the tension between the patriots' laudable goals and the misfortunes that they inflicted on their victims through the oldest device available to historians, high narrative. They described and explained how and why these things happened. After half a century the book remains as powerful as when it first appeared. (I have assigned it every time I have taught the Revolution at both the undergraduate and the graduate level; nearly every time, the students have voted it the best book assigned in the course.)

At Brown, Morgan guided ten graduate students to their doctoral degrees, most of whom studied some aspect of the Revolutionary era, several with a Rhode Island focus. Nearly all of them went on to distinguished professional careers. But then Hedges resigned the chairmanship in a curricular dispute, and Yale offered Morgan a professorship. Hedges urged him to accept the position, and in 1955 the Morgans moved to New Haven, where, in 1965, Morgan became Sterling Professor of History.

*The Birth of the Republic, 1763–1789* (1956) was published shortly after Morgan moved to Yale, and to many graduate students at the time it confirmed Morgan's reputation as a historian of the Revolution. When I went to Yale in 1959, I had read his two books on the Revolution but had never heard of *The Puritan Family,* which had been released in a very limited edition and would not be available in paperback until 1966. But the Puritans had never been far from Morgan's historical imagination, and he soon returned to them. In 1958 he published *The Puritan Dilemma: The Story of John Winthrop,* the best selling of all his books and also the top seller in the series in which it appeared, the Library of American Biography, edited by Oscar M. Handlin, a friend since their graduate school days together at Harvard.

*The Puritan Dilemma* has probably had a broader and more lasting impact on historians and the general public than anything else Morgan has written. (Even a rock band, performing in Madison, Wisconsin, in the late 1960s, went by that name.) The book, reissued recently in a second edition, remains one of the most effective introductions to the otherwise alien world of Puritan values. It is brief and yet remarkably thorough, at least in its coverage of the 1630s, connecting the struggles of the Puritans to a universal theme, announced in the title. The "central Puritan dilemma" was, Morgan insists, "the problem of doing right in a world that does wrong." He used this theme to explore the difficulties of what Perry Miller had identified as "non-separating Congregationalism," Winthrop's form of Puritanism. Separatists, who rejected the Church of England as a false church, might escape England and the world to practice their convictions in isolation. But Winthrop had to try to change a sinful world from which he refused to flee.

Ezra Stiles, who served the Congregational church in Newport before

he became president of Yale, provided an interesting link for Morgan between Brown and Yale. Morgan acquired a fascination for Stiles's papers
while researching *The Stamp Act Crisis* and drafted a lengthy biography
that he finally published in 1962 as *The Gentle Puritan.* This book provides
a broad window into the cultural world of the last half of the eighteenth
century, but Stiles actually disappointed Morgan. Stiles was, as Morgan
once told me, paraphrasing Morison, a "gonna man." He was always *going
to* do some vast and impressive project, but he never quite completed any
of them. "You can't really get across propositions about intellectual history very well in the biography of a minor figure—at least that's how it
seemed to me after I got the thing done," he later reflected. "I was quite
satisfied with it, actually—I'm as satisfied with that book as with any I've
written," he admits. "But it was not [the compelling] way of telling people
about the New England mind in the eighteenth century that I thought it
would be."[2]

New York University then invited Morgan to give the Anson Phelps
Stokes Lectures, a prestigious series that takes place every three years. The
lectures, published in 1963 as *Visible Saints: The History of a Puritan Idea,*
have been his most thoughtful and original contribution to Puritan studies. He began with an elegant idea and stated it simply. "Christianity teaches that God is good and man is bad," he wrote, "that God is in fact so good
and man so bad that man deserves eternal damnation." He then traced
the Puritan attempt to bring the "visible church" of those Christians still
living into as close a conformity as possible with Augustine's "invisible
church," those whom God has elected to save—past, present, and future.
A purified church was a central preoccupation of the movement.

But, of course, we already knew that much, no matter how eloquently
restated. Morgan rapidly moved onto new ground. He showed that no Puritans before the 1630s had thought to test the validity of someone else's
conversion experience. That shift, he argued, occurred in North America
and probably first appeared in response to John Cotton's ecstatic sermons in Boston in the mid-1630s. The new practice probably helped
drive Thomas Hooker from Massachusetts and turn him into a principal
founder of Connecticut. It set the New England churches upon the path
to the Half-Way Covenant of 1662, which Morgan interpreted as a stronger
affirmation of the Puritan vision than any of the alternatives available to

---

2. *William and Mary Quarterly* 44 (1987): 351.

contemporaries, an interpretation many still find compelling. In a spare narrative of about 150 pages, he used the theme of visible saints to tie together most of the tensions that afflicted serious Puritans into the Great Awakening of the 1740s. Like *The Stamp Act Crisis,* this slender volume retains its power. When, for the first time in perhaps fifteen years, I assigned it to my graduate seminar in the fall of 1999 (the more recently published alternatives were temporarily unavailable), the students were awed by how much *Visible Saints* explained in its few pages.

When Morgan decided to take a break and spend 1961–1962 in Switzerland, he assured friends that he had no great project currently in mind now that he had finished *Gentle Puritan* and *Visible Saints.* He thought he had earned a year of relaxation and general reading. Yet when he returned to New Haven, he brought with him the draft of another book on Puritans, *Roger Williams: The Church and the State* (1967), a project that had begun as a review essay and somehow seemed to grow. Morgan had brought to Switzerland a recent reissue of Williams's writings, edited by Perry Miller, with a volume of additional material that Miller put together. Once again the sources surprised Morgan. A systematic reading of Williams convinced him that he had not properly understood the man when he wrote *The Puritan Dilemma.* In many respects the Williams book became an exercise in self-correction.

But Morgan was already beginning to move in quite a different direction. Yale students in his graduate seminar in 1959 all read Max Weber's *The Protestant Ethic and the Spirit of Capitalism,* a study that Morgan has always admired and continues to defend. Around 1963 he confided that he intended to write a book on the work ethic in American history and apply Weber to the South as well as to New England. One of his better known essays, "The Puritan Ethic and the American Revolution," which appeared in the *William and Mary Quarterly* in 1967, began to explore this theme and even placed Thomas Jefferson and other Virginians within this framework. This effort quickly drew a rather sharp rejoinder from his colleague and friend C. Vann Woodward, who published "The Southern Ethic in a Puritan World" in the same journal a year later. Woodward doubted that the Puritan ethic would ever tell us much about the eighteenth-century South.

Morgan was already reaching the same conclusion by a different route. As part of his grand project he immersed himself in Elizabethan materials and in the early records of Virginia. Here, too, he was surprised by his sources. He found no trace of a Puritan work ethic in early Virginia. But rather than just abandon the project, he began to rethink his understanding of colonial Virginia. He offered a preview in "The Labor Problem at Jamestown, 1607–1618," which appeared in the *American Historical Review* in 1971, and then he placed his findings in a much broader framework in his presidential address for the Organization of American Historians, which was published as "Slavery and Freedom: The American Paradox" in the *Journal of American History* a year later. He pulled all of his evidence together in his most profound book, published in 1975, *American Slavery, American Freedom: The Ordeal of Colonial Virginia,* a study that combines meticulous research into very difficult local sources with perhaps the most disturbing big question that American history raises. He saw an organic link, not everywhere but certainly in Virginia, between slavery and freedom. By enslaving their poor, Virginians did not have to treat them as political actors and could be eloquent in praise of the liberty enjoyed by those who actually were free.

That result was the product of a tangled history of more than a century from the founding of Jamestown in 1607 to the establishment of a secure world of great plantations in the eighteenth century. Successful Virginians found ways to make other people work for them, a quest that took hold with the emergence of tobacco as a cash crop before 1620. Why planters gradually shifted from indentured servants, who eventually became turbulent freedmen, to African slaves, who served for life, became a major theme of the book. Morgan broadened and restated the central problem in his closing lines: "Was the vision of a nation of equals flawed at the source by contempt for both the poor and the black? Is America still colonial Virginia writ large? More than a century after Appomattox the questions linger."

By then Morgan was already turning to the last big project of his professional career, a study of the political fictions that have organized public life in the Anglo-American world and how they have changed over the last four centuries. Specifically, why did the divine right of kings yield priority to the sovereignty of the people in the two centuries after about 1640? Both ideas, he insists, are fictions invoked by the many to control, or at least limit, the powers of the few who do the actual governing. Those who preached the divine right of kings hoped it would persuade rulers to behave according to established standards of Christian morality. In our republican world, the few still make nearly all of the actual decisions about governance, but the idea of a sovereign people, especially when organized as the electorate, has real power to limit their behavior. *Inventing the People: The Rise of Popular Sovereignty in England and America* was published in 1988, a few years after Morgan's retirement.

On June 22, 1983, after Helen's death in September 1982, Ed married Marie Carpenter Caskey, a formidable historian in her own right and the author of *Chariot of Fire: Religion and the Beecher Family* (1978). Although now in his mideighties, he remains active, frequently contributing thoughtful essays to the *New York Review of Books.* In collaboration with Marie, he has published, in March 2000, a comprehensive review of the twenty-four-volume *American National Biography,* the successor to *The Dictionary of American Biography.*

Morgan's prose is special. Some insist that he writes as well as Morison, and others that he writes even better. Historians should direct their prose, he has advised, at an audience of "ignorant geniuses." They should never condescend to their readers, many of whom are smarter than they are. "But, on the other hand, don't assume that [the reader] knows anything, because whatever you write should be self-contained, in the sense that it should supply the reader with everything needed to understand what you're trying to say." Good history, he insists, resembles good fiction. It "gives vicarious experience, and I think that history at its best is vicarious experience." "You're born in a particular century at a particular time," he explains, "and the only experience you can have directly is of the place you live and the time you live in. History is a way of giving you experience that you would otherwise be cut off from."

Morgan's histories convey a lot more than vicarious experience. His one- or two-sentence summaries of complex issues have become famous. Some of his best aphorisms include the pithy conclusions of many of his chapters. *American Slavery, American Freedom* has several examples. In recapitulating the lessons that the Roanoke colony can teach us, he observed, "Doubtless the expectations had been too high, but it is always a little sad to watch men lower their sights. And Roanoke was only the beginning." In setting up the Jamestown venture, he declared, "The Virginia Company had sent the idle to teach the idle. And they had sent, as it turned out, a quarrelsome band of gentlemen and servants to bring freedom to the free. It was a formula for disaster." Or, in laying out the dilemma that British policies posed for the colonists during the Stamp Act crisis, he suggested that the settlers might have to decide "whether they would be men and not English or whether they would be English and not men." He concluded that book with a graceful line about Collector John Robinson. After describing Robinson's revenge against his tormentor, James Otis, Jr., Morgan wrote, "Having completed his part, John Robinson sailed for England with his bride and drifted out of the stream of history."

During Morgan's Yale career, thousands of undergraduates passed through his two-semester early American history sequence, which became one of the most popular courses in the history department. Morgan has always taken seriously the advice that Morison gave him in 1942. "Now listen: don't ever teach just graduate students. You've got to teach undergraduates, and you've got to keep on teaching undergraduates. It's the only way to keep you honest." Constant contact with undergraduates, Morgan believes, helped to cleanse his prose of the technical jargon that characterizes most historical writing. But a strong commitment to undergraduate teaching did not drive him away from graduate students. At Yale he also supervised about fifty doctoral students, many of whom, as with the Brown contingent, have built substantial careers of their own.

Morgan's undergraduate lectures were always highly polished but were never mere set pieces. He spoke from notes, not a written text, and he always maintained eye contact with his class. Clarifying Puritan beliefs and values for a twentieth-century audience was always a challenge. In one class, someone asked him how anyone could accept Calvinist predestination and live with the results. Morgan responded by scrapping his lecture and taking on the whole class. "If you believe in God," he shot back, "you must accept predestination. The only alternative is moral cowardice." For the rest of the hour he demolished one counterargument after another, insisted that the very idea of an omnipotent God has vast consequences for anyone who takes it seriously, and forced the students to recognize, at a minimum, that Calvinism has coherence and a tight intellectual integrity, and once had enormous powers of persuasion.

Morgan put immense time and energy into his course. For example, during my last year at Yale, Morgan asked James H. Hutson and me to serve as his graders. At the fall midterm, the three of us read and swapped half a dozen exams to try to settle upon reasonably uniform standards of evaluation. Jim and I then split the pack of more than a hundred papers, graded them, and brought them to Morgan at the end of the week. At the first lecture the following week, he handed them back. But he first explained that he had read more than half of them himself and had revised the grades, usually downward by as much as a full letter grade. "Your graders seem much impressed with your accomplishments," he explained, "but I have a higher opinion of your abilities." He then announced that for the rest of the year he would handle all appeals about any grade that we assigned but that he reserved the right to lower as well as raise what we gave. Jim and I were mortified, of course, but after completing the final set of papers in May, we noticed one obvious benefit. Nobody had challenged a single grade we assigned. Whether or not Morgan had so intended, he had conferred on us an almost sovereign power.

Morgan's graduate seminar was an intellectual delight. I had begun graduate study at Notre Dame, where my mentor, Marshall Smelser, gave me *The Stamp Act Crisis* to read for a research paper. The book pleased me so much that I transferred to Yale and persuaded Smelser to support my move, which he generously did. Eager to confront the Revolution, I anticipated Morgan's seminar with keen interest. But Morgan guided us through the Puritans before he finally turned me loose on the Revolution in the spring. We spent at least a month of the fall term reading Perry Miller— a revelation to me—and each of us had to master the full body of writings of some prominent Puritan. I chose John Cotton. When we moved on to the Revolution, Morgan used a different pedagogical device. To introduce us to the widest variety of source material, he assigned each student, or in some cases a pair of students, a small research project on which we were to report, briefly, the following week. My first topic was newspaper coverage of the Albany Congress in 1754. There was none. Did Morgan already know that? I'm still not sure. My most interesting assignment came the day I challenged him, mildly, on the distinction between internal and external taxes, which in *The Stamp Act Crisis* he associates with a self-interested rather than a principled resistance to British taxes. Merchants, I suggested, were probably less concerned about high principles than were others who denounced parliamentary taxation. After all, hardly any of them complained about the Revenue Act of 1766, which imposed a penny duty on every gallon of imported molasses, French or British, entering a colonial port. They were happy to have the duty lowered from the three-penny duty that the Sugar Act imposed only on foreign molasses, which accounted for about 90 percent of colonial imports of that product. "I'll bet a much higher percentage of them became Loyalists than we find in the population at large," I argued. "OK," he smiled, "that's your project for next week." When I did successfully show that quite a high percentage of merchants turned Loyalist, he treated my report as a research triumph, however incomplete. But he has never retreated on the significance, or insignificance, of the internal-external dichotomy.

Morgan treated his graduate students as individuals with different needs. On one occasion, I had made an appointment to discuss portions of my dissertation with him. As I climbed the steps toward the second floor of the Hall of Graduate Studies a little ahead of schedule, I heard his voice—angry, censorious, and loud enough to make out from quite some distance, although his door was closed. He was accusing another graduate student of malingering, and from what I could tell—the student's male voice was faint and shamed, and I did not recognize whose it was—Morgan cut off the excuses before the student could finish. "I want you to report to me every week from now on, and you had better bring with you concrete evidence of what you've accomplished," he ordered.

My first reaction was selfish. Realizing that I had not consulted with him for a month or perhaps two and that I may have watched too many Ingmar Bergman movies when I could have been in Sterling Library, I thought, "Morgan's really in a foul mood and is going to give me hell. He might eat me alive." My second thought was about the student in his office. Any minute now he would come through that door, and my presence outside would embarrass him, whoever he was. So I went back downstairs, rounded a corner, and waited until I was fifteen minutes late. Then, nervously, I returned to Morgan's office. When I entered he was cheerful, affable, unruffled. Reflecting on the experience afterward, I realized that he had been responding to a very specific situation and that, if anything, he may have been overrating my own self-discipline all along, for he never pressed me about my progress.

On a personal level, Morgan was always quite informal. He and Helen lavishly entertained the students in his seminar one memorable Sunday afternoon, and on several occasions he invited me to their home for lunch or just to visit. Once, during the history department's annual faculty–graduate student softball game (this occurred before slow-pitch became the preferred form), I was pitching for the students. One of my teammates, I think it was Robert E. Pope, dared me to brush Morgan back with a high, hard one. I threw one high and tight, but not too hard, and Ed ducked out of the way. He got back up and lined the next pitch for a clean single to center field. He then smiled at me, a little triumphantly, from first base. When I later described the incident to Helen, she remarked, "My Ed is fearless." As usual, Helen got it right.

# David M. Potter

## by Howard Temperley

A t the time of his death in 1971, David Potter had the unusual distinction of holding the two highest positions available to members of his profession: the presidencies of both the American Historical Association and the Organization of American Historians. The photograph that appeared alongside his obituary notice in the *Journal of American History* shows him in a typical pose: crew-cut, bow-tied, head slightly cocked to one side, brow wrinkled, as if about to respond to a question with one of his famously well-constructed answers. In the accompanying article Edmund S. Morgan, a Yale colleague, is quoted as describing him as "the wisest man I ever knew." Others recalled that during the turbulent 1960s when he chaired the Department of History at Stanford his was always the voice of moderation and reason. No discussion was ever complete, another recalled, if he was present and had not spoken. Writing in *The Times* of London an Oxford friend, H. G. Nicholas, ascribed to him "a high degree of the rare historical virtue of humility." All bore witness to the fact that in addition to his achievements as a scholar he had a remarkable capacity for inspiring devotion.[1]

Potter was born in Augusta, Georgia, in 1910. Although the Civil War had ended almost two generations earlier, it remained a bitter memory. He recalled growing up with "a feeling that in an indirect, nonsensory way" he could actually remember what was still referred to simply as "The War." On Memorial Day, held on a different date from that observed in the North, he saw large numbers of men in gray proudly marching through town in celebration of the battles the South had lost. It left an indelible

---

1. Don E. Fehrenbacher, Howard R. Lamar, and Otis A. Pease, "David M. Potter: A Memorial Resolution," *Journal of American History* 58 (September 1971): 307–10, and obituary, 533–35; Carl N. Degler, "David M. Potter," *American Historical Review* 76 (October 1971): 1273–75; obituary, *London Times* February 26, 1971.

impression, although what in later years struck him most was the irony that neither the war itself nor its long aftermath gave southerners much cause for celebration.[2]

After attending the local high school, Potter left home in 1928 to go to Emory University in Atlanta. By the early 1930s Emory was a lively place. New ideas were afloat, even in the Deep South. In the *American Mercury,* Potter read H. L. Mencken's strictures on lynching, peonage, chain gangs, sharecropping, child labor, illiteracy, judicial corruption, bigotry, bible thumping, and other wickednesses and the absurdities of the Bible Belt. In Atlanta, too, there were signs that times were changing. The city had lately become the headquarters of Will W. Alexander's Commission on Interracial Co-operation, the aim of which was to stir consciences with regard to the manifest injustices under which African Americans labored. As a member of the Emory debating team, Potter came to know its coach, Glenn Rainey, an influential graduate student engaged in writing a dissertation on the Georgia riots of 1906, an episode that revealed southern racism at its most abhorrent. Rainey's liberal views ultimately resulted in a resolution being passed in the Georgia legislature denouncing him by name. Potter later recalled that Rainey's probing questions led a good many students, including presumably himself, to realize for the first time that the South's racial system was not, like the laws of nature, something to be taken for granted.[3]

After graduating from Emory, Potter went "up North" to Yale in 1932 for his graduate training. There he found himself in a very different world, where liberal sympathies prevailed and southern ways were commonly regarded with a mixture of condescension and ridicule. Nevertheless, the director of graduate studies in history turned out to be a fellow Georgian, Ulrich B. Phillips, with whom Potter soon established a close relationship. Until only recently southern history had been regarded as hardly worth

2. Potter, *The South and the Sectional Conflict* (Baton Rouge: Louisiana State University Press, 1968), v–vi.

3. Potter, "C. Vann Woodward," in *Pastmasters: Some Essays on American Historians,* ed. Marcus Cunliffe and Robin W. Winks (New York: Harper and Row, 1969), 376. Potter and Woodward were contemporaries as undergraduates at Emory, 1928–1932, and both belonged to the debating team. There is a useful essay on David Potter by Sir Dennis Brogan in the same volume (316–44). See also C. Vann Woodward, *Thinking Back: The Perils of Writing History* (Baton Rouge: Louisiana State University Press, 1986), 9–27, which describes the intellectual milieu of southern university life in the early 1930s that he and Potter encountered.

studying, most of what had been written being seen as more noteworthy for its celebration of local worthies and expressions of sectional pride than for its objective treatment of the South's past. There were also the sentimental illusions of the sword-and-magnolia cult and special pleadings on behalf of the Lost Cause with which to contend.

Potter soon learned that Phillips had made a start at rectifying this situation, first at the University of Michigan and subsequently at Yale. Apart from his tendency to view slavery almost exclusively from the standpoint of the masters, he had largely emancipated himself from the prevailing southernisms of his day. His career, as a southerner who had chosen the North as his intellectual arena, in many ways foreshadowed Potter's own. At Yale he offered courses on the antebellum South, sectional issues, and the southern economy—in fact on virtually all of the southern topics about which Potter subsequently taught and wrote. But for Phillips's death from cancer in 1934 (again the parallels are close) he would presumably have been Potter's dissertation supervisor. As a tribute to their friendship Potter compiled a bibliography of Phillips's writings which appeared in the *Georgia Historical Quarterly* later that same year.[4]

After a further two years at Yale, his dissertation still incomplete, Potter returned to the South to teach, first at the University of Mississippi and subsequently in Houston at what was then known as Rice Institute. Having been away for four years, he was more than ever struck by the region's contradictions and anomalies. One was the patently false image the South had of itself as being an agrarian society quite distinct from the capitalist North. Backward though it remained in many respects, the South impressed Potter as being every bit as oriented toward satisfying the demands of world markets as were other parts of the country. Odder still for Potter was the ability of southerners to think of themselves as committed to upholding the principles of social equality while obstinately remaining committed to preserving distinctions of race. The attention Potter devoted to these matters—the discrepancy between southern myth and reality and between southerners' views of themselves and how they were viewed by others—presumably contributed to the exceptional degree of

---

4. Potter, *Sectional Conflict*, v; Wood Gray, "Ulrich Bonnell Phillips," in *The Marcus W. Jernigan Essays in American Historiography,* ed. William T. Hutchinson (Chicago: University of Chicago Press, 1937), 354–73.

self-awareness he reveals in his writings. It can hardly have been entirely by coincidence that the deconstruction of popular myths about the South and the historian's need for self-scrutiny became two of the dominant themes in his work.[5]

Of more immediate concern, however, was a northern lack of perceptiveness or, more precisely, the extraordinary failure of the Republicans to grasp what was happening during the five-month interval that separated Lincoln's election in November 1860 from the firing on Fort Sumter. The seeming paralysis that gripped the Republican Party as the nation drifted toward war was the subject of his Yale dissertation and, in due course, of his first book. As a result, Potter found himself dealing once more with the sort of confusion and denial that occur in human affairs when reality and the perceptions of reality fail to coincide—a subject that had hitherto received little attention. Perhaps this oversight was largely because historians, viewing events in retrospect, had tended to assume that by November 1860 war was unavoidable. Lincoln's election, as they saw it, was simply the last straw. From their perspective, they could see evidence of impending conflict as far back as they cared to look: the Missouri Crisis, the Nullification Crisis, the annexation of Texas—one sectional confrontation after another like so many signposts all pointing in one direction. As in some Greek tragedy, it seemed to them as if events had acquired a momentum of their own.

But as Potter was astute enough to recognize, several things were wrong with this view. For a start, it failed to take note of all the signs that did *not* point in the direction specified. Anyone looking for evidence to support the notion of an irrepressible conflict could, of course, find it, but if that was all they were looking for they would miss acts and facts no less worthy of close study. In the first paragraph of *Lincoln and His Party in the Secession Crisis* (1942), Potter quotes a section from an editorial that had appeared in an obscure South Carolina newspaper in 1851. It mentioned the forts around Charleston and prophesied with eerie precision how a war between the North and the South would break out. The point of choos-

---

5. Potter, *Sectional Conflict*, v–vi. See also the three essays grouped together under the general heading "The Nature of Southernism" in *Sectional Conflict*, 3–86. For his views on historical method, see his essay "Explicit Data and Implicit Assumptions" in *History and American Society: Essays of David M. Potter*, ed. Don E. Fehrenbacher (New York: Oxford University Press, 1973), 4–26.

ing this example, however, was not to do what a naive historian might have done, namely use one lucky shot to prove the war's inevitability, but rather to contrast it with all the statements made by equally qualified observers that were wide of the mark.[6]

As Potter later argued at more length in his essays on historical methodology,[7] there is no surer way of distorting one's understanding of the past than by viewing it as though it were destined to arrive at some preordained conclusion known to the historian but not to the participants. This approach misrepresents the past because it fails to take into account how the people concerned viewed the problems confronting them and thus why they chose the solutions they did. Historians who rely on hindsight have a way of imposing their own views on the past instead of listening to what people of the time actually said. Starting out with their eyes firmly fixed on the known outcome they make it appear altogether more predetermined than it actually was.

Those public men who participated in the constitutional crisis of 1860–1861, as Potter pointed out, did not know that there would be a civil war. Had they known, and had they had any inkling that it would be as costly as it eventually turned out to be, they would not have behaved as they did. To be sure, there had been talk of secession and war for thirty years, but precisely for that reason the possibility of either occurring had begun to seem increasingly remote. Potter is good at listening to what people said, and what he shows is that the Republicans believed they had heard cries of "Wolf!" altogether too often. Time and again southerners had threatened drastic action, and time and again the same thing had happened— they and their northern Democrat collaborators had got what they wanted and walked off arm in arm to divide the spoils. Northern leaders thought the time had come to call the South's bluff and put an end to such shenanigans.

There were other reasons the Republicans failed to take southerners' threats seriously. Among them was a belief that a large section of the South's own population, most notably the former Whigs, actually op-

---

6. *Lincoln and His Party in the Secession Crisis* (New Haven: Yale University Press, 1942), vii–viii, 1. In 1942 the country was preoccupied with the war, but the scholarly community was quick to discern the merits of Potter's book. A leading scholar, Wood Gray, praised it as an "admirable study [that] ought to suggest to historians . . . other supposedly exhausted fields might repay cultivation" (*American Historical Review* 47 [1943]: 591–92).

7. *History and American Society*, 3–108.

posed secession. In this respect the northerners were not entirely mistaken. Lincoln's opponents in the late election, Douglas, Bell, and Breckinridge, had all declared their support for the Union. In the past, southern conservatives had always managed to control the fire-eaters. South Carolina had been a hotbed of radicalism for as long as anyone could remember but had signally failed to ignite the other states. Now, admittedly with more backing from elsewhere in the region, but with southern opinion still deeply divided, was the outcome likely to be any different?

We now know, of course, that it would be, but listening to the babble of voices it is plain that this was something about which even the secessionists themselves had doubts. Moreover, as Potter shows, what people said was not always quite what they meant. Northerners who spoke of allowing the seceding states to depart in peace were not for the most part proposing that they be allowed to do so, but rather were issuing them a challenge in the expectation that it would be refused. This is evident from the way the speakers' attitudes changed when it became clear that their challenge would actually be taken up. Piecing the story together, showing the mounting sense of panic as the crisis deepened, as politicians rushed about, newspaper editors changed their tack, and public opinion wavered, is something Potter does remarkably well.

Behind all these comings and goings, however, stood the still mysterious figure of the president-elect. Until Potter drew attention to it, Lincoln's role in these events had largely been ignored. His election had, of course, precipitated the crisis. But while Washington buzzed like a beehive with proposals and counterproposals, he remained aloof and virtually incommunicado in Springfield, Illinois. Asked what he thought of events, he responded by saying that he stood by his party's electoral platform and that he had already made his personal views clear in his speeches. Strictly speaking, he was still a private citizen. Yet, as Potter shows, at no time during his presidency were his actions as important as those he made during the four months between his election and his inauguration. Despite his lack of public utterances, he was firmly in control of his party's policies throughout that time thanks to his contacts with Thurlow Weed and William Seward.

Although Lincoln is remembered as the Great Emancipator and a stalwart war leader, he aspired to be neither. The image of the president-elect that emerges from Potter's pages is of a very different figure—inexperienced, misguided as to the gathering strength of the secession movement, and stubbornly intent on defending the Republican platform on which he was elected. Right up to the firing on Fort Sumter, in spite of mounting evidence of the need to make concessions, he clung to the notion that southern Unionists would somehow come to the nation's rescue. So confident was he of the moderates' support that he used the full weight of his authority to prevent even so much as a gesture of good will from being made toward those on whose support his hopes were pinned. He rejected Sen. John J. Crittenden's proposed compromise along with all the other ideas floated. There were, to be sure, strong arguments against these proposals, most notably the far-fetched fear that a latitudinal division between slave and free territories (such as the Missouri Compromise line of 36° 30′) would encourage southern expansion into Central America and the Caribbean. Even so, the possibility remains that some agreement about slavery in the territories could have been cobbled together.

As things turned out, the Union was preserved and slavery was abolished, but at an appalling cost. As Potter points out in his 1962 edition of *Lincoln and His Party,* for every eight slaves freed, one young northerner or southerner died. Whether the same ends could have been achieved by other means, had Lincoln used his influence more adeptly, Potter does not say. Nevertheless, as he shows, there is enough evidence of conciliatory sentiment North and South, and even within the Republicans' own ranks, for a plausible case to be made. Such an outcome would not have solved the underlying problems that had led to the crisis any more than did the Compromise of 1850, but by adept statesmanship crises can be managed and wars delayed or avoided. In his introduction to the 1962 edition Potter cites the Cold War as an example. Had he lived longer he might have used the same example to show that if wars are delayed long enough sometimes even the underlying problems disappear.

How to weigh Lincoln's own and his party's contribution to the coming of the war in relation to all the other factors involved is a matter on which historians will continue to differ. Subsequent research, however, has failed to modify to any significant degree the account Potter gives of the way events unfolded. The subsequent discovery of Lincoln's letter to Governor Pickens of South Carolina informing him of the intention to supply provisions to Fort Sumter actually strengthens Potter's claim that, far from seeking to provoke a war on northern terms, Lincoln did everything he could, short of acquiescing to the breakup of the Union, to prevent the outbreak of war. But as is made plain in Potter's second book, *National-*

*ism and Sectionalism in America, 1775–1877: Select Problems in Historical Interpretation* (1947), the significance attached to the events of 1860–1861 depends on the questions asked and the view taken of developments stretching right back to the origins of the republic.[8]

*Nationalism and Sectionalism* was a pioneering work to the extent that it was one of the first contributions to what subsequently became an avalanche of "problem books." Today it looks a little dated, mainly because on a number of peripheral questions—for example, the scale and duration of the Atlantic slave trade—the information it contains is patently wrong. However, in terms of its imaginative selection of documents and Potter's often lengthy commentaries on them, it remains as fresh and pertinent as ever. Given that his perennial concern was not simply with reaching conclusions but with demonstrating how they were reached, the format of the problem book suited his purpose ideally. As a teacher he had an extraordinary ability to take a question, however stumblingly expressed, rephrase it so as to ensure that he had fully grasped what the questioner intended, break it down into its constituent parts, and then proceed to answer each part in logical sequence. In *Nationalism and Sectionalism* he displays the same skill, supplying the evidence in documentary form, outlining the standpoints from which it may be viewed, indicating the deductions that might be drawn, but leaving the final choice of a conclusion to the reader.

Formidable as Potter's powers of discrimination were in such matters, his third major work, *People of Plenty: Economic Abundance and the American Character* (1954), tested them to their limits (and, some have argued, beyond).[9] In terms of approach and subject matter, *People of Plenty* represented a significant departure from anything he had previously attempted. The book was the result of a seemingly innocuous invitation from the Charles R. Walgreen Foundation to deliver a series of six lectures on that old chestnut: the American character. As he disarmingly explains, his purpose in accepting had been "only to join the mixed lot of scholars,

---

8. *Nationalism and Sectionalism* (New York: Henry Holt, 1949) was coedited with Thomas G. Manning, as was its sequel, *Government and the American Economy: 1870 to the Present* (New York: Henry Holt, 1950). Although the volumes were a joint venture, it is reasonable to assume that each coeditor took primary responsibility for the one relating to his area of expertise.

9. Robert M. Collins, "In Retrospect: David M. Potter's *People of Plenty* and the Recycling of Consensus History," *Reviews in American History* 16 ( June 1988): 321–35.

maiden ladies, itinerant lecturers, professional pundits, and overnight experts whose writings have adorned the subject."[10] Being a perfectionist, however, Potter quickly found that he could not rest content with the sort of random generalizations they supplied. There had to be a more disciplined approach—in short, a method.

Reflection quickly persuaded him that in this respect history offered little help. Historians were more concerned with getting on with the job than with wasting time on methodology. The results of this approach were not reassuring. What he found was that while expressing doubt as to whether such a thing as national character existed, they continued to invoke such abstract concepts as "the American tradition" and "the American mind," precisely as though it did. What they came up with as a result was a hodge-podge of miscellaneous observations based on assumptions that were unexamined, half hidden, and largely inchoate. The fact was that no one could write a history of the United States or any other nation on the assumption that the people concerned were simply any old people, no different in their views, aspirations, and lifestyles from any other random cross section of the world's population. The very concept of nationhood required the recognition of there being an identifiable group of people with at least some shared aspirations and characteristics.

In contrast to history, Potter found the newer social sciences—psychology, sociology, and anthropology—altogether more open about their methodologies. They had, moreover, experience in dealing with much the sort of problems he now confronted. In the postwar years their prestige was high, so high that for a time it seemed that a whole new science of human behavior was in the making. Potter accordingly set about enlisting their methods to help him with putting into manageable order the mélange of ideas associated with the notion of national identity that his readings had revealed.

This was an ambitious undertaking. The problem with the concepts on which these new disciplines are based is that, on close examination, they turn out to be extremely difficult to pin down. Central to the whole enterprise is the concept of culture, which, as defined by anthropologists, denotes an entire way of living. It is no accident, therefore, that this notion has proved more readily applicable to small, relatively static communities

10. *People of Plenty* (Chicago: University of Chicago Press, 1954), vii.

of a kind fast disappearing, but still found in remote parts of the world, than to large, modern, rapidly changing societies like the United States. Accounting for change, however, is what historians are supposedly good at doing. Might it be possible, Potter wondered, to marry history to the behavioral sciences and thereby throw light on modern societies also?

*Culture* is a word with many meanings. As commonly used, it denotes no more than the seemingly unrelated hodgepodge of beliefs and practices occurring within a given society. In this sense it differs little, if at all, from what social commentators commonly refer to as manners, habits, mores, or simply character and refer to in the random way Potter decries. More strictly employed, however, the word carries the additional implication that at some deeper level the assumptions and practices of a society are all interconnected. It was the notion of employing the concept of culture in this second sense that caught Potter's imagination, namely the idea that for a society to be understood fully, it needs to be seen as a totality and its features regarded as parts of a transcendent whole.

As evidence that such totalities exists, Potter cites Freud, to whom he attributes the ability of "piercing through the superficial zones of intellect and reason to the vasty, irrational deeps of the id and ego beneath."[11] Freud, of course, is concerned with the psychology of individuals rather than of whole cultures. But, taking his integrative concept of personality as a starting point, Potter was intrigued to discover that social psychologists such as Erich Fromm and Karen Horney used it as a basis for positing a similarly integrative concept of culture—and, by extension, of national character. Looked at in this way, national character was formed by culture acting on and shaping individual personalities.

In the 1950s these ideas appeared more plausible than they do in 2000. It is surprising, nevertheless, to find a scholar as skeptical of the working methods of his own and other disciplines as Potter still so willing to accept lock, stock, and barrel those of the behavioral scientists. We may speculate that, aware of his own lack of training in the areas concerned, he felt in no position to call into question the behavioral approach. Even so, the respectfulness of his attitude contrasts oddly with what he had to say about the practices of scholars working in more familiar fields, such as economists, whose favored working model he notes with characteristic

11. Ibid., 33.

acerbity as being "a desert island occupied by economic men in a number not greater than could be counted on the fingers of one hand."[12] He makes no similar comments about the models used by Freud and the behavioral scientists. He was, of course, trying to make a case and aware that he was venturing into unfamiliar territory. But that plainly made the quest all the more exciting, particularly on his discovering that the findings of the disciplines concerned, disparate though they were, dovetailed remarkably neatly. It is significant, all the same, that he never tried to psychoanalyze Lincoln and was unfailingly dismissive of the attempts of those who sought to explain the culture of the South in holistic terms.[13]

The social science ideas of the 1950s are no longer held in high regard.[14] In certain respects, therefore, *People of Plenty* represents a failed shotgun marriage. Nevertheless, the boldness and novelty of the attempt were in tune with the spirit of the times and gained Potter a wide readership. The book appealed particularly to those engaged in setting up the new American studies programs, for whom culture was an important unifying concept. In the 1950s and 1960s such programs were springing up not only in the United States but elsewhere around the world thanks to American beneficence and Cold War pressures. Universities outside the United States that had not previously taught American subjects often found it administratively convenient to group history, literature, and political science together in a single American studies department.[15] As a result, *People of Plenty*—along with other interdisciplinary works such as Henry Nash Smith's *Virgin Land* (1950) and Leo Marx's *Machine in the Garden* (1964)—became a key text for a generation of non-Americans intent on studying the United States.

But what principally assured the book's success was the fact that it dealt with what in the 1950s appeared to be America's principal defining characteristic, namely its economic abundance. What fascinated the rest of the world, and stirred the imaginations of Americans too, was the sight of a

12. Ibid., xiv.

13. See, for example, "The Historian's Use of Nationalism and Vice Versa" and the other essays grouped under the general heading "The Nature of Southernism" in Potter, *Sectional Conflict,* 3–86; also *The Impending Crisis, 1848–1861,* ed. Don E. Fehrenbacher (New York: Harper and Row, 1976), 32.

14. Richard Pells, *The Liberal Mind in a Conservative Age: American Intellectuals in the 1940s and 1950s* (New York: Harper and Row, 1985).

15. This was typically the case all over Europe. On the United Kingdom, see Howard Temperley, "American Studies in Britain," *American Quarterly* 18 (summer 1966): 251–69.

nation that was not only rich, but richer than any nation had been in the whole of history. After the Depression and the war years the spectacle was dazzling. Potter himself spent 1947–1948 as the visiting Harmsworth Professor at Oxford. This was at a time when the British were subject to even worse shortages and more draconian rationing than during the war years. Elsewhere in Europe people were starving. Even the most cursory glance at the statistics was enough to reveal the scale of the contrast. Americans' per capita income was three times that of the French and four times that of the West Germans. With only 7 percent of the world's population, the postwar United States possessed half of the world's manufacturing capacity along with an even larger share of its automobiles, refrigerators, television sets, and all the other goods modern industry produced.

Putting these elements together, Potter showed that Americans took for granted much that others saw as far beyond their reach and in the process acquired attitudes that by any standards but their own appeared wasteful, if not positively profligate. He was also able to demonstrate how abundance affected the everyday behavior and attitudes of individuals in ways of which they were unaware, like assuming there would be seats on a train, that wealth was infinitely expandable, and that there were other ways of helping the poor than by milking the rich. Not all of the effects of American affluence, however, were benign. Among its most characteristic and least beneficent manifestations was the influence of the American advertising industry, the rise of which Potter saw as reflecting the shift from a production to a consumer economy. Advertising's role—unlike those of the school and the church, which sought to inculcate attitudes and beliefs deemed of social value—was to stimulate people's anxiety and greed. Americans mistook the world's envy of their material success for a desire to acquire democratic institutions analogous to those of the United States and supposed that, if they did, affluence would automatically ensue. Far from celebrating his nation's capitalistic achievements, Potter was concerned over what he saw as the growing dangers of unbridled materialism and mass conformity. For all its sophistication, *People of Plenty* has more than a little in common with Sloan Wilson's *Man in the Gray Flannel Suit* (1955), William H. Whyte's *The Organization Man* (1956), Vance Packard's *The Hidden Persuaders* (1957), and the other popular jeremiads of the period in drawing attention to the doubts and uncertainties evoked by what to outside observers looked like America's unparalleled good fortune.

Today all this appears distinctly dated. Jeremiads are no longer in fashion, and the abundance of the 1950s is no longer the glittering vision it once seemed. To Americans, now much richer than forty years ago, it no longer even looks like abundance. More important, other nations have since been catching up, so that much of what Potter describes is simply the everyday experience of people throughout the developed world and to that extent not peculiarly American. This is a development that, far from undercutting his argument, illustrates his claim that there is nothing fixed or immutable about either culture or character, as both are in part reflections of the circumstances in which people live and thus apt to change as circumstances change.

Although it draws attention to the various forms of abundance Americans have encountered in the course of their history, *People of Plenty* is essentially a statement about the postwar United States. It remains a classic, full of brilliant insights, but inevitably reflective of the limitations of viewpoint characteristic of its day. By the early 1960s the rediscovery of poverty, arising in part from the publication of Michael Harrington's *The Other America* (1962), made its single-minded emphasis on affluence appear outdated. The same may be said of its concern with mass conformity and the sinister influence of advertising, both of which, in the light of the political and social turbulence of the 1960s, seem distinctly anachronistic.

In later years Potter returned more than once to the issue of national character, most notably in his 1963 Commonwealth Lectures, edited by his Stanford colleague and friend Don E. Fehrenbacher and published posthumously as *Freedom and Its Limitations in American Life* (1976). Here the principal focus is not on Americans' affluence but on their notions regarding the complex and ambiguous relationship between freedom and coercion. Americans, he notes, cherish a view of themselves as being both the freest people on earth and the most committed to equality. Yet, as he points out, freedom and equality are incompatible principles in that the unhindered pursuit of one prevents the achievement of the other.

To get around this difficulty, Americans have defined equality and freedom in a characteristically American context. Thus they have tended to interpret equality as meaning equality of opportunity rather than equality of condition, and freedom as freedom from any officious kind of coercive authority rather than as a right to do anything one pleases. The Declaration of Independence was drafted because Americans were no longer prepared to put up with the authoritarian behavior of George III and his ministers, and they have remained instinctively hostile to displays of rank and practices requiring the giving and receiving of orders ever since. Yet all societies, the United States included, need ways of making people do what is necessary. Where Americans differ from others is in their anxiety to disguise hierarchical relationships by emphasizing the importance of team membership and avoiding as far as possible situations that require the pulling of rank. When compulsion does become necessary, they summon up imperatives of an indirect and less personal kind such as the dictates of the market. Just as Americans' belief in freedom favored free enterprise, so free enterprise helped bolster their belief in individual freedom by substituting the laws of economics for the authority of men. On the other hand, as Potter also shows, Americans' commitment to freedom has seldom stood in the way when a majority wished to legislate on moral issues. In this regard they have been no less willing than other peoples to encumber themselves with restrictions and prohibitions.

At the time of his death in 1971 Potter still had not completed his magnum opus, a history of the coming of the Civil War for Harper's New American Nation series, on which he had worked for the previous seventeen years. Throughout that time he had allowed himself to be continually distracted by other commitments. As he wrote to his editor at Harper's in 1962, "My position is quite like that of a defaulting debtor who has no assets on which his creditors can foreclose. . . . Like all debtors I have had more than one creditor, and have been trying more or less desperately to pay the smaller creditors because I thought they could be taken care of more easily." However, with these "smaller creditors" paid off, he henceforward intended to devote himself single-mindedly to his "first creditor."[16]

In spite of this assurance, Potter continued to take on new writing assignments and administrative responsibilities—among them the Commonwealth Lectures and the chairmanship of the Stanford history department. If anything, he was even more amenable to distractions than before. Whether this was evidence of human weakness or creative exuberance is hard to say. Plainly it was not time wasted, for his reputation as a historian rests almost as much on the two dozen or so essay-length arti-

16. Potter's long travails with Harper over *The Impending Crisis* are described by Don E. Fehrenbacher in his "Editor's Preface" to *Freedom and Its Limitations in American Life* (Stanford: Stanford University Press, 1976), vii–xi.

cles he produced over these years as on his longer works. One collection of these pieces, *The South and the Sectional Conflict,* put together by Potter himself, was published in 1968. It was followed by a posthumous volume, *History and American Society,* edited by Don E. Fehrenbacher and published in 1973. Together they provide an overview of the three principal areas to which he devoted his attention: the coming of the Civil War, approaches to the writing of history, and the distinguishing characteristics of American society.

Potter later incorporated many of the ideas first set out in his essays into his work for Harper. Despite the many distractions, he had never put the manuscript aside for long, working away at it in the intervals between other assignments. In the process it had grown larger than originally planned, but by the time of his death eighteen of its twenty chapters were substantially complete. Luckily the two remaining ones related to the issues already covered in *Lincoln and His Party,* leaving little room for doubt as to how he intended to conclude. Like his two other posthumous books, *The Impending Crisis, 1848–1861* (1976) was completed and seen through the press by Fehrenbacher, himself a distinguished Civil War scholar. In it Potter displays, albeit on a larger canvas, the same ability to see issues through the eyes of participants that he had shown in his earlier works. Evident, too, is his awareness of the many paradoxes of the period, among them the way developments that might have been expected to promote pride and unity, such as the nation's westward march, instead fueled sectional jealousy and discord. Critics hailed it as an outstanding work of scholarship, a judgment reinforced by the awarding of a Pulitzer Prize.

Potter's writings are not without their own paradoxes. One is that, although remembered as a historian of the South, he has remarkably little to say about African Americans. He does not attempt to identify with them or to consider how events looked from their standpoint. The nearest he gets to admitting the possibility of their playing an active role in the South's affairs is in his essay "John Brown and the Paradox of Leadership among American Negroes," in which he takes Brown to task for attempting to organize a rebellion on their behalf without going to the trouble of informing them of his intention.[17] Otherwise, he tends to see them as "a

---

17. *Sectional Conflict,* 201–18.

kind of peasantry," whose status left them essentially powerless.[18] As with the traditional view of the peasants of the middle ages, African Americans are significant for being fought over rather than for any contribution they themselves made to the onrush of events. How they lived and what they thought appears to have concerned him little.

Puzzling, too, is the relationship between Potter the historian of the sectional struggle and Potter the analyst of postwar American culture. One way of accounting for the discrepancy is in terms of the contrasting demands of the two subject areas in which he worked, history and American studies. Unlike history, already well established as a discipline, American studies in the 1950s and 1960s was new, uncertain of its status, and actively searching for ways of looking at the United States that would encourage scholars from different disciplines to coordinate their efforts. As chairman of the Yale American studies program, Potter found this a matter of practical as well as theoretical concern.

Like Frederick Jackson Turner, who in certain aspects he resembles, Potter sought an explanation for what he saw as the distinguishing features of American society in his own day and came up with an answer that incorporated various ideas associated with the forward-looking approach of the time as well as other, more familiar ideas, including Turner's own. Both he and Turner emphasized the importance of shared values and experiences, but where Turner saw the dominant shaping influence as being that of the frontier, Potter saw the powerful effects of abundance. Potter also went a step further by introducing the notion of culture into the equation, thereby invoking the idea that the United States represented if not exactly an organic whole at least something closely akin to it. This fitted the needs of the emerging American studies movement as well as impressing many as an apt description of the America of the Eisenhower years. It proved distinctly less well fitted to the America of the 1960s and 1970s when the country seemed to be coming apart, scholars in the American studies movement despaired of ever finding a method, and students began referring to their nation as "Amerika."[19]

Writing about the 1850s, Potter was at pains to emphasize that those liv-

18. *Nationalism and Sectionalism,* 156, 166.

19. Collins, "In Retrospect," 325–28. See also the reviews of *People of Plenty* by George Caspar Homans, *New England Quarterly* 27 (December 1954): 553–54, and Irvin G. Wyllie, *Journal of Economic History* 15 (1955): 189–90.

ing at the time did not foresee that the country was about to be torn apart. Writing in the 1950s about the America of the postwar years, he was likewise unaware of an impending crisis. This, however, in no way diminishes his stature as a historian or even as a commentator on the prevailing social attitudes and tendencies of his own time. In drawing attention to the effects of affluence—both its good features and its downside in the form of social alienation, crude materialism, and mass conformity—he was ahead of most of the intellectuals of his generation. In a small way, too, he helped pioneer women's studies.[20] His belief in the achievements and potential of the behavioral sciences was characteristic of the period. So, too, was his political conservatism as reflected in his failure to take note of the many Americans who had *not* benefited from the postwar boom and for one reason or another—lack of skills, poor education, physical disability, racial discrimination, geographical location, age—were unlikely ever to do so. In all these ways he reflected the strengths and weaknesses of the social thinking of the time. As a commentator on the antebellum years, however, he remains unequaled.

But to say that there are two David Potters would be misleading, as many of the same characteristics are to be found throughout his work. He always expressed himself with directness and economy and was mindful of the need to make explicit the logical steps by which he arrived at his conclusions. He was also invariably meticulous in the way he gave full credit to those whose views he discussed, never twisting, exaggerating, or misconstruing what they had to say so as to strengthen the case he wished to advance. This he did with such scrupulousness that, even where the purpose was to take issue, his restatement of a case often made it appear more plausible than the original. His concern with fairness and his refusal to cut corners, whether employed with regard to issues from the past or to the views of other scholars, help explain why his treatment of familiar topics so often yielded unexpected results. Although the topics he chose and the authorities on which he relied differed widely, there are certain qualities—among them his respectful handling of sources, openness to alternative ways of looking at issues, and lucidity of exposition—that are easily recognizable in everything he wrote.

He died in 1971, while still at the height of his powers. His presidential

---

20. See "American Women and the American Character," first presented as a lecture at Stetson University, 1959, in *History and American Society,* 277–303.

addresses to the Organization of American Historians and the American Historical Association were never delivered. Leaving aside his edited works, three of his six books, thanks to the labors of Don E. Fehrenbacher, appeared after his death.[21] It is a pity he did not live to enjoy their acclaim.

21. For a full listing of writings by and about Potter, compiled by George Harmon Knoles, see *Freedom and Its Limitations,* 65–89.

# Arthur M. Schlesinger, Jr.

## by Daniel Feller

For nearly half a century, Arthur Meier Schlesinger, Jr., has held a unique place among American historians. As a scholar he has been versatile and prolific, the author of foundational works on Jacksonian America, Franklin Roosevelt and the New Deal, and John and Robert Kennedy. He is without peer as a narrative stylist, and his books have found a large audience while meeting the highest academic standards. Yet Schlesinger has always been controversial, for his scholarship seeks overtly, even ostentatiously, to serve political ends. He has dedicated himself to an instrumentalist approach to history, to the uncovering of useful lessons for the present from the study of the past. He believes that history can inform policy making and that it is the civic duty of the historian to make sure that it does, even to the point of becoming a policy maker himself. "If intellectuals decided to abandon government to non-intellectuals," he has said, "they would have only themselves to blame for the result." He has also said that political liberals, of which he is one, come in two kinds. "On the one hand are the politicians, the administrators, the doers; on the other, the sentimentalists, the utopians, the wailers." Schlesinger himself has always aimed to be a doer.[1]

Accordingly he has lived in the public eye, writing for publications from *Partisan Review* and the *New Republic* to the *New York Times*, the *Wall Street Journal*, *Esquire*, *Vogue*, *Parade*, and *Family Weekly*. He has served two full generations as a kind of public preceptor and all-around cultural commentator, speaking as the nation's wise counsel and even as its conscience. He knows the ways of power and celebrity firsthand: he has reviewed books and movies, counseled a president, graced the cover of *Time*,

---

1. *A Thousand Days: John F. Kennedy in the White House* (Boston: Houghton Mifflin, 1965), 744; *The Vital Center: The Politics of Freedom* (Boston: Houghton Mifflin, 1949), 159.

and been interviewed by *Playboy.* He is perhaps the most widely known historian in the country, and surely one of the most respected. Yet his scholarship has also suffered persistent attack for intellectual shallowness, for a distorting present-mindedness, and for subservience to expedient ends. Schlesinger's career exemplifies the rewards and risks that await the historian in politics.

Schlesinger's pedigree and upbringing perfectly prefigured his career. He was born on October 15, 1917, in Columbus, Ohio. Both parents were historians and liberal political activists. Arthur Meier Schlesinger, Sr., a professor at Harvard after 1924, aimed to enlarge the scope of history "to include the totality of human experience."[2] He did pathbreaking work in social, urban, and cultural history and coedited the landmark History of American Life series. His wife, Elizabeth Bancroft Schlesinger, was a pioneering women's historian and a relative of George Bancroft, a nineteenth-century scholar and statesman who wrote the ten-volume *History of the United States,* served as a diplomat abroad, and was secretary of the navy under President James K. Polk.

Young Schlesinger attended Phillips Exeter and then Harvard, graduating in 1938. His undergraduate thesis on Orestes Brownson, a contentious Jacksonian intellectual with shifting views in politics and religion, was published in 1939 as *Orestes A. Brownson: A Pilgrim's Progress.* A three-year membership in Harvard's Society of Fellows allowed Schlesinger to continue academic work without taking a Ph.D. He served in the Office of Strategic Services in World War II and in 1945 published his second book, *The Age of Jackson,* which won a well-earned Pulitzer Prize.

*Orestes A. Brownson* was a precocious achievement. *The Age of Jackson* was simply stunning. Masterfully crafted and magisterially self-assured, rich in detail and broad in scope, it was the kind of book that might cap a distinguished scholarly career. Written when Schlesinger was in his midtwenties, it remains perhaps his most impressive accomplishment and is still the one indispensable work in its field, a singular distinction for a book now more than fifty years old.

At one level, *The Age of Jackson* was an exercise in simple revisionism. Where scholars of Turnerian bent had traced the Jacksonian political explosion to origins in frontier democracy, Schlesinger found its roots in the

2. Arthur M. Schlesinger, *In Retrospect: The History of a Historian* (New York: Harcourt, Brace and World, 1963), 199.

developing class struggle of the industrializing East. But Schlesinger did much more than relocate the Jacksonian constituency and reinterpret its program. The book was aptly titled: it was neither a study of Jackson himself (who retires from the scene less than halfway through) nor a simple political narrative but a panoramic portrait of an era, with politics as the center stage on which its defining social conflict was fought out. And that conflict, the class struggle for supremacy between "the business community and the rest of society," though it took new shape in Jacksonian America, formed according to Schlesinger a central theme throughout the whole of American history.[3]

Here Schlesinger drew on some ideas of his father's, his own previous work on Brownson, and his experience of economic depression and war to elucidate a grand thesis. The signal fact about America was the ability of its democracy to weather domestic and international crisis without sliding into revolution or dictatorship. The anchor of that success, the very "foundation for liberty," was the maintenance of an ongoing "struggle among competing groups for the control of the state." Historically, the leading contenders had been a business class wielding the clout of concentrated wealth and a popular majority periodically rallying behind a strong executive to restrain business's power and right its abuses. Complete victory for either side in this contest would have put in jeopardy either economic or political freedom, capitalism or democracy. But held within bounds by constitutionalism and pluralism, the struggle preserved them both. A political equilibrium was maintained by cyclical rotations in power between Federalist/Whig/Republican business "conservatives" and reforming agrarian (or laboring) Democratic "liberals." Thomas Jefferson's presidency marked one epoch of popular ascendancy over business, Jackson's a second, and Franklin Roosevelt's a third.[4]

Schlesinger celebrated Andrew Jackson for his practical, experimental approach to problems, his energetic leadership, and his championship of the common people against the rich and powerful. The New Deal parallels were obvious. Indeed, in *The Age of Jackson* Schlesinger revealed much of himself, sounding his admiration for politically engaged intellectuals like Brownson and Schlesinger's own kinsman George Bancroft, and trumpeting the virtues of patriotism and liberalism. Asides and footnotes

3. *The Age of Jackson* (Boston: Little, Brown, 1945), 307.
4. Ibid., 505.

praised Franklin Roosevelt and gibed at communist fellow travelers and wartime conscientious objectors.

Full of sharp vignettes and memorable characters, *The Age of Jackson* was a literary tour de force. It unveiled also its author's astonishing range. In chapters on law, religion, literature, and economic and social theory, Schlesinger endowed Jacksonian Democracy with an intellectual content no historian had found before. He made it a movement not only of politics but also of ideas. He set the terms of a debate that has continued ever since, over whether Democrats and Whigs really did represent distinct class interests in society. Schlesinger's own partisanship both enlivened his analysis and demeaned it. His treatment of Whig leaders and Whiggery descended to caricature, while he damned as cowards or hypocrites those thinkers, clerics, and reformers who shirked responsibility by avoiding politics or who dared to enlist on the anti-Democratic side.

From a later historiographical vantage, perhaps most damaging to *The Age of Jackson*'s credibility were the subjects Schlesinger simply chose to leave out. In 527 pages of text there is barely a mention of Indian removal, surely an essential element in Jackson's Democracy. Antislavery appears as a mere sideshow, a conceit of religious zealots and interlopers, until taken up and made politically effective in the 1840s by Democratic partisans. Tracing the roots of Republican antislavery to "the straight Jacksonian tradition," Schlesinger claimed Abraham Lincoln, who had been a fervent Whig, as a lineal heir of Andrew Jackson. (He would later add Theodore Roosevelt.)[5] Such manipulations lent credence to a charge that would dog Schlesinger throughout his career: that his work is more apologia than analysis, his history mere grist for his political mill.

After World War II, Schlesinger joined his father on the Harvard history faculty, becoming a full professor in 1954. He entered politics in 1947 as a founding member of the Americans for Democratic Action, which he called "a group of pragmatic liberals opposed to all dogmatisms, conservative, socialist, or communist, and dedicated to piecemeal and gradual reform."[6] In *The Vital Center* (1949), his first book on current affairs, he filled out the dimensions of his middling creed.

With the Great Depression and World War II now past, Schlesinger

5. Ibid., 433.
6. This characterization appears in *The Politics of Hope* (Boston: Houghton Mifflin, 1963), 120.

urged liberals to reposition themselves for the new challenges of affluence at home and communism abroad. At one end of the political spectrum was the business community, indispensable for its economic role yet too selfish and stupid for responsible civic leadership. At the other extreme was communist totalitarianism and its unwitting domestic abettors, the muddle-headed, soft-hearted "progressives" exemplified by Henry Wallace, who Schlesinger compared to northern "doughface" apologists for slavery in the years before the Civil War.

The middle ground was occupied by the liberals, the anticommunist "free left." They were hardheaded realists in foreign relations and "humane, experimental, and pragmatic" in their domestic policy. They believed in "the integrity of the individual, in the limited state, in due process of law, in empiricism and gradualism." For Schlesinger, liberalism was not a set of doctrines but an absence of doctrine, a principled yet always flexible response to particular problems as they arose. As he said in a new preface to *The Vital Center* in 1962, "if liberalism should ever harden into ideology, then, like all ideologies, it would be overwhelmed by the turbulence and unpredictability of history." Marx's "fatal error" had been to understate the adaptability of liberal democracy, its capacity to right the capitalist ship through moderate redistribution of wealth and cushioning of the business cycle. Spurning "the dogmatists, the philosophers of either/or," liberals had created the "mixed society," which surpassed and would outlast its competitors of left and right. "Both classical socialism and classical capitalism were products of the nineteenth century, and their day is over."[7]

*The Vital Center* was both a call to arms and a biting polemic, exhibiting the breadth of Schlesinger's reading and the sharpness of his pen. Blending historical and literary allusions, pairing Lincoln with Dostoyevsky, Nathaniel Hawthorne with the Moscow show trials, it showed Schlesinger's talent for firing a moderate cause with radical fervor. Schlesinger took liberal democracy—a creed whose hallmarks were caution and restraint, skepticism of absolutes and whole truths, and satisfaction with compromises and halfway solutions—and made it a "fighting faith." Prophetically, the domestic terms of that faith in 1949 moved beyond sustaining prosperity to include a revival of community spirit and

---

7. *The Vital Center: The Politics of Freedom,* 2d ed. (Boston: Houghton Mifflin, 1962), 130, xv, 156, ix–xiii.

institutions, a firm defense of civil liberties in the face of anticommunist hysteria, and "an unrelenting attack on all forms of racial discrimination." In foreign affairs, the liberal way meant enlightened internationalism, expressed through containment of communism and a friendly helping hand to the peoples of the underdeveloped world.[8]

Having laid out an agenda for the next two decades of American liberalism, Schlesinger returned to history with the multivolume *Age of Roosevelt*. Three volumes—*The Crisis of the Old Order, The Coming of the New Deal,* and *The Politics of Upheaval*—appeared in rapid succession from 1957 to 1960 and carried the story through 1936. (Despite a promise renewed in 1988, the series remains unfinished.) Here was *The Age of Jackson* over again, but on a grander scale. Again Schlesinger unfolded a stirring saga, his kaleidoscopic narrative enlivened with vivid episodes and brilliant character sketches. The prologue set at the inauguration was familiar: a nation steeped in crisis; a capital city sunk in gloom; a rugged, confident hero emerging to lead the people out of darkness. Like the old Jeffersonians in 1829, the Progressive keepers of the democratic flame awoke from exile in 1933 to rally around the new savior, while crabbed conservatives wrung their hands and cried of doom.

Like *The Age of Jackson*, Schlesinger's New Deal trilogy married narrative history of the highest order to a conception of politics as an intellectual activity. Schlesinger's central concern was with neither social conditions nor the mechanics of governance but with what he later called "the battlefield of ideas," where people in power strove to grasp the essence of problems and to work out their solution in public policy. He attended especially to the philosophical groundings of New Deal programs and to the interplay of views and personalities around the president. Schlesinger identified two distinct New Deals. The first, until 1935, was patterned on Theodore Roosevelt's New Nationalism and pointed toward central economic planning. The second drew from Woodrow Wilson's New Freedom and the works of John Maynard Keynes and sought to restore competition while stimulating growth. What held them together was not theoretical consistency but an improvisational outlook that refused the alternatives of socialist compulsion or heartless, mindless laissez-faire. "The distinction of the New Deal lay precisely in its refusal to approach social problems in terms of ideology. . . . The great central source of its energy was

8. Ibid., 191.

the instinctive contempt of practical, energetic, and compassionate people for dogmatic absolutes. Refusing to be intimidated by abstractions or to be overawed by ideology, the New Dealers responded by doing things." Again Schlesinger affirmed "that a managed and modified capitalist order achieved by piecemeal experiment could best combine personal freedom and economic growth"; again he assailed utopians and purists who would rather dream and theorize than work to make the real world better. Rooseveltian pragmatism, guided by the president's great faith in the people and theirs in him, rescued capitalism from its own follies and preserved American democracy as a beacon to the world.[9]

Despite its obvious slant, *The Age of Roosevelt* was an impressive achievement. Utilizing interviews and manuscript sources still held in private hands, it brought the New Deal out of memory into history. In forging a grand and compelling synthesis out of the confusion of fairly recent events, Schlesinger framed the terms for subsequent debate over the New Deal. For a second time he had set the template for the understanding of an era.

Meanwhile, he was living his activist creed, serving as a speechwriter for Adlai Stevenson during his presidential bids of 1952 and 1956. In 1960, Schlesinger signed on early with the campaign of John F. Kennedy, whom he had long known as a Massachusetts congressman and senator. After the election Robert Kennedy offered him a post as special assistant to the president, to "serve as a sort of roving reporter and trouble-shooter." Schlesinger accepted and became for the next three years an actor in his own history, one of the influential "men around the president" he had described in Roosevelt's and Jackson's White House. Kennedy saw the parallel, telling Schlesinger, "when I read your Roosevelt books, I thought what towering figures those men around Roosevelt were. . . . Then I read Teddy's book [Theodore White's *The Making of the President: 1960*] and realized that they were just [Theodore] Sorensen and [Richard] Goodwin and you."[10]

In 1963, while serving with Kennedy, Schlesinger published *The Politics of Hope*, a collection of his essays from the 1950s. The title invoked his cyclical theory. The generational wheel had turned again: stagnation had given way to innovation; the liberal party of Hope—"humane, skeptical,

---

9. *The Politics of Upheaval,* American Heritage Library Edition (Boston: Houghton Mifflin, 1988), x, 647–48.
   10. *A Thousand Days,* 143, 481.

and pragmatic"—had displaced the conservative party of Memory.[11] The adventure was exhilarating but brief. Kennedy's assassination in November 1963 stunned Schlesinger. Resigning his White House post, he stayed in Washington to write *A Thousand Days: John F. Kennedy in the White House*, which was published in 1965 and won Schlesinger his second Pulitzer Prize, this time for biography.

Actually, *A Thousand Days* was less a biography than an insider's memoir, albeit written with a historian's perspective and precision. Drawing heavily on firsthand observation and private recollections, it omitted source citations and treated events largely through the prism of Schlesinger's personal experience. Much of the story was familiar: a set-piece prologue at the inauguration; a burst of youthful energy in government; a charismatic leader confronting a stodgy "business community"; a struggle between narrow private interest and broader visions of a just society. Working old themes, Schlesinger praised Kennedy's flexibility against Eisenhower's rigidity in subchapters headed "Dogmatism vs. Pragmatism" and "Uniformity vs. Diversity."

Most of *A Thousand Days* dealt with foreign policy, reflecting both the internationalist priorities of the Kennedy White House and Schlesinger's own sphere of action within it. Deep admiration for Kennedy suffused the narrative, untempered by major criticisms either personal or political. Schlesinger acknowledged failures at the Bay of Pigs and in Vietnam but found others than Kennedy to blame for them. He heaped superlatives on Kennedy's performance in the Cuban missile crisis and argued that by the fall of 1963 all signs pointed to a presidency of unparalleled achievement both at home and abroad. Dallas ended all that. So in contrast to *The Age of Jackson* and *The Age of Roosevelt*, *A Thousand Days* spoke more of promise than of fulfillment. Its closing note was inspirational yet bleak.

One could argue that Schlesinger never fully recovered from the despairing sense of dashed opportunity that set in after Kennedy's death. More blows followed—Vietnam, the killings of Robert Kennedy and Martin Luther King, the explosion of street violence, the election and reelection of Richard Nixon. Through all this Schlesinger's liberal centrism never swerved, but confidence and celebration gave way increasingly to doubt and disillusion. His early books had sounded the trumpet of the vital center and the politics of hope. Later titles spoke in darker tones.

11. *The Politics of Hope*, xi.

*The Bitter Heritage* (1966) was a burning indictment of American pol-icy in Vietnam. Schlesinger avoided personal censure (except upon Dean Rusk, who also fared poorly in *A Thousand Days*), but he excoriated the messianic self-righteousness that in his view had led America into a fruit-less war. Schlesinger called for an end to escalation and a search for a ne-gotiated peace. Above all, he pleaded not to "let the war in Vietman poi-son our national life." His warning went unheeded, and in 1969 Schlesinger uttered in *The Crisis of Confidence* an impassioned cry against "the down-ward spiral of social decomposition and moral degradation." With his usual incisive prose he again defended the radical middle, the posture of reason, civility, and moderation, against the rising tide of hysteria and violence.[12]

Schlesinger had always looked to the presidency as the font of creativi-ty in public life, "the most effective instrumentality of government for jus-tice and progress." Observing the impediments thrown up by Congress, the Supreme Court, and the administrative bureaucracy (whose obstruction-ism he had seen close-up in Kennedy's State Department), he had warned of the dangers of an immobilized executive. *A Thousand Days* celebrated Kennedy's "most efficacious" device of bolstering control by appointing his closest confidant (and younger brother) as attorney general. *The Crisis of Confidence* proposed to further fortify presidents with an item veto on legislation and with unilateral authority to reallocate funds and adjust tax rates. "The problem of the American Presidency in domestic affairs," Schlesinger opined in 1969, "is not too much power but too little."[13]

Then came Richard Nixon. The line between past and present, between scholarship and advocacy, never broad in Schlesinger's writings, had thinned as his history became more contemporary. In *The Imperial Pres-idency* (1973) it finally vanished altogether. Much of the book was a foot-noted historical account of presidential power and of its rapid escalation in the mid-twentieth century. But a contemporary question drove the narrative throughout: how could a now out-of-control presidency be re-strained? Schlesinger probed constitutional and institutional dimensions of the problem yet rejected most structural fixes. Good judgment and

12. *The Bitter Heritage: Vietnam and American Democracy, 1941–1966* (Boston: Houghton Mifflin, 1967), 117; *The Crisis of Confidence: Ideas, Power and Violence in America* (Boston: Houghton Mifflin, 1969), 9.

13. *The Imperial Presidency* (Boston: Houghton Mifflin, 1973), 404; *A Thousand Days*, 692; *The Crisis of Confidence*, 290.

good will, a commitment to openness and shared decision making on both sides, could restore balance between Congress and the White House. Most presidential powers (except some pertaining to internal security) were necessary and not intrinsically dangerous if properly checked and held in responsible hands.

The partisan thrust in this analysis was barely concealed. In *The Crisis of Confidence* Schlesinger had acknowledged what he called "a troubling question": had scholars hitherto "promoted the cult of the strong Presidency because, up to 1965, strong Presidents had been mostly doing things that historians and political scientists had mostly wanted done?"[14] Critics could ask the same of *The Imperial Presidency,* where the most dangerous openings to executive tyranny were laid not at Roosevelt's door or Truman's or Kennedy's, but at Eisenhower's. Democratic expansions of presidential power, though sometimes affording mischievous precedents, were not themselves abusive. But Nixon's aggressive infringements on the constitution were truly "revolutionary."

Nixon resigned in 1974, and four years later Schlesinger completed his homage to the Kennedys with the mammoth *Robert Kennedy and His Times.* Framed as "a sort of sequel to *A Thousand Days,*" it again married the genres of history and memoir in a rich and urgent narrative. Schlesinger had been on more intimate terms with Robert Kennedy than with John, and the book edged yet closer to hero worship, palpably tinged even after ten years with grief and regret for what might have been had Kennedy lived to be president. The prologue that set the tone this time was not an inauguration but a funeral.[15]

After completing *A Thousand Days,* Schlesinger had left Washington and joined the City University of New York as Albert Schweitzer Chair in the Humanities. This affiliation served less as a reentry into academia than as a platform for continuing a wider public role. Even before his White House interlude, Schlesinger had not confined himself to the usual professorial pursuits. He had not built his reputation in the ordinary academic way, by training graduate students, pioneering a new field of study, or launching an interpretive school. He eschewed specialization, ranging broadly in periods and subjects. His books were best-sellers; his shorter pieces appeared mainly in popular magazines and quasi-scholarly venues

---

14. *The Crisis of Confidence,* 288–89.
15. *Robert Kennedy and His Times* (Boston: Houghton Mifflin, 1978), xii.

like *Foreign Affairs* rather than academic journals. He took little hand in professional organizations and rarely appeared at their conferences. Conservatives had always loathed him, and in the 1960s and 1970s his centrist politics and narrative "great-man" approach to history earned the scorn of some leftist scholars as well. Egregiously, neither the American Historical Association nor the Organization of American Historians ever made him its president.

While Schlesinger and the academic establishment thus held each other at a certain distance, he increasingly represented that establishment to the public in his roles as spokesman, critic, and impresario. His name has appeared everywhere: as general editor in the 1970s of a series of multivolume collaborative works on American political parties, presidential elections, congressional investigations, and foreign policy; as editor of an American history almanac and a picture book on presidential campaigns; as a commentator on scholarly vogues from Civil War and Cold War revisionism to statistical social science; and, in 1999, at the head of a list of historians protesting (in full-page ads) President Clinton's impeachment. Updating a project begun by his father in 1948, Schlesinger polled historians and political scientists on their rating of the presidents in 1996, and in 1998 he served on a panel that ranked the century's greatest books.

In 1986 Schlesinger published *The Cycles of American History.* A collection of reworked essays dating back to the 1950s, the volume offered a considered restatement of familiar themes. Again Schlesinger indicted dogmatism and rigidity in domestic and foreign policy and the absolutist worldview that produced them. America, he insisted, was not an agent of appointed destiny but a practical and indeterminate experiment in human self-government. In this experiment, ideology ("profoundly alien to the Constitution . . . the curse of public affairs . . . out of character for Americans") was the enemy of success; sound leadership, its guarantee. "Democracy will stand or fall on the quality of its leadership."[16] Schlesinger renewed his briefs against Cold War revisionism and the rehabilitation of Republican presidential reputations. He subpoenaed history to back his call for abolition of the vice presidency, repeal of the Twenty-fifth Amendment, and reform of the electoral college. Most of all, he developed his case for a grand cyclical theory of American political change.

Schlesinger identified several recurring historical patterns, including

16. *The Cycles of American History* (Boston: Houghton Mifflin, 1986), 67, 419.

an alternation between "experimentalist" (the Roosevelts, Kennedy) and "predestinarian" (Woodrow Wilson) leadership. But the main cycle was one first posited by his father in 1924 and reiterated in Schlesinger's Jackson, Roosevelt, and Kennedy books: a rotation between "public purpose and private interest" as the guiding force in politics, between an active government and a stand-pat one, between liberalism and conservatism. This succession was generational, turning full circle roughly every thirty years. Reform eras began around 1900, 1930, and 1960; another was due in 1990.[17] Still the cycle's duration could vary with its intensity: a spate of unusually active liberalism might exhaust public energies and thus give way to an elongated conservative interval while people recouped for the next round of reform. The pattern was also dialectic rather than cyclical, in that conservatism consolidated rather than reversed the preceding liberal gains, while each liberal wave carved its own new policy agenda.

Invoked through all his work and finally restated in formal guise, Schlesinger's cyclical analysis may be taken as his chief contribution to historical theory. The thesis obviously has many problems both evidential and definitional, enough to ask whether Schlesinger's pattern is rather forced upon events than based upon them. Deployed by less artful hands, a scheme that fastens disparate eras and presidencies onto a single template would seem flatly ahistorical. A cynic looking at Schlesinger's Jackson, Roosevelt, and Kennedy books might say that the cycle theory of history merely serves up recycled histories. Even accepting the cyclical premise, it remains unclear whether change is driven by generational turnover, which would make it essentially deterministic, or by the happenstance of presidential leadership. Schlesinger has suggested both. In *The Politics of Hope* he thanked John F. Kennedy "for vindicating the cyclical theory of American politics." Yet elsewhere he has referred to the cycle not as a contingent prospect but as established reality.[18]

The cyclical theory reaffirmed Schlesinger's lifelong commitment to the now much criticized presidential synthesis—the idea that power em-

17. The senior Arthur Schlesinger first announced this cyclical theory in a talk in 1924 and published it in a 1939 *Yale Review* article entitled "Tides of American Politics." Schlesinger's prediction of liberal phases lasting fifteen or sixteen years and recurring every thirty years purportedly helped persuade Franklin Roosevelt to seek a third term in 1940 and John F. Kennedy to seek the presidency in 1960. Schlesinger, *In Retrospect,* 108, 127, 190–91.

18. *The Politics of Hope,* xii.

anates from the center, and that a strong leader can give shape to an era. The very titles *Age of Jackson* and *Age of Roosevelt* bespoke assumptions about how to periodize American history and about what within it was most important. "Leadership," said Schlesinger in *Cycles*, "is really what makes the world go round."[19] He had always believed in a strong executive, and one could argue that this conviction predetermined what he would find in history. His books stressed presidential initiative while minimizing the roles of the Congress, states, communities, interest groups, organizations, or popular movements. His use of presidential inaugurations as generational break points left little room to acknowledge continuity or evolution from one administration to the next, and his metropolitan vantage point tended to exclude historical trends and circumstances that occurred outside the presidential purview.

Unlike most historians, Schlesinger has staked his credibility as much on the prescience of his forecasts as on the soundness of his narratives.[20] In this he has in the main been fortunate. He has lived to witness the triumph of his vital center over its rivals of left and right, though its very preemption of the field has threatened to unmoor his liberalism in a postideological era. As nondemocratic and noncapitalist alternatives have receded and lines of political demarcation have blurred, Schlesinger's liberalism, itself more a posture than a policy, has lost much of its programmatic coherence. The liberal turn in the cycle that he anticipated for around 1990 has failed to make its appearance, at least in any recognizable form; and the reorientation of politics around questions of culture and identity has left Schlesinger's inclusive centrism looking, at least to its critics, very much like querulous conservatism.[21] In *The Disuniting of America: Reflections on a Multicultural Society* (1991), Schlesinger lashed out at the intrusion of ethnic tribalism into American history education and defended the melting pot as both valid history and vital aspiration. Condemning the subordination of history to political or social ends, Schlesinger still

---

19. *The Cycles of American History,* 419.

20. This is a criterion he accepted: "However hard it may be to define with precision the role of history in public policy, it is evident that this role must stand or fall on the success of history as a means of prediction—on the proposition that knowledge of yesterday provides guidance for tomorrow" (*The Bitter Heritage,* 81).

21. In a new 1999 foreword to *The Cycles of American History,* Schlesinger attributed "the prolongation of the conservative phase of the cycle" to the shift from the Industrial Revolution to the Computer Revolution, which would henceforth establish its own, as yet undiscernible, cyclical rhythm.

upheld its utility in furthering "the quest for unifying ideals and a common culture." Although "history as a weapon is an abuse of history," "honest history is the weapon of freedom."[22]

In *Disuniting,* as indeed in all his works, Schlesinger damned sectarian dogmas while somewhat naively identifying his own values as unarguable nonideological truths. Schlesinger has always claimed the political center for his heroes and himself, branding positions to either side as extremist and utopian. Yet where the center is depends, of course, on how one sets the spectrum. In practice, the flexibility and reasonableness that Schlesinger championed seemed always to sanction his own policy preferences. To see always from the middle, or to believe that one does, is not necessarily to see most clearly. Schlesinger's self-declared freedom from ideology has served to shield his own premises from the kind of critical self-scrutiny that might have tempered some of his judgments. And in the stridency of his polemics, he has risked becoming the very exclusionist he abhors. While decrying the rigidity of either/or, he has himself traded heavily in dualisms: young/old, pragmatic/dogmatic, realist/utopian, liberal/conservative. With great zeal and righteousness he has condemned the zealous and self-righteous. Meditating on the uses and abuses of history in *The Bitter Heritage,* Schlesinger warned that knowledge of the past furnished no certain prescriptions for future action. At best it could warn off arrogance and instill in its place a cautionary humility when facing the inscrutable complexity of human affairs. This was wise counsel; yet his own practice has not always been so modest.

Hailed and assailed, honored and resented, Schlesinger has long been an inescapable public figure. To celebrate the end of the century, President Clinton invited a select group of "American Creators" to the White House Millennium Dinner on December 31, 1999. The guest list included actors and actresses, musicians, singers, dancers, playwrights, athletes—and a historian, Arthur M. Schlesinger, Jr. In the twilight of his career, he has become as durable an icon of American liberalism as the presidents he chronicled so compellingly.

22. *The Disuniting of America: Reflections on a Multicultural Society* (New York: W. W. Norton, 1992), 19, 72, 52.

# C. Vann Woodward

## by Robert H. Ferrell

Comer Vann Woodward's life has virtually spanned the twentieth century—born in 1908, he celebrated his ninety-first birthday in November 1999. And it has been a life marked by the signs of achievement. As a historian, he has received more recognition, one might contend, than almost all of his contemporaries. He has held the presidencies of the three major historical associations: the oldest and most prestigious, the American Historical Association; the Organization of American Historians, whose ponderous title distinguishes its members from scholars of other historical subjects; and the Southern Historical Association, the only regional group that for generations has achieved national support and published its own journal. For his books he has been awarded the Pulitzer Prize for history as well as the Bancroft Prize. His entry in *Who's Who* lists a galaxy of lesser awards. His honorary degrees number twenty, extraordinary for a historian, and surpassed only by Arthur M. Schlesinger, Jr., and John Hope Franklin.

An essential part of Vann Woodward's background—he early dropped his first name in favor of an initial—was his birth and upbringing in the small towns of Arkansas. There was never any doubt, for him or for anyone else, that he was a southerner. Arkansas had gone with the Confederacy in 1861, even though it was not a part of the Old South. The Lost Cause was something that he grew up with. The town in which he was born, Vanndale, called attention to the heritage of a southern family, that of his mother. When the Woodwards moved to Morrilton and Arkadelphia it was more of the same, the small-town South. This legacy proved ineradicable and eventually pointed the way to his academic specialization.

What the background made possible, attendance at Emory University in Atlanta reinforced. Woodward had spent two years at a college in Arkadelphia known as Henderson-Brown, a struggling place that enrolled

130 students, and then went to Emory on the urging of his uncle Comer, for whom he had been named, who was dean of students at Emory and professor of sociology.[1] The change offered the advantage of friends with wider interests, for Emory was a much larger institution. There he met such individuals as David M. Potter, who would also become a well-known historian, would serve as Woodward's predecessor at Yale University, and like him would receive the Pulitzer.

Meanwhile, Woodward's family had moved to Oxford, Georgia, where his father served as head of Emory's former campus, which had become a junior college. There the Woodwards met the Odum family. The well-known southern regional sociologist Howard W. Odum taught at the University of North Carolina, and in 1934 he would arrange for Vann Woodward to receive a graduate fellowship at Chapel Hill.

After taking a bachelor's degree at Emory, Woodward taught English composition for two years at Georgia Tech in Atlanta. Teaching brought contact with a very interesting Atlantan, Will W. Alexander, head of the Commission on Interracial Cooperation, and proximity brought not merely acquaintance but friendship with J. Saunders Redding, a young man who taught at the all-black Atlanta University. Redding was the first African American with whom Woodward broke bread and whom he came to know well. The novelty, he wrote years later, was difficult to believe. "I had grown up with black people all around, and since they were always there I shared to some extent the common illusion that I was already familiar with them and their problems. What I was thoroughly familiar with was one side of the universally prevailing system of racial subordination— the white side and white attitudes."[2]

The years at Georgia Tech were separated by a year of study at Columbia University in New York City, where he received an M.A., and by two summer trips to Europe, during which he learned more about racism. At Columbia he met members of the city's black community. During an excursion to the Soviet Union he encountered criticism of the South's behavior over "the Scottsboro boys," blacks in Alabama who were tried and convicted on a racially trumped-up charge of rape. In Berlin he lived with

1. Few historians have had books written about them during their lifetimes, but Woodward did. See John Herbert Roper, *C. Vann Woodward: Southerner* (Athens: University of Georgia Press, 1987).
2. *Thinking Back: The Perils of Writing History* (Baton Rouge: Louisiana State University Press, 1986), 14.

a Jewish family whose members speculated uneasily about the political future of their country—the year was 1932—as the National Socialists were increasing in strength; optimistically, they felt that the avowed racism of the Hitler movement would not turn into public policy. These experiences gave the young Woodward unusual insights into human perceptions of race and politics as driving forces in history.

Moving to North Carolina in 1934, Woodward needed no further encouragement to take an interest in his native South. He already knew Odum, and at Chapel Hill he met Odum's equally well known colleague, Rupert B. Vance. The year before the move, Woodward had begun work on a biography of the Georgia political leader Tom Watson, whose papers were at Chapel Hill. For his dissertation supervisor he chose the historian Howard K. Beale, to facilitate getting his doctorate "out of the way," to use a phrase familiar to all graduate students. At North Carolina he saw that Odum and Vance were more conservative than he had thought, while the approach of Beale, a civil libertarian, was more attractive to him personally.

Howard Beale proved a good choice for his dissertation supervisor. An accomplished historian, Beale liked the South but not its racial customs. He did not understand why the South was the way it was, and in his 1930 book *The Critical Year,* dealing with the months after the Civil War, he drew the usual scene of a prostrate South victimized by the industrial Northeast, with the South a rural place in league with the West but nonetheless victimized.[3] Studying the southern fire-eater Watson, Woodward already was becoming unsure of this theme of southern innocence and basic rural instincts. Beale let him go his own way, and his principal contribution to the emerging dissertation probably was literary: in later years he would teach a large group of talented graduate students at the University of Wisconsin and instruct every one of them in the art of good writing.

Woodward earned his doctorate in 1937. The next year saw the publication of *Tom Watson: Agrarian Rebel.* During World War II he served in the navy, working in Washington on navy historical projects that inspired

3. Beale saw "an agrarian South . . . contending for those time-honored principles of frontier individualism and plantation aristocracy which had dominated an America that was passing" (David M. Potter, "C. Vann Woodward," in *Pastmasters: Some Essays on American Historians,* ed. Marcus Cunliffe and Robin W. Winks [New York: Harper and Row, 1969], 379).

him to write his own account of the greatest navy confrontation with Japan during the Pacific war, *The Battle for Leyte Gulf* (1947).

The postwar era found him teaching at Johns Hopkins in Baltimore, with easy access to the vast collections of the Library of Congress, and returning to the study of the South. Thirteen years after the publication of *Tom Watson* he brought out, in 1951, a monograph on the Compromise of 1877, *Reunion and Reaction,* and—later the same year—*Origins of the New South: 1877–1913,* a book in a series of volumes on the South.[4] Together with *Watson* these two works on southern history made his scholarly reputation.

In producing these books, Woodward was up against the prevailing interpretation of why the South was such a special region. The interpretation was more than a view justified by the South's historians; it was the belief of its intellectual leaders in a long past that, although they refused to admit it, had made racism, as the Yale historian Ulrich B. Phillips drew it, the central theme of southern history. Southern leaders offered a black-and-white version of what really happened. They announced Reconstruction as an anomaly, imposed by the North and by, even worse, such northern extremists as Representative Thaddeus Stevens of Pennsylvania, who spent his dying moments either contemplating the grave—Stevens seemed to enjoy such speculation—or pondering how, avoiding death for a moment or two, he could impose further penalties on the South. According to the southern version of history Stevens had much support. He certainly did within his congressional district, where he was so firmly in the affections of voters that even after his death they voted him another term in the House! Fortunately (according to the go-along historians) after the departure of federal troops from the south came the Redeemers, southern conservatives, who took back government from the North and brought the South law and order, which prevailed into the twentieth century.

The reality, as Woodward saw it, was that the South's leaders after Reconstruction were far less interested in law and order than in reviving conservatism to protect their own economic interests. The monograph on the 1877 compromise pointed out unexpected reasons for the fraudulent confirmation of Rutherford B. Hayes as president of the United States, prin-

---

4. The publisher for the Watson was Macmillan, the *Origins* volume appeared in a series sponsored by Louisiana State University Press, and *Reunion and Reaction* was brought out by Little, Brown, with a revised edition published by Oxford University Press in 1991.

cipally the proposed construction of a railroad grandiloquently designated the Texas and Pacific. *Origins of the New South* surveyed the entire era, pooh-poohed the notion of the New South highlighted by its title, and stressed a return to the Old South. To make certain of their control the Redeemers turned racist. They enlisted the poor whites against the crackers' natural allies, the equally downtrodden blacks, and sponsored segregation including disfranchisement. The result was a curious arrangement for the combination of former Whigs, essential compromisers, and the virtually new class of businessman Redeemers that lasted well into the 1940s. Woodward already had described this scene in the latter half of the Watson book, where he traced how the politician's resort to conservatism and racism resulted in Watson's unabashed, uncontrite rise to the U.S. Senate. In the books of 1951 he again showed how the South had redrawn its history to suit conservative convenience.

Southern history would never be the same. It was the details of the two books of 1951 that proved so damning. Woodward made sure that he sought out the available sources, including newspapers and private papers deposited in the Library of Congress and in state historical societies and private depositories; his investigations took him to the South and North and even to the West. The depth of his research was especially in evidence in *Reunion and Reaction,* its theme made clear in its title, which relied on detailed analyses that over the next half century proved unassailable save for hemstitching by a few scholars. The Compromise of 1877 lasted far longer, Woodward demonstrated, than the compromises of 1820, 1833, 1850, and of course the fourth effort at compromise that brought the nation into the Civil War. The *Origins* book similarly rested on unprecedented research.

At that juncture the historian's career took a turn from scholarship to advocacy. In the autumn of 1954, by chance the same year as the historic decision in *Brown v. Board of Education,* Woodward gave a series of lectures at the University of Virginia, published the following year under a provocative title, *The Strange Career of Jim Crow.* The book was an outright indictment of what had befallen blacks in the South. It sold modestly through the rest of the decade and then in the early 1960s came into its own, as sales rose dramatically from dozens of copies into the hundreds of thousands. Its author claimed the sales concerned him, for he feared many people bought the book, read a few pages, and set it on a coffee table. So he told everyone who would listen, and by the 1960s that was many, what the book was about: racism. He professed concern about misinterpretation. Then tongue in cheek he remarked that to be the author of a book that sold was better than to be the author of one that did not, and although he did not say so he clearly believed that the devil could take the hindmost. He updated the book in several editions, correcting or modifying a few errors or seeming errors. But in the main the message of *Jim Crow* remained as it had been presented in the lectures at Charlottesville.

The activism bothered his friend Potter, who had been enthusiastic about the Watson book, proclaiming it "the best and most revealing biography that has been written of any Southerner living in the period since the Civil War."[5] He sniffed at *The Strange Career,* willing to say only that it contained nothing new. Yet the usually acute Potter should have understood not merely what Woodward had done but why he had done it. The Arkansas historian had not in any sense written the book to advance his career. Certainly the uses the civil rights movement made of his thesis, of his books of research, was gratifying. When, after accompanying Dr. Martin Luther King on the march from Selma to Montgomery, Woodward stood outside Alabama's capitol and heard King quote from *The Strange Career,* the historian took a considerable pleasure from hearing his own words and from watching the hard faces of Alabama onlookers, who he felt sure hated the very notion of a fellow southerner providing grist for the mill of that black troublemaker King. But apart from the momentary gratification he realized that here, in the rights movement, was a fulfillment of his long-held hope for justice for American blacks, South and North. The book was testimony to what he believed, and opposition to what he had grown up with in Vanndale and Morrilton and Arkadelphia.

In *The Strange Career* and the books of collected essays that followed, bearing such titles as *The Burden of Southern History* (1966) and *Thinking Back* (1986), the scholar rejected the role of publicist and became an activist based on his own historical research. Woodward believed history demonstrated a course the South needed to follow. He deplored the region's dual fascination with slavery and the cotton gin, the temptation that by 1880 reduced the region to a per capita property evaluation of $376 compared to $1,186 in states outside the South. The answer, he said, did not lie in dreaming about the Lost Cause, nor in complaining about the ills of Reconstruction, which were hardly as important as critics claimed,

5. "C. Vann Woodward," in *Pastmasters,* 383.

nor in making light of what he believed to have been a most promising fusion of poor white purposes with those of the former slaves in the Populist movement. "It is altogether probable," he insisted, "that during the brief Populist upheaval of the nineties Negroes and native whites achieved a greater comity of mind and harmony of political purpose than ever before or since in the South."[6] The racism that set in during the 1890s as a cover for continuing the Redeemer program had been carried to absurd lengths, such as separate Bibles for whites and blacks to kiss before testimony at court trials, not to mention the silliness of separate cars for travelers on trains (or at the least separate seats), separate buses, even separate taxicabs. All this segregation played on the ignorance of streetcar conductors, ordinary workmen, and others who were unaware of the South's history and wanted only to separate themselves from poor blacks. When racism was sanctioned by city ordinances and state laws, when the U.S. Supreme Court in the 1880s and 1890s not merely went along with this nonsense but lent the majesty of its opinions to segregation, the result was altogether unfair to blacks, the vast majority of whom could not vote. It called out for remedy.

Bringing the South into the mainstream of American life—economically, politically, socially—required evenhandedness in Woodward's criticism, which was to say tact, and he displayed a great deal of it. By no means, he wrote, was the South entirely to blame for what had happened. For a while he turned his attention to comparative history and related that the South should have compared itself with other parts of Plantation America, seeing what manumission with payment rather than expropriation, and generally a more understanding attitude by northerners toward the plight of moneyed slaveholders and other property holders, might have accomplished in terms of better post-freedom economics.[7] If the

6. *The Strange Career of Jim Crow* (New York: Oxford University Press, 1955), 64.

7. C. Vann Woodward, ed., *The Comparative Approach to American History* (New York: Basic Books, 1968). He admitted that the essays in this volume, the content of which he left up to the authors because he had chosen them for their interest in the approach, were mixed. In his own writings Woodward necessarily could not take the comparative approach beyond generalities, because research would have involved thorough knowledge of Spanish or Portuguese and of an enormous literature. He encouraged a book on the freeing of Russian serfs in 1861, and a decade later the book appeared. But as he remarked in a review essay it was apparent that freeing the serfs by edict was different from what befell southern slavery, that the experiences of serfs and slaves had been far different if only because serfs were usually distant from the masters who lived in cities, and because the serfs being white could blend into peasant Russia and escape as families or groups, sometimes

South compared its history to the horrendous histories of other areas of slavery in the New World, people could see that life for southern slaves was not so bad. In the South slaves multiplied rapidly, their numbers increasing year by year. In most portions of Plantation America the death tolls were unbelievably high, requiring incessant importations. All the while the North, he pointed out, behaved shamelessly toward blacks in its midst as well as toward southerners who, according to northern lights, had acted wrongly toward their human chattels. In his youth, probably because of his experience at his first college, the tiny Methodist Henderson-Brown, he had observed how religion in the South allied with segregation and accepted it, and for years thereafter he probably believed that southern religion was a sham. But so was northern religion; in one of the most basic Protestant principles, which is that conviction of sin is necessary for salvation. In the early 1950s he came to admire the writings of Reinhold Niebuhr, whose politics were much to his taste, and the idea of sin reentered his thoughts and was quickly applied in his essays to the proud North.[8]

The criticism of the North as he drew it was undeniable in its particulars. His basic authority was Tocqueville, who in 1831 wrote that "The prejudice of race appears to be stronger in the states that have abolished slavery than in those where it still exists." He brought in the most recent scholarship, notably the work of Pulitzer Prize–winning historian Leon F. Litwack, who wrote in *North of Slavery: The Negro in the Free States, 1790–1860* (1961) that "the inherent cruelty and violence of southern slavery requires no further demonstration, but this does not prove northern humanity." Only 6 percent of blacks lived in the five states of New England (except Connecticut) that by 1860 permitted them to vote. Until 1855 even

---

by the thousands. In these senses the comparative approach mostly yielded marked differences. Freedom in 1861 produced few changes in Russian history.

8. I find Woodward's excitement over Niebuhr in the 1950s akin to my own in the same period and in some ways just as innocent, for a historian's judgment of the theologian may have verged on misinterpretation. I once heard Niebuhr give two sermons at the Yale chapel. The first was a marvelous sermon, I thought, the kind of admonitory exposition one goes to church to hear. My friends from the Divinity School turned up their noses. The next night came the theology, which bored me to tears, while the divinity people thought it marvelous. Woodward (and I) nonetheless became converts, with Woodward's enthusiasm lasting longer: "He wrote . . . with the calm of a philosopher and the serenity of a learned theologian, and I read him eagerly. Furthermore, he had a grasp on history and he addressed precisely those contemporary American delusions, temptations, and obsessions that absorbed and alarmed me" (*Thinking Back,* 105).

slavery-hating Massachusetts refused to allow blacks to serve on juries. As for the underground railroad, so much talked about, the critical Woodward pointed out the work of the historian Larry Gara, who showed that the railroad was largely a myth, that few blacks reached the North with or without its assistance, that the number of slaves given manumission during the same era was double that of fugitives, and that for the most part fugitives never got out of the slave states.

Similarly, in an essay published in 1951 he turned to the subject of John Brown. He was appalled that New England intellectuals had cast Brown in the role of a martyr, even though he was a wanton murderer. He demonstrated Brown's essential inhumanity. Almost certainly insane, Brown established himself as a Kansas murderer before obtaining private northern support for his rebellion in 1859 at Harpers Ferry. The killings that accompanied his capture of the federal arsenal were cheered by all the good antislavery enthusiasts of Boston and environs. The catalog of contemporary praise in Woodward's essay is shocking: William Ellery Channing, Bronson and Louisa May Alcott, Longfellow, William Cullen Bryant, Lowell, Wendell Phillips, and Theodore Parker all pronounced the mad Brown, as Parker put it, "not only a martyr . . . but also a SAINT." Thoreau ventured that Brown's methods were "nothing; the spirit is all," meaning that the means justified the end.[9]

From Brown the historian's list of northern prejudices reached into the twentieth century, from the race riots of 1919, more than a dozen of them, during what John Hope Franklin described as the greatest period of interracial strife the nation ever witnessed, to the flourishing of the revived Ku Klux Klan in the early 1920s, to the race riots of World War II, to the burning of northern cities in riots of the mid-1960s and the subsequent rise of black separatism (which Woodward deplored).

The developing Cold War reminded him to emphasize in several of his essays that the South had known tragedy. The North and the rest of the country had experienced bad moments but by and large nothing comparable to the crushing defeat in the Civil War, followed by the penniless years of Reconstruction and the penury for generations of southerners thereafter, down to his time. The United States of the post-1945 years bothered him in its luxury, although he could not have imagined the wealth of

9. *The Burden of Southern History* (Baton Rouge: Louisiana State University Press, 1966), 54.

the 1990s, far exceeding that of the 1950s and early 1960s. He disliked the spread-eagle postwar patriotism, especially the Republican sentiments of the era of President Dwight D. Eisenhower. He detested the bicentennial celebrations of 1976 and 1987 and the braggadocio that accompanied them. All this led to thoughts about the recent fate of many peoples in Europe and elsewhere and the need of southerners to warn their countrymen against overconfidence.

Pointing out what the South might contribute to the betterment of the American mind-set, the historian of the South did not fail to mention such national troubles as Vietnam, the illegalities of President Richard M. Nixon, and the trading of missiles to Iran to provide money for the Nicaraguan Contras under a conservative Republican president, Ronald Reagan.

He recalled the South's neighborliness—a trait sometimes known, if with black assistance enslaved or hired, as hospitality—a habit of people helping each other rather than engaging in national schemes. Southern hospitality stood a light year apart from Republican rascality. The small-town nature of so much southern life was something to cherish, not poke fun at. In the midst of all this distressing behavior after World War II, Woodward averred, the South surely could change its ways without further criticism.

Woodward, then, not merely produced an outstanding foundation for his thesis about the South but followed with books and essays that ensured his reputation when the civil rights movement adopted him, as he already had adopted its advocates. Predictably, further support came from a growing body of publications in which his Hopkins graduate students took facets of his interpretation and developed them. They divided the South into subregions, or applied his theories in the several states, or used them to examine major cities. His move in 1961 from Hopkins to Yale, where he received a Sterling professorship, brought more graduate students. The 1960s marked a time when colleges and universities, including private institutions, received federal money and tripled their enrollments; in the major institutions and the minor ones, too, Woodward's followers and former students saw to it that his thesis flourished.[10]

---

10. Woodward received more than the usual number of published accolades for his scholarship. In 1982 a festschrift was edited by J. Morgan Knauser and James M. McPherson: *Region, Race, and Reconstruction: Essays in Honor of C. Vann Woodward* (New York:

The spread of Woodward's ideas also was assisted by one of the historian's marked traits, his ability to deflect criticism. Perhaps this quality came from his southern courtliness, which allowed him to disarm critics by gentleness rather than through crashing contention. He instinctively knew that a gentle answer turned away wrath and wrote in an essay of employing "the past subjunctive" against critics. He accepted something in their points, admitted the possibility of two or more views, questioned something. Sometimes he would disarm critics with a point of humor.

Only in an open argument with University of Michigan historian Dwight L. Dumond did he become sarcastic, which was uncharacteristic behavior on his part. In a 1961 book that appeared in the same year as the works by Litwack and Gara, Dumond made it all easy. In passage after passage he flat-footedly announced the South's guilt, which by itself was enough to arouse Woodward. In addition he had refused to consult secondary works or monographs, such as Woodward's, using only what he described as source materials—that is, documents. Woodward referred to Dumond as "professor" and carefully took him apart. When he did not cite his own writings to prove his points he used those of Litwack and Gara.

In such manner the years passed, including those after retirement in 1977, forced by Woodward's arrival at the Yale retirement age of sixty-eight. But withdrawal from teaching did not mean, as it does for many academicians, withdrawal from scholarly interests. In 1981 Woodward published a volume of 886 pages that contained the text of the well-known diary of the southerner Mary Chesnut. Suddenly he found himself in another controversy.

He managed the controversy over the Chesnut diary in a masterful manner. In his gentlemanly, genial way the tall, lanky, retired professor, speaking slowly, haltingly, softly as was his way, perhaps with a trace of a smile, confessed his concern, even worry, about the publication of his edition. But one has the impression that he may not have found the diary fracas obnoxious, if only because the edition received the Pulitzer Prize for history in 1982. Admittedly this was part of the controversy that surrounded its appearance. A few critics disliked the awarding of the prize to

---

Oxford University Press). Fifteen years later came the Roper account of his life and work, an unprecedented tribute to an active scholar. In 1997, Roper also edited a symposium, *C. Vann Woodward: A Southern Historian and His Critics* (Athens: University of Georgia Press).

an edited book rather than one produced by an author. There was talk about the fact that the diary was a rewritten version of a wartime diary, done in the 1880s. At least one reviewer likened the award to a Pulitzer that had gone to a Washington reporter the year before who later admitted making up the winning story out of the whole cloth. Woodward acknowledged that there might have been some peculiarity in a prize for an edition but vigorously defended publication of a diary that was abridged. The contemporary diary, he said, contained personal observations unpublishable even years thereafter; also, the passage of years allowed the author to see the South's plight more clearly, to give a judgment earlier denied. To reduce the temperature of purist critics he then joined with Mary Chesnut's biographer, Elizabeth Muhlenfeld, to bring out an edition of the wartime diary.[11]

Woodward's most recent book, *The Old World's New World*, was published jointly in 1991 by the New York Public Library and Oxford University Press. It is a series of lectures on American history, with due attention to the lecturer's principal point of inquiry during his long years of scholarship.

One comes full circle to C. Vann Woodward's enormous reputation because his scholarship, before and after World War II, replaced the nostalgic and historically irrelevant interpretation of the southern past. Hard facts, diligent research, and brilliant insights challenged the shopworn myths, casting them into the dustbin of history. The literature of the Lost Cause, the wrongfulness of Reconstruction, the righteousness of the Redeemers, the forgetfulness of the Populists—all were cover-ups for the ensuing racism. The genteel southerner, now resident in Yankee New Haven, could look back over his years with satisfaction that the nation and the profession are richer for his lifetime of achievement.

Woodward died on December 17, 1999, shortly after this article was drafted.

---

11. *The Private Mary Chesnut: The Unpublished Civil War Diaries* (New York: Oxford University Press, 1984). The Pulitzer book was *Mary Chesnut's Civil War* (New Haven: Yale University Press, 1981).

# About the Contributors

Catherine Clinton is a writer and historian whose books include *Fanny Kemble's Civil Wars* and *Taking Off the White Gloves: Southern Women and Women Historians.*

Paul K. Conkin will shortly retire as Distinguished Professor of History at Vanderbilt University. Before moving to Vanderbilt in 1979, he was the Merle Curti Professor of History at the University of Wisconsin-Madison.

John Milton Cooper, Jr., served on the editorial board of the Woodrow Wilson Papers. He is the E. Gardner Fox Professor of American Institutions at the University of Wisconsin in Madison.

Daniel Feller is Professor of History at the University of New Mexico. He is the author of *The Public Lands in Jacksonian Politics* (1984) and *The Jacksonian Promise: America, 1815–1840* (1995), and the editor of Harriet Martineau's *Retrospect of Western Travel* (2000).

Robert H. Ferrell is Professor Emeritus of History at Indiana University in Bloomington. He is the author or editor of numerous books, including *Harry S. Truman: A Life, The Strange Deaths of President Harding, The Dying President: Franklin D. Roosevelt, 1944–1945,* and *Truman and Pendergast.*

Paul Finkelman is the Chapman Distinguished Professor of Law at the University of Tulsa College of Law. He has published more than seventy scholarly articles and is the author or editor of more than a dozen books, including *A March of Liberty: A Constitutional History of the United States* (2d ed., 2001, with Melvyn Urofsky), *Dred Scott v. Sandford: A Brief Histo-*

ry (1997), *Slavery and the Founders: Race and Liberty in the Age of Jefferson* (1996), and *An Imperfect Union: Slavery, Federalism and Comity* (1981, rpt. 2000). He received his Ph.D. in history from the University of Chicago in 1976, where he studied with John Hope Franklin.

Lewis L. Gould wrote his dissertation under Lamar's direction at Yale. He is the Eugene C. Barker Centennial Professor Emeritus at the University of Texas, and his most recent book is *Lady Bird Johnson: Our Environmental FIrst Lady* (1999).

John M. Murrin was a Morgan student at Yale. He has taught American colonial and revolutionary history at Princeton University since 1973. He is a coauthor of *Liberty, Equality, and Power: A History of the American People* and in 1999 was president of the Society for Historians of the Early American Republic.

Jack Pole has taught at Churchill College, Cambridge; St. Catherine's College, Oxford; and elsewhere throughout the world. His publications include *Political Representation in England and the Origins of the American Republic* (1966), *The Pursuit of Equality in American History* (1978), *Paths to the American Past* (1979); and *The Gift of Government* (1983).

Jack N. Rakove wrote his dissertation at Harvard under Bailyn's direction. He is the Coe Professor of History and American Studies at Stanford, and his book *Original Meanings: Politics and Ideas in the Making of the Constitution* received the 1997 Pulitzer Prize in History.

Robert Allen Rutland is Research Professor of History at the University of Tulsa. He is also the author of numerous books, including *The Democrats: From Jefferson to Clinton, The Republicans: From Lincoln to Bush,* and *James Madison: The Founding Father.*

Howard Temperley studied with Potter while writing his dissertation at Yale. He is professor emeritus at the University of East Anglia (U.K.) and served as chairman of the British Association for American Studies. His books include *British Antislavery, 1833–1870* and *White Dreams, Black Africa: The Antislavery Expedition to the Niger, 1841–1842.*

# Acknowledgments

A salute of gratitude goes to the more than two dozen historians who bravely offered their thoughts on who should be included in *Clio's Favorites*. Their friendly and professional counsel turned an idea into reality. Special mention is due Robert Ferrell, Jack Greene, William Harbaugh, Michael Kammen, Linda Kerber, Leonard Levy, Merrill Peterson, James Morton Smith, and Paul H. Smith. The director of the University of Missouri Press, Beverly Jarrett, has been supportive at all phases of publication, as has the managing editor, Jane Lago. Their decision to place footnotes at the bottoms of the pages (where they belong) was a victory of good judgment over production costs. And all of the authors deserve thanks, too, for their willingness to write an essay, pay attention to deadlines, and have faith in the project.

# Index